Brain–Computer Interfaces 2

Series Editor
Maureen Clerc

Brain–Computer Interfaces 2

Technology and Applications

Edited by

Maureen Clerc
Laurent Bougrain
Fabien Lotte

WILEY

First published 2016 in Great Britain and the United States by ISTE Ltd and John Wiley & Sons, Inc.

ISTE Ltd
27-37 St George's Road
London SW19 4EU
UK

www.iste.co.uk

John Wiley & Sons, Inc.
111 River Street
Hoboken, NJ 07030
USA

www.wiley.com

Library of Congress Control Number: 2016945318

British Library Cataloguing-in-Publication Data
A CIP record for this book is available from the British Library
ISBN 978-1-84821-963-2

Contents

Chapter 4. BrainTV: Revealing the Neural Bases of Human Cognition in Real Time 65

Jean-Philippe LACHAUX

Chapter 5. BCIs and Video Games: State of the Art with the OpenViBE2 Project 85

Anatole LÉCUYER

Chapter 8. Technical Requirements for High-quality EEG Acquisition 143

Emmanuel MABY

Chapter 9. Practical Guide to Performing an EEG Experiment 163

Emmanuel MABY

Chapter 13. OpenViBE Illustration of a P300 Virtual Keyboard 227

Nathanaël FOY, Théodore PAPADOPOULO and Maureen CLERC

Chapter 14. Recreational Applications of OpenViBE: Brain Invaders and Use-the-Force 241

Anton ANDREEV, Alexandre BARACHANT, Fabien LOTTE and
Marco CONGEDO

Chapter 17. Conclusion and Perspectives 311

Maureen CLERC, Laurent BOUGRAIN and Fabien LOTTE

Foreword

A Brain–Computer Interface (BCI) records brain signals, translates them into commands that operate a variety of devices, and provides feedback to the user about how intentions are transformed into actions. These three essential components, forming a closed-loop system, define the core components of a BCI. Their natural target population has traditionally been people with motor disabilities that have lost control of their body but have preserved cognitive functions, and BCIs have been intended to act as alternative assistive devices for them. However, in recent years the scope of a BCI has widened to include restoration or rehabilitation of motor and even cognitive functions for patients after some kind of central nervous system injury, brain state monitoring for healthy subjects, and new tools for studying human brain functions.

An anecdotal, even fringe, field of research at the confines with science fiction when it appeared, BCIs have grown over the last 40 years from early prototypes in a handful of locations to more than 3,000 research labs and nearly 150 companies working in BCI-related areas nowadays. The complexity of today's BCI systems, which are moving beyond constrained laboratory conditions, calls for truly multidisciplinary efforts spanning clinical research to computer science and human–computer interfaces, from neuroscience to biomedical and neuroengineering, from rehabilitation to robotics and virtual reality, and from human psychology to material and electrical engineering.

This wide range of fields that contribute to BCI makes it difficult, if not impossible, to have a unified view covering all the facets of this fascinating scientific and translational enterprise. Thus, a certain bias is always present and openly acknowledged in our research. This book is no exception. It is edited by signal processing and machine learning specialists. Yet, aiming to become a reference for the French-speaking research community, it gathers a collective body of expertise from all the fields involved in BCI research and practice. We consider this challenge that the editors have successfully tackled, as the book covers state-of-the-art research and results in a way that all other communities can relate to. Furthermore, the curious layperson – I hope you are if you want to live long with a healthy brain! – can also profit from a significant number of chapters that do not require any specific background.

The book is organized into seven parts, distributed between two volumes.

Following on from the first volume (*Foundations and Methods*), this second volume (*Technology and Applications*) clearly exposes the field of BCI from the standpoint of end users (mainly people with physical disabilities) and practitioners. Part 1 presents a large variety of domains, clinical and non-clinical. Academic and clinical researchers, but also BCI enthusiasts, will find Part 2 a precious resource for setting up a BCI platform, both at the hardware and at the software level. Special emphasis is placed on the OpenViBE software platform in Part 3. Finally, Part 4 concludes the second volume of this reference book by addressing key societal issues regarding ethics and acceptability, which should concern any informed citizen – from the researcher to the experimental subject, from the clinician to the end user and from the philosopher to the policy maker.

Brain–Computer Interfaces by Clerc, Bougrain and Lotte is the first BCI book for and by the French-speaking community. Here, it is also translated in English as it has important lessons for all BCI researchers and practitioners worldwide. I am certain that this book will appeal to each of them as it has done to me. Enjoy it.

José DEL R. MILLÁN
Geneva
Switzerland
May 2016

Introduction

A Brain–Computer Interface (BCI) is a system that translates a user's brain activity into messages or commands for an interactive application. BCIs represent a relatively recent technology that is experiencing a rapid growth. The objective of this introductory chapter is to briefly present an overview of the history of BCIs, the technology behind them, the terms and classifications used to describe them and their possible applications. The book's content is presented, and a reading guide is provided so that you, the reader, can easily find and use whatever you are searching for in this book.

I.1. History

The idea of being able to control a device through mere thought is not new. In the scientific world, this idea was proposed by Jacques Vidal in 1973 in an article entitled "Toward Direct Brain–Computer Communications" [VID 73]. In this article, the Belgian scientist, who had studied in Paris and taught at the University of California, Los Angeles, describes the hardware architecture and the processing he sought to implement in order to produce a BCI through electroencephalographic signals. In 1971, Eberhard Fetz had already shown that it was possible to train a monkey to voluntarily control cortical motor activity by providing visual information according to discharge rate [FET 71]. These two references show that since that time, BCIs could be implemented in the form of invasive or non-invasive brain activity measurements, that is, measurements of brain activity at the neural or scalp levels. For a more

Introduction written by Maureen CLERC, Laurent BOUGRAIN and Fabien LOTTE.

comprehensive history of BCIs, the reader may refer to the following articles: [LEB 06, VAA 09].

Although BCIs have been present in the field of research for over 40 years, they have only recently come to the media's attention, often described in catchy headlines such as "writing through thought is possible" or "a man controls a robot arm by thinking". Beyond announcements motivated by journalists' love for novelty or by scientists and developers' hopes of attracting the attention of the public and of potential funding sources, what are the real possibilities for BCIs within and outside research labs?

This book seeks to pinpoint these technologies somewhere between reality and fiction, and between super-human fantasies and real scientific challenges. It also describes the scientific tools that make it possible to infer certain aspects of a person's mental state by surveying brain activity in real time, such as a person's interest in a given element of a computer screen or the will to make a certain gesture. This book also details the material and software elements involved in the process and explores patients' expectations and feedback and the actual number of people using BCIs.

I.2. Introduction to BCIs

Designing a BCI is a complex and difficult task that requires knowledge of several disciplines such as computer science, electrical engineering, signal processing, neuroscience and psychology. BCIs, whose architecture is summarized in Figure 1.1, are closed loop systems usually composed of six main stages: brain activity recording, preprocessing, feature extraction, classification, translation into a command and feedback:

– *Brain activity recording* makes it possible to acquire raw signals that reflect the user's brain activity [WOL 06]. Different kinds of measuring devices can be used, but the most common one is electroencephalography (EEG) as shown in Figure I.1;

– *Preprocessing* consists of cleaning up and removing noise from measured signals in order to keep only the relevant information they contain [BAS 07];

– *Feature extraction* consists of describing signals in terms of a small number of relevant variables called "features" [BAS 07]; for example, an EEG signal's strength on some sensors and on certain frequencies may count as a feature;

– *Classification* associates a class to a set of features drawn from the signals within a certain time window [LOT 07]. This class corresponds to a type of identified brain activity pattern (for example the imagined movement of the left or right hand). A classification algorithm is known as a "classifier";

– *Translation into a command* associates a command with a given brain activity pattern identified in the user's brain signals. For example, when imagined movement of the left hand is identified, it can be translated into the command: "move the cursor on the screen toward the left". This command can then be used to control a given application, such as a text editor or a robot [KÜB 06];

– *Feedback* is then provided to the user in order to inform him or her about the brain activity pattern that was observed and/or recognized. The objective is to help the user learn to modulate brain activity and thereby improve his or her control of the BCI. Indeed, controlling a BCI is a skill that must often be learned [NEU 10].

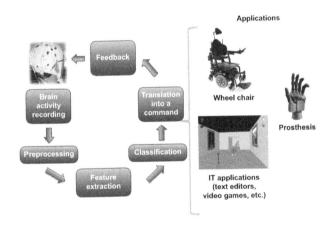

Figure I.1. *Architecture of a BCI working in real time, with some examples of applications*

Two stages are usually necessary in order to use a BCI: (1) an offline calibration stage, during which the system settings are determined, and (2) an online operational stage, during which the system recognizes the user's brain activity patterns and translates them into application commands. The BCI research community is currently searching for solutions to help avoid the costly offline calibration stage (see, for example, [KIN 14, LOT 15]).

I.2.1. *Taxonomy of BCIs*

BCIs can often be classified into different categories according to their properties. In particular, they can be classified as active, reactive or passive; as synchronous or asynchronous; as dependent or independent; and as invasive, non-invasive or hybrid. We will review the definition of those categories, which can be combined when describing a BCI (for example a BCI can be active, asynchronous and non-invasive at the same time):

– *Active/reactive/passive* [ZAN 11b]: an active BCI is a BCI whose user is actively employed by carrying out voluntary mental tasks. For example, a BCI that uses imagined hand movement as mental command is an active BCI. A reactive BCI employs the user's brain reactions to given stimuli. BCIs based on evoked potentials are considered reactive BCIs. Finally, a BCI that is not used to voluntarily control an application through mental commands, but that instead passively analyzes the user's mental state in real time, is considered a passive BCI. An application monitoring a user's mental load in real time to adapt a given interface is also a passive BCI;

– *Synchronous/asynchronous* [MAS 06]: user–system interaction phases may be determined by the system. In such a case, the user can only control a BCI at specific times. That kind of system is considered a synchronous BCI. If interaction is allowed at any time, the interface is considered asynchronous;

– *Dependent/independent* [ALL 08]: a BCI is considered independent if it does not depend on motor control. It is considered dependent in the opposite case. For example, if the user has to move his or her eyes in order to observe stimuli in a reactive BCI, then BCI is dependent (it depends on the user's ocular montricity). If the user can control a BCI without any movement at all, even ocular, the BCI is independent;

– *Invasive/non-invasive*: as specified above, invasive interfaces use data measured from within the body (most commonly from the cortex), whereas non-invasive interfaces acquire surface data, that is, data gathered on or around the head;

– *Hybrid* [PFU 10]: different neurophysiological markers may be used to pilot a BCI. When markers of varied natures are combined in the same BCI, it is considered hybrid. For example, a BCI that uses both imagined hand movement and brain responses to stimuli is considered hybrid. A system that combines BCI commands and non-cerebral commands (e.g. muscular signals) or more traditional interaction mechanisms (for example a mouse) is also considered hybrid. In sum, a hybrid BCI is a BCI that combines brain signals with other signals (that may or may not emanate from the brain).

I.2.2. *BCI applications*

Throughout the last decade, BCIs have proven to be extremely promising, especially for handicapped people (in particular for quadriplegic people suffering from locked-in syndrome and stroke patients), since several international scientific results have shown that it is possible to produce written text or to control prosthetics and wheelchairs with brain activity. More recently, BCIs have also proven to be interesting for people in good health, with, for example, applications in video games, and more generally for interaction with any automated system (robotics, home automation, etc.). Finally, researchers have shown that it is also possible to use BCIs passively in order to measure a user's mental state (for example stress, concentration or tiredness) in real time and regulate or adapt their environment in response to that state.

I.2.3. *Other BCI systems*

Let us now examine some systems that are generally related to BCIs. Neuroprostheses are systems that link an artificial device to the nervous system. Upper limb myoelectric prostheses analyze electric neuromuscular signals to identify movements that the robotic limb will carry out. Neuroprostheses are not BCIs if they do not employ brain activity, but rather, the peripheral nervous system activity. Exoskeletons also make it possible to bring life to a limb by equipping it with mechanical reinforcement, but to date they are very seldom activated by brain activity[1]. Cochlear implants and

---

1 However, the MindWalker project has started research in that direction; see https://mindwalker-project.eu/.

artificial retinas can be compared to neuroprostheses since they connect a device that replaces a defective organ with the central nervous system. However, these kinds of implants differ from BCIs in their directionality, since they do not measure neural activity, but rather stimulate it artificially.

I.2.4. Terminology

Several other terms are employed to refer to BCIs. In this regard, the term "brain–machine interface" refers to the same idea, although the term is more often used when the brain measurements are invasive. Although more rarely, the term "direct neural interface" is also sometimes used to designate BCIs. In this book, the term "brain–computer interface" will be employed because it underscores the idea that the processing chain is not fixed; this is to say that the system may adapt to evolutions in brain signals and the user's preferences through learning. The acronym BCI will also largely be used throughout the book, since it is the most commonly employed.

I.3. Book presentation

This book seeks to give an account of the current state of advances in BCIs by describing in detail the most common methods for designing and using them. Each chapter is written by specialists in the field and is presented in the most accessible way possible in order to address as large an audience as possible. This book, Volume 2 (Technology and Applications) follows Volume 1 (Foundation and Methods).

I.3.1. Volume 2: Technology and Applications

BCI applications are abundant. Part 1 of the book, entitled "Fields of Application", focuses on applications in the clinical and video-game fields. The scope of clinical applications includes consciousness disorders, motor rehabilitation, verbal communication and presurgical diagnosis of epilepsy. Examining these applications makes it possible to better understand the future and current limits of BCIs.

The Part 2, entitled "Practical Aspects of BCI Implementation" explains the inherent difficulties of this task. This section's first chapter (Chapter 6) studies the expression of patients' needs, which drives the development of BCIs devoted to them. Next, we move on to study platforms that employ EEG. The role that sensors play in this technology is explained, as well as the material and software requirements they involve. Finally, some recommendations for developing EEG experiments are presented.

The Part 3, entitled "Step by Step Guide to BCI Design with OpenViBE" explores the software implementation and execution of the methods proposed in this book. It first presents the main existing software platforms, placing special emphasis on OpenViBE, an open source software that makes it possible to quickly design BCIs and to perform real-time processing for neuroscience[2]. The following chapters illustrate several practical applications through OpenViBE, allowing readers to experiment with the concepts presented in the book by downloading scenarios and signals, or even to begin their own research in the field.

The book ends with Part 4 entitled "Societal Challenges and Perspectives", which opens up the debate about the use of BCIs from ethical, philosophical and societal perspectives. The insights that the humanities and societal sciences can bring to the field of BCIs are extremely important as not to lose sight of the fact that new technologies must always be developed with the greatest possible respect for animals, humans and society at large.

I.3.2. *Reading guide*

This book is intended for anyone seeking to understand BCIs, their origins, how they work, how they are used and the challenges they face. It may prove useful for people approaching the field in order to carry out research (researchers, engineers, PhD students, postdoctoral fellows) but also for present and future users (patients, medical practitioners, video game developers and artists), as well as for decision makers (investors, insurance experts and legal experts).

In order to facilitate the reading of this multidisciplinary book, we have provided an icon signaling the scope of each chapter's content. Chapters that are essential for understanding how BCIs work are denoted with ♥ . Those

---

2 http://openvibe.inria.fr.

chapters compose a common core of indispensable knowledge, which can be complemented by more specialized notions in:

– neuroscience 🧠

– math and computer science ⚡

– clinical fields ⚕

– technological fields ⚙

– societal fields ⚖

We suggest the following reading combinations according to readers' profile or to their field of specialization:

– general public: ♥

– patients: ♥ + ⚕ + ⚖

– medical/clinical practitioners: ♥ + ⚕ + 🧠

– neuropsychologists, cognitive neuroscientists: ♥ + 🧠 + ⚙

– mathematicians, computer scientists: ♥ + ⚡

– electrical engineers, mechatronic engineers: ♥ + ⚙ + ⚡

– investors, insurance experts and legal practitioners: ♥ + ⚖

I.4. Acknowledgments

This book is the collective work of a very large number of colleagues from very different disciplines, which would not have been possible without their contributions. We would like, therefore, to thank all the authors, and to all the colleagues and friends who have helped us in writing this book. We are indebted to Flora Lotte for creating the cover illustration.

I.5. Bibliography

[ALL 08] ALLISON B., MCFARLAND D., SCHALK G. *et al.*, "Towards an independent Brain–Computer Interface using steady state visual evoked potentials", *Clinical Neurophysiology*, vol. 119, no. 2, pp. 399–408, 2008.

[BAS 07] BASHASHATI A., FATOURECHI M., WARD R.K. *et al.*, "A survey of signal processing algorithms in Brain–Computer Interfaces based on electrical brain signals", *Journal of Neural Engineering*, vol. 4, no. 2, pp. R35–57, 2007.

[FET 71] FETZ E.E., FINOCCHIO D.V., "Operant conditioning of specific patterns of neural and muscular activity", *Science*, vol. 174, 1971.

[KÜB 06] KÜBLER A., MUSHAHWAR V., HOCHBERG L. *et al.*, "BCI meeting 2005-workshop on clinical issues and applications", *IEEE Transactions on Neural Systems and Rehabilitation Engineering*, vol. 14, no. 2, pp. 131–134, 2006.

[KIN 14] KINDERMANS P.-J., TANGERMANN M., MÜLLER K.-R. *et al.*, "Integrating dynamic stopping, transfer learning and language models in an adaptive zero-training ERP speller", *Journal of Neural Engineering*, vol. 11, no. 3, 2014.

[LEB 06] LEBEDEV M., NICOLELIS M., "Brain-machine interfaces: past, present and future", *Trends in Neurosciences*, vol. 29, no. 9, pp. 536–546, 2006.

[LOT 07] LOTTE F., CONGEDO M., LÉCUYER A. *et al.*, "A review of classification algorithms for EEG-based Brain–Computer Interfaces", *Journal of Neural Engineering*, vol. 4, pp. R1–R13, 2007.

[LOT 15] LOTTE F., "Signal processing approaches to minimize or suppress calibration time in oscillatory activity-based Brain–Computer Interfaces", *Proceedings of the IEEE*, vol. 103, no. 6, pp. 871–890, 2015.

[MAS 06] MASON S., KRONEGG J., HUGGINS J. *et al.*, "Evaluating the performance of self-paced BCI technology", report, Neil Squire Society, 2006.

[NEU 10] NEUPER C., PFURTSCHELLER G., "Neurofeedback Training for BCI Control", in GRAIMANN B., PFURTSCHELLER G., ALLISON B. (eds), *Brain–Computer Interfaces*, Springer, 2010.

[PFU 10] PFURTSCHELLER G., ALLISON B.Z., BAUERNFEIND G. *et al.*, "The hybrid BCI", *Frontiers in Neuroscience*, vol. 4, p. 3, 2010.

[VAA 09] VAADIA E., BIRBAUMER N., "Grand challenges of Brain–Computer Interfaces in the years to come", *Frontiers in Neuroscience*, vol. 3, no. 2, pp. 151–154, 2009.

[VID 73] VIDAL J.J., "Toward direct brain–computer communication", *Annual Review of Biophysics and Bioengineering*, vol. 2, no. 1, pp. 157–180, 1973.

[WOL 06] WOLPAW J., LOEB G., ALLISON B. *et al.*, "BCI Meeting 2005 – workshop on signals and recording methods", *IEEE Transaction on Neural Systems and Rehabilitation Engineering*, vol. 14, no. 2, pp. 138–141, 2006.

[ZAN 11] ZANDER T., KOTHE C., "Towards passive Brain–Computer Interfaces: applying Brain–Computer Interface technology to human-machine systems in general", *Journal of Neural Engineering*, vol. 8, 2011.

PART 1

Fields of Application

Brain–Computer Interfaces in Disorders of Consciousness

1.1. Introduction

The notion of an altered state of consciousness describes a large spectrum of pathological states in which the patient is not able to interact with his or her environment by means of speech or gesture. Even if there remain active residual cognitive processes, or if the patient retains some degree of self or environmental awareness, he or she is unable to communicate. These minimal fragments of consciousness can pass unobserved clinically due to motor deficits, sensory disorders, fatigability, cognitive disorders or fluctuations in wakefulness. Caring for patients with altered states of consciousness presents challenges at multiple different levels, not just ethical, but practical, human, and economical, affecting everything from diagnosis to treatment-related decision making. Today, research on altered states of consciousness is a dynamic field of neuroscience with the two-part objective of shedding light on poorly understood neural mechanisms of consciousness, and finding ways to assess patients' levels of consciousness or even restore basic communication whenever possible.

The purpose of this chapter is to provide a brief overview of studies in electrophysiology and neuroimaging that represent advances in terms of both

Chapter written by Jérémie MATTOUT, Jacques LUAUTÉ, Julien JUNG and Dominique MORLET.

care for patients with altered states of consciousness and the way that we view these patients, followed by a presentation of the most recent works performed in this field together with a future outlook based on brain–computer interface (BCI) techniques. In the first section, we show how resting brain signals and passive responses to stimuli can provide the basis for a hierarchical approach to the functional assessment of patients, from the prognosis of coma awakening to the differential diagnosis between different levels of consciousness. In the second section, we present paradigms for eliciting voluntary participation from the patient. The goal of these so-called "active" paradigms is to determine the patient's level of consciousness, as well as his or her capacity to cooperate. Finally, in the third section, we show how the ability to measure brain function in real time could soon make it possible to monitor patients' cognitive functions for diagnostic purposes, restore some form of communication with certain patients and perhaps even assist in their rehabilitation.

1.2. Altered states of consciousness: etiologies and clinical features

1.2.1. *From coma to awakening*

Coma is defined as a severe disorder of consciousness with full loss of awareness and the incapacity to respond to external prompts. Coma occurs following significant brain lesions that are usually the result of traumatic brain injury or cerebral anoxia, but may also arise from other origins such as metabolic, infectious or toxic disorders. Coma is characterized by functional alterations to attention and wakefulness mechanisms in the ascending reticular formation [ZEM 97]. Both the ability to wake (arousal) and the substance of consciousness (awareness) are lost. This acute phase of coma may last from several days to several weeks, during which the future progression of the coma is difficult to predict. If a patient survives the acute phase of the coma, he/she enters a phase in which the eyes are open with the appearance of wakefulness, but with no communication. If no objective signs of a reaction to stimuli are observed, the patient is said to be in a vegetative state (VS, or "unresponsive wakefulness syndrome", see [LAU 10]). In some cases, this VS can last for months or even years – this state is given the name of permanent vegetative state (see [LAU 04]). If the patient is able to follow simple commands or shows purposeful non-reflex behavior, the state is described as a minimally conscious state (MCS, see [GIA 02]). MCS can refer to a wide range of situations, depending on the nature and the extent of the observed responses. For this reason, some authors distinguish between MCS+ for patients with responses said to be high level (e.g. intelligible verbalization) and MCS- for patients with only low-level responses (e.g. localization of a pain stimulus) [BRU 11].

In the best-case scenario after awakening from coma, the patient recovers to a fully conscious state, with variable degrees of long-term functional consequences. The potential to improve relational capabilities and the timescales of these improvements vary strongly from patient to patient. They are in particular strongly linked to the etiology of the coma. The clinical progression of traumatic comas is generally more favorable than that of anoxic comas, with a faster and stronger recovery of consciousness. One very specific and infrequent postcoma state is locked-in syndrome (LIS, see [BAU 79]), which arises as a result of lesions on the brainstem. This is not a consciousness disorder, as patients awaken from coma fully conscious, but with full paralysis in all voluntary muscles except for the eyelids. Patients' cognitive abilities generally remain intact, but their means of communication are extremely limited, or even non-existent (complete locked-in). Degenerative neurological diseases such as amyotrophic lateral sclerosis (ALS) can also lead to a LIS after paralysis develops progressively in the patient's muscles without affecting his/her consciousness [HAY 03].

1.2.2. *The importance of differential diagnosis*

In a postcoma state, wakefulness is restored but the capacity to interact with others, self-awareness and awareness of surroundings might remain affected to a greater or lesser extent. The patient's state can be thought of as part of a continuum of states of consciousness ranging from fully non-responsive (VS) to a regular state of consciousness (LIS), with MCSs in between.

Establishing a differential diagnosis between VS and MCS, or in other words discerning the presence of some conscious awareness in patients unable to communicate, is particularly crucial. The right diagnosis is the first step toward the right course of treatment. An optimal regime of care should involve interacting with the patient whenever possible, for both basic everyday life situations and consequence-heavy decision making. Clinical assessment involves observing the patient's spontaneous behavior as well as behavioral changes in response to various stimuli. The goal is to detect a motor response consistent with the given command, an oriented response to sound or pain, an intelligible verbalization or visual tracking or fixation, all of which are signs of emerging consciousness. The differential diagnosis between VS and MCS is somewhat unreliable, as it is difficult to distinguish subtle indications of consciousness from purely automatic responses, and because of the limitations posed by the patient's state. It has been estimated that up to 43% of patients with disorders of consciousness may have been incorrectly diagnosed as vegetative [SCH 09]. Indeed, these patients can suffer from peripheral or cortical sensory deficits, neuromuscular deficits and other pathological conditions that disguise their state of consciousness. Assessment is repeated multiple times to account for possible fluctuations in wakefulness. Carefully structured scoring tests have been validated in an attempt to standardize this clinical evaluation process. One commonly used test is the Coma Recovery Scale Revised [GIA 04, SEE 10], which explores the patient's auditive, visual, motor and oromotor/verbal capacities in depth, as well as communication and wakefulness. The application of these kinds of test should improve the precision of the diagnostic process, but due to the difficulties described above, a standard measure of consciousness does not exist.

1.3. Functional assessment of patients with altered states of consciousness (passive paradigms)

1.3.1. *Prognosis of coma outcome*

For therapeutic, ethical and economical reasons, establishing a prognosis for both survival and awakening during the acute phase of coma is the most urgent medical objective. The prognosis depends on the etiology of the coma, the severity and extent of brain lesions, and the patient's clinical functional state. The criterion used to evaluate prognostic techniques is the clinical outcome of the patient 6 months or 1 year after coma onset. Classically, patient states after coma are evaluated according to the Glasgow Outcome Scale [JEN 75], which originally comprised three levels of awakening (no disability, moderate or severe disability), VS and death. This system has the benefit of being simple, but although it may be used to describe the functional state and overall level of dependency of the patient, it does not provide further information about potential intermediate disorders of consciousness such as MCSs [GIA 02].

1.3.1.1. *A multimodal approach in search of objective criteria*

For many years, the prognosis of coma was based on a collection of clinical observations and tests performed with anatomical neuroimaging and electrophysiology. The techniques applied in routine clinical procedures are particularly effective at predicting the most unfavorable developments (persistent coma or death). The most commonly used methods in the context of clinical assessment during the acute phase are the pupillary light reflex and the Glasgow Coma Scale [TEA 74, YOU 09]. The latter is based on ocular, verbal and motor responses. A patient who does not open his/her eyes and neither responds nor produces a motor response is given the minimum score of 3. A healthy, conscious subject receives a score of 15. Anatomical neuroimaging (by X-rays, computed tomography scan or by magnetic resonance imaging (MRI)) has excellent spatial resolution. It allows the localization and severity of cortical lesions to be assessed and any damage to the basal ganglia to be detected [YOU 09, GRE 14]. Diffusion MRI (diffusion-tensor imaging, (DTI)), a biomarker of the severity of damage to white matter bundles, was recently used to successfully establish a prognosis for traumatic [GAL 12] and anoxic comas [LUY 12].

1.3.1.2. *The essential role of electrophysiology*

Electrophysiology offers excellent temporal resolution, which facilitates an approach to the patient's functional state [GUE 10]. It is non-invasive and inexpensive, and can be applied directly at the patient's bedside by means of scalp electrodes. The electrophysiological tests routinely applied with comatose patients are resting electroencephalograms (EEG) and evoked potentials (EPs).

Resting EEG is an indicator of cortical electrical activity. Its visual inspection is commonly used in intensive care units to identify typical scenarios with unfavorable prognosis ("malignant" EEGs, which include isoelectric patterns, strongly discontinuous patterns, patterns with periodic epileptic graphoelements and patterns with stationary slow waves indicating defective thalamocortical coupling). Conversely, signs of a good prognosis include EEG traces that are only slightly slowed, with graphoelements indicative of sleep, fluctuating over time and/or reactive to auditory or nociceptive stimuli. However, there is a wide range of intermediate situations in which visual inspection is not very informative for the prognosis.

EPs characterize modifications in electric brain activity in response to sensory stimuli. As they have very low amplitude relative to background EEG, EPs are identified by averaging the signals over repeated stimuli. Components are characterized by their poststimulus latency. Early latencies indicate sensory processing at subcortical and cortical levels. Cognitive processes evoke later responses and are referred to as event-related potentials (ERPs). Somatosensory cortical responses (somatosensory EPs (SEPs), approximately 30 ms after stimulus onset), and to a lesser extent short-latency brainstem auditory evoked responses (BAEPs, within 10 ms poststimulus) and middle-latency primary cortical auditory responses (MLAEPs, within 100 ms) are interpreted as strongly predictive of unfavorable developments when absent. Hence, in axonic comas, SEPs are used to identify patients prone to high mortality rate and possibly guide a decision to limit active therapeutics [MAD 96]. Traumatic comas are less black-and-white. An observed absence of SEPs may still be compatible with favorable developments, particularly in children [JAV 12]. Focal lesions can modify these cortical potentials without endangering vital processes. Conversely, the presence of SEP and/or MLAEP components in a coma does not guarantee that consciousness will recover [LOG 03].

1.3.1.3. *The benefit of event-related potentials*

For over 20 years, the absence of primary sensory EPs (in particular, SEPs) in comas has been used to predict unfavorable developments. More recently, interest has grown in "cognitive" EPs with later latencies (ERPs) in comatose patients, with the expectation that they might prove useful for predicting favorable outcomes [LEW 06, MOR 14]. Auditory paradigms with more sophisticated stimuli than the simple clicks used for BAEPs and MLAEPs evoke responses that reflect the successive cortical stages of information processing. One commonly employed paradigm is the "oddball" paradigm, which supplies repeated (standard) sounds that are occasionally randomly replaced by other (deviant) sounds. This paradigm appeals to both the encoding of acoustic input in the auditory cortex, indexed by the fronto-central N1 sensory response around 100 ms [NÄÄ 87], and an automatic mechanism for detecting the violation of an established pattern, indexed by the mismatch negativity (MMN). The MMN appears around

120 ms and has generators in the auditory and frontal cortices [NAA 78, GIA 90]. Its presence during coma is a very specific marker of awakening [KAN 93, KAN 96, FIS 99, FIS 04, FIS 06]. In postcoma states, it is a strong marker of improvement [KOT 05, WIJ 07]. Finally, the infrequent occurrence of an unexpected stimulus in an *oddball* paradigm triggers attention orienting, characterized by the *novelty* P3 component between 250 and 300 ms [FRI 01]. Moreover, calling the patient's first name among other simple sounds triggers a particularly robust *novelty* P3. The detection of this wave during coma is strongly correlated with awakening 3 months after coma onset [FIS 08].

1.3.2. *Functional patterns in postcoma states*

Experimental study of conscious perception in healthy subjects has shown that it is associated with the activation of large networks of interconnected brain areas [ZEM 01]. A number of studies in neuroimaging and electrophysiology have explored brain function in postcoma states, and have attempted to identify functional patterns that might be used to distinguish patients diagnosed as minimally conscious (MCS) from patients with no signs of consciousness (VS).

Positron emission tomography (PET) had previously shown that glucose metabolism is globally diminished in patients in a VS as compared to healthy subjects [BEU 03], with particular deficits in corticocortical and thalamocortical connectivity [LAU 99]. DTI shows significant differences between VS and MCS in white matter, in the subcortex and the thalamus [FER 12]. In VS patients, auditory or pain stimuli only activate the sensory cortices, as observed with PET [LAU 00, LAU 02] and functional MRI (fMRI) [DI 07], whereas MCS patients exhibit stronger connectivity between secondary auditory regions and temporal and frontal associative cortices, as observed with PET [BOL 04, BOL 05]. An fMRI study on 41 patients showed that hierarchically assessing speech processing, from low-level hearing to high-level comprehension, is beneficial for both diagnosis and prognosis [COL 09]. The activation of the default mode network by means of personal questions is stronger in MCS than in VS patients [QIN 10, HUA 14]. The deactivation of this network after stimulation is thought to indicate the interruption of introspective processes. It was found to be reduced in MCS patients and absent in VS patients [CRO 11].

Recent quantitative methods enable the assessment of the frequency content of resting EEG and its fluctuations in time and space. In group studies, these methods succeeded in differentiating vegetative from MCS patients (see [LEH 12b] for a review). Disordered states of consciousness are associated with slowed basic rhythms. VS compared to MCS patients show an increase in the lowest frequencies (1–4 Hz delta band) and a decrease in the alpha band (8–12 Hz) [LEH 12a, SIT 14, FIN 12]. Patients' behavioral assessments are strongly negative correlated with brain signal complexity, which   can   be   identified   by   various   measures   of entropy [SIT 14, GOS 11, WU 11]. A reduction in brain connectivity, as evaluated by different approaches, is more strongly apparent in VS than MCS patients [LEH 12a, KIN 13]. Effective connectivity may also be observed with transcranial magnetic stimulation (TMS) in combination with high-density EEG. The perturbational complexity index was recently suggested as a measure of complexity of brain responses to TMS perturbations in order to evaluate a patient's level of consciousness [CAS 13].

For EPs, we saw earlier that the presence of an MMN in response to deviant stimuli indicates the preservation (or recovery) of elementary automatic processes and is a predictor of a potentially favorable outcome. However,   MMN   alone   is   not   sufficient   to   assess   patients' consciousness [MOR 14]. A more in-depth exploration based on realistic generative models of the neural dynamics underlying these evoked responses ("dynamic causal modeling") compared the effective connectivity of VS and MCS patients, and control subjects, showing disruptions to top-down connections (from frontal to temporal cortex) in the group of vegetative patients [BOL 11]. Event-related potentials with higher latencies, in particular the P300 and N400 components, have also been tested with the objective of detecting residual cognitive functions in patients with altered states of consciousness. The P300 (or P3, around 300 ms after stimulus onset) can be evoked by infrequent stimuli. It contains at least two subcomponents, the frontocentral P3a associated with involuntary detection processes, and the parietal P3b associated with attention-related differentiation [POL 07]. The P3b is the typical signature of attention-related processing when the deviant stimulus is designated as the target, but it can also arise without instructions when the deviant stimulus is particularly infrequent and noticeable, or is associated with some special meaning [FRI 01]. In healthy subjects, calling the subject's first name triggers a P3, both while awake and while asleep, when presented as part of a series of other names [PER 99] or simple sounds [HOL 06, EIC 12, EIC 13]. When presented in a series of simple sounds, it triggers a *novelty* P3, which indicates attention orienting. We saw earlier that the presence of this wave during a coma is a good indicator of favorable outcome [FIS 08]. In some patients with persistent disorders of consciousness, it was observed but did not correlate with the level of consciousness established by behavioral assessment [FIS 10]. When spoken together with other first names, the subject's first name triggers semantic recognition processes and evokes an augmented P3 that has been observed primarily in patients with minimal states of consciousness and patients with LIS, but which has also been observed in some VSs [PER 06]. The N400 is evoked by words (read or heard) inconsistent with their semantic context (word out of place in a sentence, pairs of non-matching words), while awake [KUT 00] and asleep [PER 02]. This response was observed in patients with minimal states of consciousness, but also in patients thought to be in a VS [KOT 05, SCH 04]. A recent study investigated the response to words presented in semantically matching and non-matching pairs to a group of patients (15 VS and 15 MCS) [ROH 15]. The study was able to distinguish a response resembling a N400 in both groups, and a more delayed parietal positivity in the MCS group only, suggesting that the N400 might represent an unconscious response to semantic violations, whereas delayed parietal positivity might represent conscious processes. Both of the two components were difficult to detect on an individual level, even in healthy, conscious subjects. Still, it is interesting to note that the three patients in which they were successfully identified were minimally conscious, and that two of them subsequently regained consciousness.

Long-latency potentials (P3 and N400) are indicative of cognitive processes that are activated without explicitly demanding the patient's attention. These potentials appear as false positives when the clinical behavioral assessment is considered as the ground truth. The existence of these false positives highlights the ambiguity of the results. On the one hand, we know that clinical observations tend to underestimate the level of consciousness of some patients. On the other hand, while the mechanisms underlying these responses have been studied in depth in healthy subjects, they are less known in patients with disorders of consciousness. For example, a recent study based on oscillatory responses to out-of-place words showed that these words had a specific effect on MCS patients that was absent in VS patients but distinct from the effect observed in healthy subjects [SCH 11].

The neuroimaging and electrophysiology tests presented above observe the brain in a resting state or in response to stimuli. They allow the functional state of the patients' brain to be evaluated and are capable of detecting cognitive functions that are more or less intact. Their validity as a clinical tool for assessing the patient's individual level of consciousness depends on both the reliability of the reference diagnosis based on clinical observations, and our understanding of conscious perception in healthy subjects.

1.4. Advanced approaches to assessing consciousness (active paradigms)

"Can you hear me?" Only an explicit answer from the patient would prove that he/she has heard and understood the question, and therefore is conscious. If the patient is unable to answer by behavioral means, his/her cerebral responses may be observed instead. These responses should be voluntary, and not the result of a reflex. They need to unambiguously prove that the patient is deliberately participating in the task and has understood the instructions. To this effect, recent studies have attempted to implement "active" paradigms in patients with disorders of consciousness, with the goal of evaluating their level of consciousness. The general idea is to compare two conditions corresponding to two different mental tasks. Motor imagery tasks and stimulus-counting tasks have been suggested. Neuroimaging (fMRI) and electrophysiology (EEG and ERPs) techniques have been applied in this context.

The first demonstration was provided by Owen *et al.* in a vegetative patient 5 months after severe head trauma [OWE 06]. The patient was asked to consecutively perform two mental imagery tasks, including one motor (playing tennis) and one spatial (moving from room to room within her house). fMRI showed persistent and distinct response patterns to each instruction during the 30 s of the task, similar to those observed individually in healthy subjects [BOL 07]. The patient had therefore understood the stated instructions and had responded. This result was reproduced in five patients (four VS and one MCS) among 54 (23 VS and 31 MCS) in a multicentric study [MON 10]. It should be noted that in two out of the four VS diagnosed patients who managed to willfully modulate their brain activity, additional clinical tests ultimately revealed evidence of consciousness that had previously been missed. Subsequently in one patient, answers to yes/no questions were successfully obtained by using the cerebral responses to the same tasks (tennis/spatial navigation) as a binary code. So far, classical forms of bedside communication had not been possible with this patient. A variant of the fMRI motor imagery task was tested more recently on a small group of patients [BAR 11, BAR 12]. The patients were instructed to alternate between imagining themselves swimming and resting. In 14 healthy subjects, blood oxygen level dependent responses in the supplementary motor area were successfully used to identify periods when the subject was performing the task and to answer binary or multiple-choice questions [BAR 11]. The results obtained in six of the patients highlight the dissociation between the results of motor imagery and behavioral assessments. They also show the utility of extending the analysis to the whole brain, rather than simply focusing on motor regions [BAR 12]. Indeed, cortical reorganization can occur in patients with severe traumatic lesions.

Motor mental imagery can also modulate EEG power in the *mu* (7–13 Hz) and *beta* (13–30 Hz) bands over motor regions (see Chapter 4 of Volume 1), In five control subjects and three patients, modulations of the EEG between 4 and 24 Hz were compared during a motor task (swimming), spatial navigation task (moving through the house) and resting. One MCS and one LIS patient managed to modulate their EEG, proving that they were performing the task, but these modulations were different from those observed in healthy subjects [GOL 11]. Another team performed the study with the instructions: "each time that you hear the sound, imagine clenching your right fist, then relax" and "imagine wiggling your toes, then relax". One initial study considered 16 patients diagnosed as vegetative. Three patients modulated their EEG consistently in response to instructions [CRU 11]. In a second study with 23 MCS patients, five did perform the task [CRU 12a]. The etiology of the coma appears to play an important role: the comas of the five patients able to perform the task were traumatic in origin. The results of the eight patients with other etiologies were all negative [CRU 12a]. A simplified version of this paradigm was successfully tested in a patient who had been in a VS for 12 years [CRU 12b]. Only four electrodes were used, and the instructions ("move your right/left hand", "relax") were often repeated in order to reduce the required mental effort. This simple 20-min EEG procedure, which managed to elicit willful responses from patients unable to communicate, could potentially be used routinely in clinics to assess consciousness.

Another way of revealing the capability of a patient to cooperate is to draw his/her attention to designated target stimuli among other stimuli. For instance, counting target stimuli involves components of attention and working memory that are believed to play key roles in conscious processes [ZEM 05]. In terms of event-related potentials, the response to target stimuli exhibits a parietal P3 [POL 07]. In another study, the stimulation paradigm was arranged as eight randomly presented names, including the patient's name [SCH 08]. During two phases of active listening, patients had to count the number of occurrences of a given name, or of their own name. The results were analyzed in groups of subjects (eight VS, 14 MCS and 12 control subjects) and individually. Like control subjects but unlike VS patients, MCS patients exhibited augmented P3 waves in response to target stimuli, suggesting willful participation in the counting task. This effect occurred later in the patients compared to the control subjects. On an individual level, the results were more nuanced, with only nine MCS patients producing significant responses to targets, in at least one of the active tasks. This poor result might be due to fatigue, or fluctuations in awareness, and the authors suggest that the recordings should be repeated to avoid false negatives [SCH 08].

A new oddball paradigm (given the name of "local-global" by its authors) allows two mechanisms elicited by the violation of a sequential rule to be highlighted [BEK 09]. The first mechanism identifies violations that are close in time, and is based on short-term sensory memory. It occurs automatically and is represented by the MMN. The second mechanism detects violations of the global structure of the sequence, further apart in time and therefore inaccessible to sensory memory. It requires the preceding stimuli to be actively maintained in working memory, and is represented by the P300 wave. In practice, the "local-global" paradigm is composed of successive chains of five brief stimuli, the first four of which are always identical. When the final stimulus breaks the pattern of the previous four, an MMN is evoked, whether or not the subject is paying attention to the stimuli ("local effect"). In each block, all consecutive chains are identical, except for 20% of them (deviant chains). In healthy subjects, a P3 is expected to be evoked by these "global" deviant chains when they are explicitly recognized and counted. However, if the subject's attention is engaged in a visual task, the chains that violate the global rule are not consciously perceived, and do not evoke a P3. When counting, this "global effect", which activates a large brain network as revealed with fMRI, is considered by the authors to be a neural signature of conscious processing. The "local-global" paradigm was initially tested with eight patients (four VS and four MCS). An automatic "local" effect was obtained in all patients, except for one VS patient. A conscious "global" effect (P3) was only observed in three MCS patients [BEK 09]. In a group of 22 patients diagnosed as vegetative, two patients responded positively to the "global" test. These two patients showed objective signs of consciousness 3 or 4 days later [FAU 11]. The specificity of the global effect as a measure of consciousness was confirmed by means of a series of 65 recordings performed in 49 coma and postcoma patients with varying etiologies [FAU 12]. The global effect was observed in seven of the 13 patients diagnosed as conscious, and in four of the 28 MCS patients. The poor sensitivity of the test (only 11 patients were responsive in the group of 41 non-vegetative patients) might be due to the fact that the test is highly demanding in terms of cognitive resources.

In summary, on the one hand, active paradigms confirm that some patients may be incorrectly identified as vegetative by clinical assessment; on the other hand, they require cognitive performances that may be out of reach of some conscious patients due to cognitive deficits inherently associated with the patients' lesions or temporary factors (level of wakefulness during the test). Determining the clinical validity of these tests is made difficult by the lack of a reference diagnosis [CRU 14].

An appropriate assessment of patients' brain functions should involve hierarchical sensory and cognitive tests followed by active paradigms, if possible repeated, so that patients who are able and willing to communicate by BCI may be accurately identified.

1.5. Toward the real-time use of functional markers

Active paradigms discussed in the previous section all rely on the willful modulation of brain activity, following a set of given instructions. Repeating this test makes it possible to establish with statistical significance whether the instructions were properly followed or not. This procedure can be used to establish that the patient is awake and conscious [OWE 06]. It can also serve as a tool for communication, allowing yes/no questions to be answered [MON 10].

1.5.1. *Real-time approaches to communication*

Thus, active paradigms possess all the ingredients of a BCI, except that they do not operate in real time. In this context, the purpose of a BCI would be to provide an operational tool, as simple and practical as possible, that may be used at the patient's bedside [LUA 15]. This is why the most commonly preferred technique is once again EEG [CRU 11]. Of course, similarly to other applications of BCI, the goal is to establish a line of communication (decode a response online) on the basis of a small number of signals, which are usually noisy. Several types of signals have already been explored in attempts to communicate with patients with disorders of consciousness. In this section, we will give three recent examples.

1.5.1.1. *Attention-related modulation of evoked auditory responses*

Lule *et al.* tested an auditory BCI based on the P300 wave and the principles of the *oddball* paradigm [LUL 13]. Sixteen control subjects and 18 patients were tested, of which two had been diagnosed with LIS, 13 with MCS and three with VS. After asking a question, four stimuli "yes", "no", "stop" and "go" were repeated in a cycle. The patients and subjects were asked to concentrate on the "yes" or "no", depending on the desired response. The target response was expected to produce a P300-type wave. A classifier was operated in real time to provide feedback informing the user of the selected answer. The BCI was calibrated prior to being used. Online, the control group achieved an average performance of 73% correct answers. One LIS patient achieved 60%, whereas none of the MCS or VS patients were able to communicate. An offline analysis made it possible to improve the performance of healthy subjects and of the two LIS patients, but on average no significant improvement was observed in the MCS and VS patients.

In a relatively similar study performed with 14 healthy subjects and two patients with ALS, Hill *et al.* showed that using words directly associated with the subject of the instruction (answer "yes" or "no") was more effective than using standard sounds such as beeps [HIL 14]. The performance achieved was around 77% of correct answers, both in the healthy subjects and the ALS patients. Note that both of these patients were still capable of communicating by other means, and that one of them was familiar with the usage of a visual BCI.

1.5.1.2. *Mental motor imagery*

Mental motor imagery is known for producing characteristic brain activity (desynchronization of the *mu* and *beta* frequency bands) in a way that is relatively similar to the activity produced when executing an actual movement [PFU 99]. Each effector's electrophysiological response has its own scalp topography when put into motion, whether mentally or physically, which may be used to distinguish a number of different commands, typically between 2 and 4 (see Chapter 4 of Volume 1). In general, these approaches require an initial calibration phase and voluntary participation from the user, similar to BCIs that use EPs.

The study by Cruse *et al.* mentioned above [CRU 11] was one of the pioneering studies in this field. Since then, two other studies, one offline and the other online, have continued to explore this kind of strategy.

The first study compared two relatively complex mental imagery tasks (doing sport and navigating through a familiar environment) with the task of attempting to move the feet and the task of performing passive movements with the feet (movements executed by the intervention of a third party) [HOR 14]. Six MCS patients participated in three recording sessions each. Although each task led at least once to classification results above chance level, these results could not be reproduced from session to session, and success rate varied from 64% to 80% for distinguishing between four different tasks.

With only three EEG sensors, the second study compared two tasks of mental motor imagery, one with the right hand, and one with the toes, in four MCS patients [COY 15]. Over several sessions, this study used an original approach to explore the impact of visual and auditory feedback on the online BCI performance, at least in three of the patients. Although no improvement over time could be proven, the performances, which were subject to strong fluctuations, sometimes significantly exceeded chance levels.

1.5.1.3. *Visual frequency markers*

A third well-known category of BCI that has recently been explored for communicating with patients with LIS or disorders of consciousness is the category of visual frequency markers (SSVEP, see Chapter 4 of Volume 1). This marking system is based on the repetition of a visual stimulus at a given frequency. The successive responses evoked by these stimuli produce a strong signal at the same frequency as the stimuli. This signal is known to be amplified when attention is focused on one such stream of stimuli.

One study recently tested a BCI with two commands, independent of the direction in which the subject is looking, based instead on the direction in which the subject's attention is focused, either toward yellow stimuli flashing at a frequency of 10 Hz, or at red stimuli flashing at a frequency of 14 Hz [LES 14]. The experiment showed that the absence of information associated with the direction in which the subject is looking led to a decrease in performance when distinguishing between the two options. Still, an online application of this interface allowed eight of 12 healthy subjects to answer yes/no questions with an average accuracy of 80%. By contrast, only one of the four LIS patients managed to communicate at a level significantly better than chance.

Finally, another study chose a hybrid visual paradigm, combining the principle of frequency markers with a P300-based approach. The objective was again to test the performance of a channel for binary communication in healthy subjects ($n = 4$), one LIS patient, but also MCS ($n = 3$) and VS ($n = 4$) patients [PAN 14]. The stimuli consisted of two pictures of faces presented simultaneously on screen, but flashing at different frequencies (6 and 7.5 Hz, respectively). One of the faces was unknown, whereas the other was the face of the BCI user. Moreover, a P300 wave could be generated by randomly and infrequently displaying a frame around the image. The dominant direction of the attentional focus in response to an explicit instruction was estimated by the combined analysis of two different types of EEG responses. While the four subjects in the control group achieved performance varying between 82% and 100%, the LIS patient achieved from 72% to 78%. Only one VS patient and one MCS patient achieved performance above chance level, namely between 66% and 78%.

1.5.2. *The benefit of BCIs in disorders of consciousness for purposes other than communication*

BCI technology now makes it possible to analyze brain activity in real time and provide feedback to the user. This allows us to imagine ways of providing means of communication to patients who are otherwise incapable of producing reproducible and interpretable voluntary actions. But the analysis of brain signals in real time can have other applications in the context of disorders of consciousness. We shall name three such applications.

First of all, real-time analysis of the resting EEG can supply markers associated with wakefulness, awareness and complexity [SIT 14], which can contribute to the diagnostic process, and additionally serve to indicate the opportune moment for testing an active paradigm or a BCI for communication.

In the context of customized medical care, real-time signal analysis, in particular of EEG, could also help to optimize the diagnosis and prognosis of VS and MCS patients. Indeed, beyond simply detecting evoked responses such as the MMN and the P300, measuring the modulations of these waves by voluntary (focusing the attention) or implicit (learning the frequency of a deviant sound) processes [LEC 15] could provide a more finely tuned and objective assessment. To achieve this, recent studies suggest that computational models of these evoked responses [OST 12, LIE 13] combined with a real-time approach could allow passive test protocols to be optimized for each individual [SAN 14].

Finally, BCIs pave the way for true closed-loop paradigms, in which the objective of sensory feedback is to facilitate the recovery of consciousness, or at the very least to improve functional markers. This would potentially be achieved over the course of a large number of sessions similar to neurofeedback protocols (see Chapter 13 of Volume 1).

1.6. Conclusion and future outlook

The clinical assessment of patients with disorders of consciousness is slowly integrating electrophysiological measures such as the analysis of resting EEG, and early-latency EPs, middle-latency EPs and other cognitive potentials such as MMN and P3. These measures have improved the process of establishing a prognosis for patients. Furthermore, more detailed and rigorous behavioral assessments have demonstrated uncertainties in the diagnostic process. Our primary objective remains to equip ourselves with objective measurement tools that will allow the functional state of patients to be assessed as precisely and reliably as possible. The studies reviewed in this chapter show that no single technique exists that can achieve this goal perfectly. Instead, a multimodal approach is now the preferred method for compiling a body of evidence containing behavioral, structural, functional, metabolic and electrophysiological information.

Just over 10 years ago, fMRI confirmed that relying on clinical assessment alone can cause diagnostic errors, showing that patients thought to be in VSs were potentially capable of responding to instructions by producing certain types of brain activity in a voluntary and reproducible manner [OWE 06]. The fallout of this study and its replications [MON 10] was spectacular, opening a new avenue of research with the goal of communicating with patients incapable of performing actions that can be interpreted as conscious. Paradoxically, it was fMRI, a technique that is seldom employed for BCIs, that set these events in motion. fMRI provides excellent spatial resolution. However, it is inconvenient, extremely limited in its use with this category of patients, and very expensive. For these reasons, subsequent research naturally turned toward less expensive and more practical bedside alternatives such as electrophysiology. A few initial studies have also considered the potential of functional near infrared spectroscopy [SOR 09].

BCIs appear to be the only alternative for overcoming the current limitations in assessing and communicating with these patients, and applications in this area are still in their infancy, with a vast amount of potential yet to be unlocked. Still, the first studies have highlighted the difficulty of the endeavor. BCIs that were implemented for simple, binary communication did not achieve the desired accuracy rate of 100% correct classification, even in healthy subjects. Also, when working with patients the performance is drastically reduced, yet the absence of a significant performance level cannot be interpreted as the absence of consciousness or of the capacity to respond [PET 15]. Today, we can say with relative certainty that any progress in the assessment of these patients will necessarily involve a combination of techniques, requiring repeated measures, or perhaps an optimized choice of when to perform optimized measurements, and the adaptation of BCI paradigms to suit each patient as best as possible [KÜB 14].

The most recent research in this area has shown that the best experimental protocols for revealing intact cognitive processes in patients remain to be discovered, which might potentially involve exploring the personal and emotional aspects of cognition. fMRI has recently shown that decoding techniques can be used to evaluate the perception of the emotional content of a film or a story [NAC 15]. With EEG, playing the patient's favorite music tracks before electrophysiological assessment could potentially allow the responses evoked by sounds in an *oddball* paradigm to be more easily detected [CAS 15].

1.7. Bibliography

[BAR 11] BARDIN J.C., FINS J.J., KATZ D. I. *et al.*, "Dissociations between behavioural and functional magnetic resonance imaging-based evaluations of cognitive function after brain injury", *Brain: A Journal of Neurology*, vol. 134, pp. 769–782, 2011.

[BAR 12] BARDIN J.C., SCHIFF N.D., VOSS H.U., "Pattern classification of volitional functional magnetic resonance imaging responses in patients with severe brain injury", *Archives in Neurology*, vol. 69, pp. 176–181, 2012.

[BAU 79] BAUER G., GERSTENBRAND F., RUMPL E., "Varieties of the locked-in syndrome", *Journal of Neurology*, vol. 221, pp. 77–91, 1979.

[BEK 09] BEKINSCHTEIN T.A., DEHAENE S., ROHAUT B. *et al.*, "Neural signature of the conscious processing of auditory regularities", *Proceedings of National Academy of Sciences USA*, vol. 106, pp. 171–189, 2009.

[BEU 03] BEUTHIEN-BAUMANN B., HANDRICK W., SCHMIDT T. *et al.*, "Persistent vegetative state: evaluation of brain metabolism and brain perfusion with PET and SPECT", *Nuclear Medicine Communications*, vol. 24, pp. 643–649, 2003.

[BOL 04] BOLY M., FAYMONVILLE M.E., PEIGNEUX P. *et al.*, "Auditory processing in severely brain injured patients: differences between the minimally conscious state and the persistent vegetative state", *Archives in Neurology*, vol. 61, pp. 233–238, 2004.

[BOL 05] BOLY M., FAYMONVILLE M.E., PEIGNEUX P. *et al.*, "Cerebral processing of auditory and noxious stimuli in severely brain injured patients: differences between VS and MCS", *Neuropsychological Rehabilitation*, vol. 15, pp. 283–289, 2005.

[BOL 07] BOLY M., COLEMAN M.R., DAVIS M.H. *et al.*, "When thoughts become action: an fMRI paradigm to study volitional brain activity in non-communicative brain injured patients", *Neuroimage*, vol. 36, pp. 979–992, 2007.

[BOL 11] BOLY M., GARRIDO M.I., GOSSERIES O. *et al.*, "Preserved feedforward but impaired top-down processes in the vegetative state", *Science*, vol. 332, pp. 858–862, 2011.

[BRU 11] BRUNO M.-A., VANHAUDENHUYSE A., THIBAUT A. *et al.*, "From unresponsive wakefulness to minimally conscious PLUS and functional locked-in syndromes: recent advances in our understanding of disorders of consciousness", *Journal of Neurology*, vol. 258, no. 7, pp. 1373–1384, 2011.

[CAS 13] CASALI A.G., GOSSERIES O., ROSANOVA M. *et al.*, "A theoretically based index of consciousness independent of sensory processing and behavior", *Science Translational Medicine*, vol. 5, p. 198ra105, 2013.

[CAS 15] CASTRO M., TILLMANN B., LUAUTÉ J. *et al.*, "Boosting cognition with music in patients with disorders of consciousness", *Neurorehabilitation and Neural Repair*, vol. 29, no. 8, pp. 734–742, 2015.

[COL 09] COLEMAN M.R., DAVIS M.H., RODD J.M. *et al.* "Towards the routine use of brain imaging to aid the clinical diagnosis of disorders of consciousness", *Brain: A journal of neurology*, vol. 132, pp. 2541–2552, 2009.

[COY 15] COYLE D., STOW J., MCCREADIE K. *et al.*, "Sensorimotor modulation assessment and brain-computer interface training in disorders of consciousness", *Archives of Physical Medicine and Rehabilitation*, vol. 96, no. 3, pp. S62–S70, 2015.

[CRO 11] CRONE J.S., LADURNER G., HOLLER Y. *et al.*, "Deactivation of the default mode network as a marker of impaired consciousness: an fMRI study", *PloS One*, vol. 6, p. e26373, 2011.

[CRU 11] CRUSE D., CHENNU S., CHATELLE C. *et al.*, "Bedside detection of awareness in the vegetative state: a cohort study", *Lancet*, vol. 378, pp. 2088–2094, 2011.

[CRU 12a] CRUSE D., CHENNU S., CHATELLE C. *et al.*, "Relationship between etiology and covert cognition in the minimally conscious state", *Neurology*, vol. 78, pp. 816–822, 2012.

[CRU 12b] CRUSE D., CHENNU S., FERNANDEZ-ESPEJO D. *et al.*, "Detecting awareness in the vegetative state: electroencephalographic evidence for attempted movements to command", *PloS One*, vol. 7, p. e49933, 2012.

[CRU 14] CRUSE D., GANTNER I., SODDU A. *et al.*, "Lies, damned lies and diagnoses: estimating the clinical utility of assessments of covert awareness in the vegetative state", *Brain Injury*, vol. 28, pp. 1197–1201, 2014.

[DI 07] DI H.B., YU S.M., WENG X.C. *et al.*, "Cerebral response to patient's own name in the vegetative and minimally conscious states", *Neurology*, vol. 68, pp. 895–899, 2007.

[EIC 12] EICHENLAUB J.-B., RUBY P., MORLET D., "What is the specificity of the response to the own first-name when presented as a novel in a passive oddball paradigm? An ERP study", *Brain Research*, vol. 1447, pp. 65–78, 2012.

[EIC 13] EICHENLAUB J.B., BERTRAND O., MORLET D. *et al.*, "Brain reactivity differentiates subjects with high and low dream recall frequencies during both sleep and wakefulness", *Cerebral Cortex*, vol. 24, pp. 1206–1215, 2013.

[FAU 11] FAUGERAS F., ROHAUT B., WEISS N. *et al.*, "Probing consciousness with event-related potentials in the vegetative state", *Neurology*, vol. 77, pp. 264–268, 2011.

[FAU 12] FAUGERAS F., ROHAUT B., WEISS N. *et al.*, "Event related potentials elicited by violations of auditory regularities in patients with impaired consciousness", *Neuropsychologia*, vol. 50, pp. 403–418, 2012.

[FER 12] FERNANDEZ-ESPEJO D., SODDU A., CRUSE D. *et al.*, "A role for the default mode network in the bases of disorders of consciousness", *Annals of Neurology*, vol. 72, pp. 335–343, 2012.

[FIN 12] FINGELKURTS A.A., FINGELKURTS A.A., BAGNATO S. *et al.*, "EEG oscillatory states as neuro-phenomenology of consciousness as revealed from patients in vegetative and minimally conscious states", *Consciousness and Cognition*, vol. 21, pp. 149–169, March 2012.

[FIS 99] FISCHER C., MORLET D., BOUCHET P. *et al.*, "Mismatch negativity and late auditory evoked potentials in comatose patients", *Clinical Neurophysiology*, vol. 110, pp. 1601–1610, 1999.

[FIS 04] FISCHER C., LUAUTÉ J., ADELEINE P. *et al.*, "Predictive value of sensory and cognitive evoked potentials for awakening from coma", *Neurology*, vol. 63, pp. 669–673, 2004.

[FIS 06] FISCHER C., LUAUTÉ J., NEMOZ C. *et al.*, "Improved prediction of awakening or nonawakening from severe anoxic coma using tree-based classification analysis", *Critical Care Medicine*, vol. 34, pp. 1520–1524, 2006.

[FIS 08] FISCHER C., DAILLER F., MORLET D., "Novelty P3 elicited by the subject's own name in comatose patients", *Clinical Neurophysiology*, vol. 119, pp. 2224–2230, October 2008.

[FIS 10] FISCHER C., LUAUTÉ J., MORLET D., "Event-related potentials (MMN and novelty P3) in permanent vegetative or minimally conscious states", *Clinical Neurophysiology*, vol. 121, pp. 1032–1042, 2010.

[FRI 01] FRIEDMAN D., CYCOWICZ Y.M., GAETA H., "The novelty P3: an event-related brain potential (ERP) sign of the brain's evaluation of novelty", *Neuroscience and Biobehavioral Reviews*, vol. 25, pp. 355–373, 2001.

[GAL 12] GALANAUD D., PERLBARG V., GUPTA R. *et al.*, "Assessment of white matter injury and outcome in severe brain trauma: a prospective multicenter cohort", *Anesthesiology*, vol. 117, pp. 1300–1310, December 2012.

[GIA 90] GIARD M.H., PERRIN F., PERNIER J. *et al.*, "Brain generators implicated in the processing of auditory stimulus deviance: a topographic event-related potential study", *Psychophysiology*, vol. 27, pp. 627–640, 1990.

[GIA 02] GIACINO J.T., ASHWAL S., CHILDS N. *et al.*, "The minimally conscious state: definition and diagnostic criteria", *Neurology*, vol. 58, pp. 349–353, 2002.

[GIA 04] GIACINO J.T., KALMAR K., WHYTE J., "The JFK coma recovery scale-revised: measurement characteristics and diagnostic utility", *Archives of Physical Medicine and Rehabilitation*, vol. 85, pp. 2020–2029, 2004.

[GOL 11] GOLDFINE A.M., VICTOR J.D., CONTE M.M. *et al.*, "Determination of awareness in patients with severe brain injury using EEG power spectral analysis", *Clinical Neurophysiology*, vol. 122, pp. 2157–2168, 2011.

[GOS 11] GOSSERIES O., SCHNAKERS C., LEDOUX D. *et al.*, "Automated EEG entropy measurements in coma, vegetative state/unresponsive wakefulness syndrome and minimally conscious state", *Functional Neurology*, vol. 26, pp. 25–30, 2011.

[GRE 14] GREER D.M., ROSENTHAL E.S., WU O., "Neuroprognostication of hypoxic-ischaemic coma in the therapeutic hypothermia era", *Nature Reviews Neurology*, vol. 10, pp. 190–203, 2014.

[GUE 10] GUERIT J.M., "Neurophysiological testing in neurocritical care", *Current Opinion in Critical Care*, vol. 16, pp. 98–104, 2010.

[HAY 03] HAYASHI H., OPPENHEIMER E.A., "ALS patients on TPPV: totally locked-in state, neurologic findings and ethical implications", *Neurology*, vol. 61, no. 1, pp. 135–137, 2003.

[HIL 14] HILL N.J., RICCI E., HAIDER S. *et al.*, "A practical, intuitive Brain–Computer interface for communicating 'yes' or 'no' by listening", *Journal of Neural Engineering*, vol. 11, no. 3, p. 035003, 2014.

[HOL 06] HOLECKOVA I., FISCHER C., GIARD M.H. *et al.*, "Brain responses to a subject's own name uttered by a familiar voice", *Brain Research*, vol. 1082, pp. 142–152, 2006.

[HOR 14] HORKI P., BAUERNFEIND G., KLOBASSA D.S. *et al.*, "Detection of mental imagery and attempted movements in patients with disorders of consciousness using EEG", *Frontiers in Human Neuroscience*, vol. 8, p. 1009, 2014.

[HUA 14] HUANG Z., DAI R., WU X. *et al.*, "The self and its resting state in consciousness: an investigation of the vegetative state", *Human Brain Mapping*, vol. 35, pp. 1997–2008, 2014.

[JAV 12] JAVOUHEY E., MANEL V., ANDRÉ-OBADIA N., "Les explorations neurophysiologiques chez l'enfant cérébrolésé: quand, comment?", *Réanimation*, vol. 21, pp. 347–353, 2012.

[JEN 75] JENNETT B., BOND M., "Assessment of outcome after severe brain damage", *Lancet*, vol. 1, no. 7905, pp. 480–484, 1975.

[KAN 93] KANE N.M., CURRY S.H., BUTLER S.R. *et al.*, "Electrophysiological indicators of awakening from coma", *The Lancet*, vol. 341, p. 688, 1993.

[KAN 96] KANE N.M., CURRY S.H., ROWLANDS C.A. *et al.*, "Event related potentials – neurophysiological tools for predicting emergence and early outcome from traumatic coma", *Intensive Care Med*, vol. 22, pp. 39–46, 1996.

[KIN 13] KING J.R., FAUGERAS F., GRAMFORT A. *et al.*, "Single-trial decoding of auditory novelty responses facilitates the detection of residual consciousness", *Neuroimage*, vol. 83C, pp. 726–738, 2013.

[KOT 05] KOTCHOUBEY B., LANG S., MEZGER G. *et al.*, "Information processing in severe disorders of consciousness: vegetative state and minimally conscious state", *Clinical Neurophysiology*, vol. 116, pp. 2441–2453, 2005.

[KUT 00] KUTAS M., FEDERMEIER K.D., "Electrophysiology reveals semantic memory use in language comprehension", *Trends in Cognitive Science*, vol. 4, pp. 463–470, 2000.

[KÜB 14] KÜBLER A., HOLZ E.M., RICCIO A. *et al.*, "The user-centered design as novel perspective for evaluating the usability of BCI-controlled applications", *PLoS ONE*, vol. 9, no. 12, p. e112392, 2014.

[LAU 99] LAUREYS S., GOLDMAN S., PHILLIPS C. *et al.*, "Impaired effective cortical connectivity in vegetative state: preliminary investigation using PET", *Neuroimage*, vol. 9, pp. 377–382, 1999.

[LAU 00] LAUREYS S., FAYMONVILLE M.E., DEGUELDRE C. *et al.*, "Auditory processing in the vegetative state", *Brain: A Journal of Neurology*, vol. 123, pp. 1589–1601, 2000.

[LAU 02] LAUREYS S., FAYMONVILLE M.E., PEIGNEUX P. *et al.*, "Cortical processing of noxious somatosensory stimuli in the persistent vegetative state", *Neuroimage*, vol. 17, pp. 732–741, 2002.

[LAU 04] LAUREYS S., OWEN A.M., SCHIFF N.D., "Brain function in coma, vegetative state, and related disorders", *Lancet Neurol*, vol. 3, pp. 537–546, 2004.

[LAU 10] LAUREYS S., CELESIA G.G., COHADON F. *et al.*, "Unresponsive wakefulness syndrome: a new name for the vegetative state or apallic syndrome", *BMC Medicine*, vol. 8, p. 68, 2010.

[LEC 15] LECAIGNARD F., BERTRAND O., GIMENEZ G. *et al.*, "Implicit learning of predictable sound sequences modulates human brain responses at different levels of the auditory hierarchy", *Frontiers in Human Neuroscience*, vol. 9, p. 505, 2015.

[LEH 12a] LEHEMBRE R., BRUNO M.A., VANHAUDENHUYSE A. *et al.*, "Resting-state EEG study of comatose patients: a connectivity and frequency analysis to find differences between vegetative and minimally conscious states", *Functional Neurology*, vol. 27, pp. 41–47, 2012.

[LEH 12b] LEHEMBRE R., GOSSERIES O., LUGO Z. *et al.*, "Electrophysiological investigations of brain function in coma, vegetative and minimally conscious patients", *Archives italiennes de biologie*, vol. 150, pp. 122–139, 2012.

[LES 14] LESENFANTS D., HABBAL D., LUGO Z. *et al.*, "An independent SSVEP-based Brain–Computer interface in locked-in syndrome", *Journal of Neural Engineering*, vol. 11, no. 3, p. 035002, 2014.

[LEW 06] LEW H.L., POOLE J.H., CASTANEDA A. *et al.*, "Prognostic value of evoked and event-related potentials in moderate to severe brain injury", *The Journal of Head Trauma Rehabilitation*, vol. 21, pp. 350–360, 2006.

[LIE 13] LIEDER F., DAUNIZEAU J., GARRIDO M.I. *et al.*, "Modelling trial-by-trial changes in the mismatch negativity", *PLoS Computational Biology*, vol. 9, no. 2, p. e1002911, 2013.

[LOG 03] LOGI F., FISCHER C., MURRI L. *et al.*, "The prognostic value of evoked responses from primary somatosensory and auditory cortex in comatose patients", *Clinical Neurophysiology*, vol. 114, pp. 1615–1627, 2003.

[LUA 15] LUAUTÉ J., MORLET D., MATTOUT J., "BCI in patients with disorders of consciousness: Clinical perspectives", *Annals of Physical and Rehabilitation Medicine*, vol. 58, no. 1, pp. 29–34, 2015.

[LUL 13] LULÉ D., NOIRHOMME Q., KLEIH S.C. *et al.*, "Probing command following in patients with disorders of consciousness using a Brain–Computer interface", *Clinical Neurophysiology*, vol. 124, no. 1, pp. 101–106, 2013.

[LUY 12] LUYT C.E., GALANAUD D., PERLBARG V. *et al.*, "Diffusion tensor imaging to predict long-term outcome after cardiac arrest: a bicentric pilot study", *Anesthesiology*, vol. 117, pp. 1311–21, 2012.

[MAD 96] MADL C., KRAMER L., YEGANEHFAR W. *et al.*, "Detection of nontraumatic comatose patients with no benefit of intensive care treatment by recording of sensory evoked potentials", *Archives in Neurology*, vol. 53, pp. 512–516, 1996.

[MON 10] MONTI M.M., VANHAUDENHUYSE A., COLEMAN M.R. *et al.*, "Willful modulation of brain activity in disorders of consciousness", *New England Journal of Medicine*, vol. 362, pp. 579–589, 2010.

[MOR 14] MORLET D., FISCHER C., "MMN and novelty P3 in coma and other altered states of consciousness: a review", *Brain Topography*, vol. 27, pp. 467–479, 2014.

[NAA 78] NAATANEN R., GAILLARD A.W., MANTYSALO S., "Early selective-attention effect on evoked potential reinterpreted", *Acta Psychologica*, vol. 42, pp. 313–329, 1978.

[NAC 15] NACI L., SINAI L., OWEN A.M., "Detecting and interpreting conscious experiences in behaviorally non-responsive patients.", *NeuroImage*, 2015.

[NÄÄ 87] NÄÄTÄNEN R., PICTON T., "The N1 wave of the human electric and magnetic response to sound: a review and an analysis of the component structure", *Psychophysiology*, vol. 24, pp. 375–425, 1987.

[OST 12] OSTWALD D., SPITZER B., GUGGENMOS M. *et al.*, "Evidence for neural encoding of Bayesian surprise in human somatosensation", *NeuroImage*, vol. 62, no. 1, pp. 177–188, 2012.

[OWE 06] OWEN A.M., COLEMAN M.R., BOLY M. *et al.*, "Detecting awareness in the vegetative state", *Science*, vol. 313, p. 1402, 2006.

[PAN 14] PAN J., XIE Q., HE Y. *et al.*, "Detecting awareness in patients with disorders of consciousness using a hybrid Brain–Computer interface", *Journal of Neural Engineering*, vol. 11, no. 5, p. 056007, 2014.

[PER 99] PERRIN F., GARCIA-LARREA L., MAUGUIERE F. *et al.*, "A differential brain response to the subject's own name persists during sleep", *Clinical Neurophysiology*, vol. 110, pp. 2153–2164, 1999.

[PER 02] PERRIN F., BASTUJI H., GARCIA-LARREA L., "Detection of verbal discordances during sleep", *Neuroreport*, vol. 13, pp. 1345–1349, 2002.

[PER 06] PERRIN F., SCHNAKERS C., SCHABUS M. *et al.*, "Brain response to one's own name in vegetative state, minimally conscious state, and locked-in syndrome", *Archives in Neurology*, vol. 63, pp. 562–569, 2006.

[PET 15] PETERSON A., CRUSE D., NACI L. *et al.*, "Risk, diagnostic error, and the clinical science of consciousness", *NeuroImage: Clinical*, vol. 7, pp. 588–597, 2015.

[PFU 99] PFURTSCHELLER G., LOPES DA SILVA F., "Event-related EEG/MEG synchronization and desynchronization: basic principles", *Clinical Neurophysiology*, vol. 110, no. 11, pp. 1842–1857, 1999.

[POL 07] POLICH J., "Updating P300: an integrative theory of P3a and P3b", *Clinical Neurophysiology*, vol. 118, pp. 2128–2148, 2007.

[QIN 10] QIN P., DI H., LIU Y. *et al.*, "Anterior cingulate activity and the self in disorders of consciousness", *Human Brain Mapping*, vol. 31, pp. 1993–2002, 2010.

[ROH 15] ROHAUT B., FAUGERAS F., CHAUSSON N. *et al.*, "Probing ERP correlates of verbal semantic processing in patients with impaired consciousness", *Neuropsychologia*, pp. 279–292, 2015.

[SAN 14] SANCHEZ G., DAUNIZEAU J., MABY E. *et al.*, "Toward a new application of real-time electrophysiology: online optimization of cognitive neurosciences hypothesis testing", *Brain Sciences*, vol. 4, no. 1, pp. 49–72, 2014.

[SCH 04] SCHOENLE P.W., WITZKE W., "How vegetative is the vegetative state? Preserved semantic processing in VS patients–evidence from N 400 event-related potentials", *NeuroRehabilitation*, vol. 19, pp. 329–334, 2004.

[SCH 08] SCHNAKERS C., PERRIN F., SCHABUS M. *et al.*, "Voluntary brain processing in disorders of consciousness", *Neurology*, vol. 71, pp. 1614–20, 2008.

[SCH 09] SCHNAKERS C., VANHAUDENHUYSE A., GIACINO J. *et al.*, "Diagnostic accuracy of the vegetative and minimally conscious state: clinical consensus versus standardized neurobehavioral assessment", *BMC Neurology*, vol. 9, p. 35, 2009.

[SCH 11] SCHABUS M., PELIKAN C., CHWALA-SCHLEGEL N. *et al.*, "Oscillatory brain activity in vegetative and minimally conscious state during a sentence comprehension task", *Functional Neurology*, vol. 26, pp. 31–36, 2011.

[SEE 10] SEEL R.T., SHERER M., WHYTE J. *et al.*, "Assessment scales for disorders of consciousness: evidence-based recommendations for clinical practice and research", *Archives of Physical Medicine and Rehabilitation*, vol. 91, pp. 1795–1813, 2010.

[SIT 14] SITT J. D., KING J.R., EL KAROUI I. *et al.*, "Large scale screening of neural signatures of consciousness in patients in a vegetative or minimally conscious state", *Brain: A Journal of Neurology*, vol. 137, pp. 2258–2270, 2014.

[SOR 09] SORGER B., DAHMEN B., REITHLER J. *et al.*, "Another kind of 'BOLD response': answering multiple-choice questions via online decoded single-trial brain signals", *Progress in Brain Research*, vol. 177, pp. 275–292, 2009.

[TEA 74] TEASDALE G., JENNETT B., "Assessment of coma and impaired consciousness. A practical scale", *Lancet*, vol. 2, pp. 81–4, 1974.

[WIJ 07] WIJNEN V.J., VAN BOXTEL G.J., EILANDER H.J. *et al.*, "Mismatch negativity predicts recovery from the vegetative state", *Clinical Neurophysiology*, vol. 118, pp. 597–605, 2007.

[WU 11] WU D.Y., CAI G., ZOROWITZ R.D. *et al.*, "Measuring interconnection of the residual cortical functional islands in persistent vegetative state and minimal conscious state with EEG nonlinear analysis", *Clinical Neurophysiology*, vol. 122, pp. 1956–1966, 2011.

[YOU 09] YOUNG G.B., "Coma", *Annals of the New York Academy of Sciences*, vol. 1157, pp. 32–47, 2009.

[ZEM 97] ZEMAN A., "Persistent vegetative state", *Lancet*, vol. 350, pp. 795–799, 1997.

[ZEM 01] ZEMAN A., "Consciousness", *Brain: A Journal of Neurology*, vol. 124, pp. 1263–1289, 2001.

[ZEM 05] ZEMAN A., "What in the world is consciousness?", *Progress in Brain Research*, vol. 150, pp. 1–10, 2005.

2

Medical Applications: Neuroprostheses and Neurorehabilitation

The original concept of a prosthesis – a device to replace or enhance a defective organ or missing body part – goes back to Ancient Egypt, and although Ambroise Paré suggested improvements to their design in the 16th Century, it was only recently that new kinds of assistance technology emerged because of support provided by European and American governments in the search for solutions to motor deficiencies, in particular those arising from injuries sustained in war. In France, for the last 30 years organizations such as the AFM[1] have been helping to educate the general public about rare and severely disabling genetic disorders, and raising funds for research into these conditions. One innovation exclusive to certain kinds of prosthesis is that they can now be connected to and operated by the nervous system. These devices vary in the way they measure nervous activity (scalp or intracerebral electroencephalography, electrocorticography, electromyography), on the system that is being controlled (muscles, robotic hand or arm, motorized wheelchair, exoskeleton) and the presence/absence of sensory information. From another perspective, new approaches exploring the capacity of Brain–Computer Interfaces (BCIs) to display brain activity while a motor task is being performed have been introduced in the last 15 years with the goal of re-educating deficient neural networks following a stroke or other illness.

Chapter written by Laurent BOUGRAIN.
1 Association Française contre les Myopathies (French Muscular Dystrophy Association).

Taking into account a number of projects (MAIA, Brain gate, Brain gate 2, TOBI, Tremor, MindWalker, Mundus, Way, Better, etc.) and research studies, this chapter presents and discusses the results achieved, the problems encountered and future improvements for replacing, assisting, rehabilitating locomotion and prehension, and reducing tremors.

2.1. Motor deficiencies

Motor deficiency is the loss of the capacity of the body or part of the body to move or to hold itself in a certain position. This includes difficulties with maintaining a sitting or standing position; moving around; interacting with surroundings by grasping or manipulating objects; communicating by using body muscles to write or gesture, or facial muscles to form words and facial expressions. Other aspects of motor deficiency are the loss of the capacity to perceive the outside world due to loss of head and eye movement, loss of control of chewing and swallowing, loss of heat-responsive reflexes or automatic breathing patterns and so on.

Motor deficiencies may be classified according to their origin (as listed in Table 2.1).

2.1.1. *Brain motor deficiencies*

Motor deficiencies originating in the brain can arise as the result of perinatal lesions on brain structures. These can be caused by malformations or deformations, or oxygen deprivation, leading to cerebral palsy. They can also occur after birth, following head trauma, a stroke or a brain tumor. Note that the condition known as locked-in syndrome is the result of a stroke in the brainstem, causing a near-total loss of muscle control. The consequences on the motor system are not limited to the brain, but also affect muscle tone. Unlike neurodegenerative deficiencies, these conditions do not progress over time.

2.1.2. *Neuromuscular motor deficiencies*

Many neuromuscular disorders are genetic in origin, such as muscular dystrophy, in which there is degeneration of the muscle tissue. Other neuromuscular diseases are the result of an infection or inflammation, such as Guillain–Barré syndrome, which affects the peripheral nervous system. These diseases progress over time and cause a gradual loss of muscle strength. The consequences of these conditions include orthopedic deformation, respiratory failure, cardiac failure, swallowing difficulties, dysarthria, and digestive disorders.

Affected area	Congenital	Disease	Accident
Brain	Encephalopathy, C.P.	Encephalopathy, C.V.A. Locked-in syndrome, A.L.S. (Charcot), Tumor, M.S.	Head trauma
Spinal cord	Spina bifida	M.S., Acute poliomyelitis	Para- and tetraplegia
Nerves	Charcot-Marie, Obstetric paralysis	Guillain-Barré syndrome	Peripheral paralysis in one or more limbs, or frontal paralysis
Muscles	Myopathies		
Bones and joints	Malformations, Amputation, Hip dysplasia, Bone dystrophies	Scoliosis, Rheumatic disorders, Hemophilia	Fractures, Amputations

Table 2.1. *Causes of motor deficiencies and affected areas (adapted from Annex 2 of [ASS 02]. C.P. = cerebral palsy, C.V.A. = cerebrovascular accident (stroke), A.L.S. = amyotrophic lateral sclerosis, M.S. = multiple sclerosis*

2.1.3. *Neurodegenerative motor deficiencies*

In this category, degeneration occurs in the neurons, particularly those involved in motor commands. These deficiencies include amyotrophic lateral sclerosis, also known as Charcot disease, which progressively affects the motor neurons in the brainstem or the spinal cord. Multiple sclerosis is another example of a neurodegenerative disease – an autoimmune disorder that affects myelin, the protective cover surrounding the nerve cells in the central nervous system (brain and spinal cord). This leads to a deterioration of intercell communication, which in turn affects motor and cognitive functions. Parkinson's disease also belongs to this category, originating as a dysregulation of the neurotransmitters (including dopamine) responsible for chemically transporting nervous information between neurons in the synapse. Parkinson's disease causes patients to experience strong tremors.

2.1.4. *Medullary motor deficiencies*

Just like the brain, the spinal cord is an integral part of the central nervous system (see Chapter 1 of Volume 1). It is responsible for relaying nervous impulses between the brainstem and the rest of the body inside the spine, either to generate a motor action, or to pass on sensory information. It also contains networks involved in reflexes. The spinal cord is made up of 31 medullary segments. Medullary lesions can occur either from trauma or disorders affecting the spinal cord. The number of limbs and organs affected by paralysis due to a lesion, that consequently become incapable of transmitting sensations, depends on the vertical position of the damaged segment in the spine. Paralysis in the upper and lower limbs, i.e. tetraplegia, occurs when damage is in the cervical region, located above the first thoracic vertebra. Paralysis in the lower limbs only, i.e. paraplegia, occurs when the damage is situated below C7, the seventh cervical vertebra, and above L2, the second lumbar vertebra. These kinds of paralyses, consisting of the absence of transmission, also give rise to disorders in several other organs, in particular those responsible for bladder control. Medullary lesions can be partial, in which case prompt re-education can allow some motor control and sensitivity to be recovered. Trauma or the incomplete development of the spinal column can also produce similar effects, as is the case for example in spina bifida.

2.1.5. *Osteoarticular motor deficiencies*

Motor deficiencies can originate in the bones and joints following an accident requiring amputation or a malformation resulting in a missing or deformed limb. More generally, lesions on the bones, joints, muscles or tendons can be the result of a number of different disorders, such as rheumatoid polyarthritis and brittle bone disease, or deviations, such as scoliosis.

2.2. Compensating for motor deficiency

BCIs can help to compensate for motor deficiency via methods for brain stimulation and other medical and ergotherapeutic tools. More specifically, in this chapter, among the motor deficiencies listed above, we will discuss those that affect limb control (loss of locomotion or prehension and tremors). Mobility is the most immediate need expressed by patients with motor disabilities [ZIC 09]. BCI solutions for assistive communication following deficiency affecting the control of facial muscles, the tongue, or the larynx will be presented in Chapter 3. Currently, BCIs are not capable of providing solutions for other motor deficiencies. BCIs that are used in connection with cognitive deficiencies are presented in Chapters 13 of Volume 1 and Chapter 1 of this volume.

The organization of our presentation of BCI solutions is inspired by the taxonomy proposed by J. R. Wolpaw [WOL 12], which was adopted in part by the roadmap of the BNCI Horizon 2020 project on future BCIs[2] [BRU 15]. This taxonomy distinguishes between applications aiming to *replace*, *restore*, *enhance* and *improve* motor control. Specifically, we will discuss replacing, restoring and enhancing motor functions in connection with neuroprotheses, whereas improving residual motor function will be discussed in the context of neurorehabilitation.

2.2.1. *Neuroprostheses*

In the case of damage to the spinal cord, amyotrophic lateral sclerosis, a stroke in the brainstem or amputation, there is a disruption in communication between the brain and the muscles. However, activity in the motor cortex remains intact and can be analyzed to decode the intended movement, or a relevant part of it, using sensors located close to neurons, at the surface of the cortex, or on the scalp. The information obtained from decoding can be relayed to effectors such as robotic arms, exoskeletons, a motorized wheelchair or a system of functional electrical stimulation. In each of these cases, the device may be described as a neuroprosthesis, meaning a prosthesis connected to the central nervous system [SCH 11]. Remember that a prosthesis is a device that replaces or improves a defective organ or missing body part.

---

2 http://bnci-horizon-2020.eu/.

2.2.1.1. *Replacing functions*

BCIs provide solutions for replacing certain defective functions after an accident or a disease. These solutions do not use the original functions, but rely on other means to achieve equivalent functionality.

For example, if walking is no longer possible due to a spinal cord injury, mobility can instead be achieved with a motorized wheelchair. In the same way that classical wheelchairs are controlled by hand, mouth or breath via a joystick or contactors, BCIs can use brain activity. The European Maia project[3] has explored this possibility [DEL 09]. The commands to move forward, left and right are associated with variations in the rhythm of different brain regions that could voluntarily be activated by the user (see Chapter 4 of Volume 1). Thus, the activation of a specific brain region is associated with movement in a specific direction. The regions that can be used in this way are the frontal lobe, the occipital lobe, the temporal lobe and the motor regions corresponding to the right hand, the left hand and the feet (see Chapter 1 of Volume 1). To activate each of these regions in turn, the user can perform mental calculations, visualize a rotating cube, think of words beginning with an arbitrary letter and imagine using the right hand, left hand or feet. In a learning phase, the system determines for each user which three regions are most discriminating for him or her personally. Wheelchair navigation is assisted by an obstacle avoidance system. Originally, automatically detecting the mental command was usually performed by modulating regions that are far away from each other. But the tasks for activating these regions were not directly linked to the desired direction, and were mentally very tiring. This project also developed the concept of shared control between the user and the system [CAR 12]. The system could essentially take over to automatically drive the wheelchair when the desired direction was unambiguous, or when maneuvering was difficult, for example going through a door. Currently, the objective is to allow the user to formulate only high-level commands, i.e. a general direction or a destination in the house, at which point the system will be responsible for determining the trajectory and moving the wheelchair. The wheelchair could potentially be controlled by other neurophysiological markers, such as the P300 and steady state visually evoked potential (SSVEPs) (see Chapter 4 of Volume 1), but this requires additional devices for displaying the stimuli. In any case, in order for the system to be useful, the

---

3 http://cnbi.epfl.ch/page-34069-en.html.

commands need to be high level, otherwise other methods of control like microjoysticks will always prove more effective whenever the user is capable of moving any part of his or her body.

In certain cases, the objective of locomotion can be fulfilled by a robot. For example, if the goal is to visit a location, such as a museum, a robot equipped with a camera can be controlled like a wheelchair to move through the rooms, allowing the driver to view exhibits, or hold a conversation with other people at a social event when a videoconference system is added [TON 11].

In addition to locomotion, prehension is an essential motor function. The feasibility of operating an artificial arm via neuroprosthesis has made significant progress over the last decade. By surgically implanting one or multiple electrode arrays, most commonly inside the primary motor cortex, it is possible to decode the direction of a movement using the activity of a population of neurons [GEO 86] and send commands to a robotic arm to reach out and grasp a target [HOC 12, WOD 15, AFL 15]. Electrocorticography, i.e. recording neural activity using electrodes placed on the surface of the cortex, has also been used to estimate movements [WAN 13, YAN 12] by less invasive means than electrode arrays, which can cause microfissures in the tissue and trigger a reaction to the introduction of a foreign object. Non-invasive brain imaging techniques such as electroencephalography are also used to build neuroprotheses, despite low spatial resolution and noisy signals [DEL 10].

Currently, research efforts are focusing on integrating stimuli with the somatosensory cortex or the skin to provide tactile feedback, thus creating a full loop between perception and action.

Here also, some level of control over the subject's home and social activities that would usually require the usage of the arms, e.g. written communication by e-mail or twitter and navigation on the internet, can be achieved with substitute methods[4] (see Chapter 3).

2.2.1.2. *Restoring functions*

BCIs can also help to restore or limit deficient motor function. In this context, the BCI will decode the brain activity as mentioned above in order to

---

4 http://www.gtec.at/Research/Projects/BrainAble, http://www.presenccia.org/, http://www.tobi-project.org.

trigger a functional electrical stimulus [PFU 03], which will in turn trigger the activation of muscles[5], producing a movement, potentially in combination with an orthesis. An orthesis is a structure, sometimes with joints, that safely holds a body part in functional positions. Motorized ortheses are sometimes equated with exoskeletons[6]. An exoskeleton is an electromechanical device that encases a body part, forcing it to move. Lower limb neuroprostheses are more complex to implement, as they require maintenance of balance [TAV 10]. With their help, a paraplegic patient can become able to stand up and walk, and potentially go up and down stairs, generally with crutches to maintain balance. Currently, the command is issued from a control panel. Only a few experiments have attempted to use brain commands[7] [CAS 13]. Performing exercises allows the motor and locomotor systems to be maintained and potentially reinforced. Studies on restoring motor control are therefore linked with the field of brain rehabilitation (see section 2.2.2.1).

2.2.1.3. Enhancing functions

Exoskeletons can increase the user's lifting capacity. But this kind of application has only been considered in a military context to allow soldiers to carry more supplies over larger distances. Civil applications could also be found, increasing the strength of warehouse workers and technicians by an order of magnitude.

2.2.2. Neurorehabilitation

For motor deficiencies originating in the brain, such as strokes, BCIs can be used to manage rehabilitation. Several studies have shown that after a stroke, synaptic plasticity, i.e. the ability of neurons to anatomically and physiologically reorganize themselves, makes it possible to naturally recover part of the lost motor function. BCI devices, in addition to supporting passive and/or active residual movements, can assist in the recovery of motor function.

---

5 http://www.neuralrehabilitation.org/projects/tremor/consortium.html.

6 www.mundus-project.eu/.

7 https://www.mindwalker-project.eu/.

2.2.2.1. *Improving function*

In this context, the objective is to design specific exercises for remodeling brain function. To achieve this, the task must consist of constrained movements, so that activity is restricted to the zone targeted for reorganization. Strokes generally only affect one hemisphere. One possible approach is to reduce somatosensory activity and brain activity associated with the valid limb, and increase these activities in the affected limb [MAT 12].

Motor imagery of a movement triggers the activation of damaged sensorimotor regions and stimulates their reconstruction. One of the advantages of BCIs is that they allow the function of the motor system to be observed, even without visible motion. By showing brain activity in motor regions during attempts to perform movement-based exercises, the patient can learn to improve the brain activity associated with a specific movement. There are a number of interfaces for showing neurofeedback, i.e. a visualization of this activity, in various forms. In one example, the strength of the sensorimotor rhythm observed in the brain motor region corresponding to the target body part is displayed on a diagram depicting the head and brain regions. This visualization is very realistic physiologically, but is not always easy to interpret, because variations occur very rapidly, and the activity in all parts of the brain is often shown, making it difficult to focus on visualizing the important regions. Note that this kind of display can be used pedagogically as a practical demonstration of which zones in the cortex are associated with various functions, and in particular motor functions (Figure 2.1(a)) [FRE 14]. Other types of visual feedback have also been suggested. To simplify the information presented, one example represents the strength of the sensorimotor rhythm in the target region with a simple red bar. But here too, variation often occurs too rapidly to truly and properly learn to perform the exercise. By contrast, some displays are extremely sophisticated and use virtual reality (Figure 2.1(b)). This type of technology was used to reconstruct high quality virtual forearms. The size of the forearm and the skin color could be configured to match the patient. The forearms were displayed on a flat screen positioned horizontally. The patient's forearms are placed under the screen. Thus, patients have the impression that they are moving their own arms, which reinforces the sensorimotor loop. The patient follows the instructions given by the system, for example opening and closing one hand. The virtual hands are animated to match the instructions to reinforce the connection between properly executed instructions and hand movements.

Finally, in some cases, visual feedback is presented in the form of a game to improve patients' motivation and make the experience more fun. For example, the strength of the sensorimotor rhythm controlled by the patient can be associated with the speed of a race car. Other parameters, such as the position of the car, can be automatically handled by the system.

 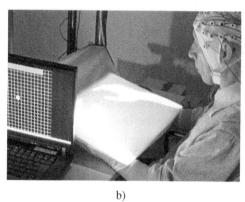

a)   b)

Figure 2.1. *Neurofeedback: a) with Teegi, users can visualize and analyze their own brain activity in real time on the model of a tangible figurine that can easily be manipulated, and interacted with; b)stroke patient is performing motor imageries of his cortically lesioned hand. Neurofeedback corresponding to complete opening or closure of the hand is given by a virtual reality system located right over patient's forearms. This system strengthens the motor cortex through neuroplasticity, on the left side a member of medical staff is observing neurofeedback related to a more precise power value of the sensorimotor rhythms of the motor imagery performed by the patient (with the kind permission of Fondazione Santa Lucia)*

2.2.2.2. *Restoring*

There are several types of assistive technology that can be implemented in parallel with brain exercises, such as exoskeletons for the arms[8] or legs[9] and functional electrical stimulation, optionally in combination with an orthesis, to maintain or potentially even reinforce the motor and locomotor systems

---

8 www.wayproject.eu/.

9 www.car.upm-csic.es/bioingenieria/better/.

(see section 2.2.1.2). A comparison of the advantages of the different assistive technologies available to stroke patients is available in [ANG 13].

2.3. Conclusions

Mobility is the most immediate need for patients with a motor disability, allowing them to recover some degree of independence [ZIC 09]. However, it seems that not all potential candidates for these new assistive technologies are capable of controlling their sensorimotor rhythms, meaning that not all patients can improve their motor capabilities in this way. One suggested explanation is that the strength of the baseline sensorimotor rhythm of these patients is low [BLA 10], which reduces the amplitude of desynchronization when performing or imagining performing a movement, making it more difficult to detect. Still, it may be possible to identify these patients beforehand, and propose secondary relaxation tasks to increase the resting strength of the signal. Although there is a real need for BCIs and a number of different applications in which they could help to compensate for motor deficiency, they have only begun to be used in the last 15 years. BCIs will not be able to provide the answer to everything, but it is clear that there has been important progress over the last few years, in particular in decoding arm movements using electrode array implants in the cortex, and that non-invasive imaging techniques are proving useful for motor rehabilitation.

The most important bottlenecks are: the creation of a lightweight, esthetic device that operates in real time at an affordable price; the design of closed-loop systems with integrated sensory feedback; and the development of paradigms of shared control between user and system to achieve motion that is more fluid and balanced, and requires less effort.

2.4. Bibliography

[AFL 15] AFLALO T., KELLIS S., KLAES C. *et al.*, "Decoding motor imagery from the posterior parietal cortex of a tetraplegic human", *Science*, vol. 348, no. 6237, pp. 906–910, 2015.

[ANG 13] ANG K.K., GUAN C., "Brain-computer interface in stroke rehabilitation", *Journal of Computing Science and Engineering*, vol. 7, no. 2, pp. 139–146, 2013.

[ASS 02] ASSOCIATION DES PARALYSÉS DE FRANCE, Déficiences motrices et situations de handicaps: aspects sociaux, psychologiques, médicaux, techniques, troubles associés, Association des Paralysés de France, 2002.

[BLA 10]   BLANKERTZ B., SANNELLI C., HALDER S. *et al.*, "Neurophysiological predictor of SMR-based BCI performance", *Neuroimage*, vol. 51, no. 4, pp. 1303–1309, 2010.

[BRU 15]   BRUNNER C., BIRBAUMER N., BLANKERTZ B. *et al.*, "BNCI Horizon 2020: towards a roadmap for the BCI community", *Brain–Computer Interfaces*, vol. 2, no. 1, pp. 1–10, 2015.

[CAR 12]   CARLSON T., DEMIRIS Y., "Collaborative control for a robotic wheelchair: evaluation of performance, attention, and workload", *IEEE Transactions on Systems, Man, and Cybernetics, Part B: Cybernetics*, vol. 42, no. 3, pp. 876–888, 2012.

[CAS 13]   CASTERMANS T., DUVINAGE M., CHERON G. *et al.*, "Towards effective non-invasive brain–computer interfaces dedicated to gait rehabilitation systems", *Brain Sciences*, vol. 4, no. 1, pp. 1–48, 2013.

[DEL 09]   DEL R MILLÁN J., GALAN F., VANHOOYDONCK D. *et al.*, "Asynchronous non-invasive brain-actuated control of an intelligent wheelchair", *IEEE Engineering in Medicine and Biology Society*, Annual Conference, vol. 2009, pp. 3361–3364, 2009.

[DEL 10]   DEL R. MILLAN J., RUPP R., MUELLER-PUTZ G. *et al.*, "Combining brain–computer interfaces and assistive technologies: state-of-the-art and challenges", *Frontiers in Neuroscience*, vol. 4, no. 161, 2010.

[FRE 14]   FREY J., GERVAIS R., FLECK S. *et al.*, "Teegi: tangible EEG interface", *UIST-ACM User Interface Software and Technology Symposium*, ACM, Honolulu, 2014.

[GEO 86]   GEORGOPOULOS A.P., SCHWARTZ A.B., KETTNER R.E., "Neuronal population coding of movement direction", *Science*, vol. 233, no. 4771, pp. 1416–1419, 1986.

[HOC 12]   HOCHBERG L.R., BACHER D., JAROSIEWICZ B. *et al.*, "Reach and grasp by people with tetraplegia using a neurally controlled robotic arm", *Nature*, vol. 485, no. 7398, pp. 372–375, 2012.

[MAT 12]   MATTIA D., PICHIORRI F., MOLINARI M. *et al.*, "Brain computer interface for hand motor function restoration and rehabilitation", in ALLISON B. *et al*, (eds.), *Towards Practical Brain–Computer Interfaces*, Biological and Medical Physics, Biomedical Engineering, Springer-Verlag, Berlin, Heildelberg, pp. 131–153, 2012.

[PFU 03]   PFURTSCHELLER G., MÜLLER G.R., PFURTSCHELLER J. *et al.*, "'Thought'-control of functional electrical stimulation to restore hand grasp in a patient with tetraplegia", *Neuroscience Letters*, vol. 351, no. 1, pp. 33–36, 2003.

[SCH 11]   SCHULTZ A.E., KUIKEN T.A., "Neural interfaces for control of upper limb prostheses: the state of the art and future possibilities", *PMR*, vol. 3, no. 1, pp. 55–67, 2011.

[TAV 10]   TAVELLA M., LEEB R., RUPP R. *et al.*, "Towards natural non-invasive hand neuroprostheses for daily living.", *IEEE Engineering in Medicine and Biology Society Annual Conference*, vol. 2010, pp. 126–129, 2010.

[TON 11]   TONIN L., CARLSON T., LEEB R. *et al.*, "Brain-controlled telepresence robot by motor-disabled people", *IEEE Engineering in Medicine and Biology Society Annual Conference*, vol. 2011, pp. 4227–4230, 2011.

[WAN 13] WANG W., COLLINGER J.L., DEGENHART A.D. *et al.*, "An electrocorticographic brain interface in an individual with tetraplegia", *PLoS ONE*, vol. 8, no. 2, p. e55344, 2013.

[WOD 15] WODLINGER B., DOWNEY J.E., TYLER-KABARA E.C. *et al.*, "Ten-dimensional anthropomorphic arm control in a human brain-machine interface: difficulties, solutions, and limitations", *Journal of Neural Engineering*, vol. 12, no. 1, p. 016011, 2015.

[WOL 12] WOLPAW J.R., WOLPAW E.W., *BCI: Principles and Practice*, Oxford University Press, Springer-Verlag, New York, 2012.

[YAN 12] YANAGISAWA T., HIRATA M., SAITOH Y. *et al.*, "Electrocorticographic control of a prosthetic arm in paralyzed patients", *Annals of Neurology*, vol. 71, no. 3, pp. 353–361, 2012.

[ZIC 09] ZICKLER C., DI DONNA V., KAISER V. *et al.*, "BCI applications for people with disabilities: defining user needs and user requirements", *Assistive Technology from Adapted Equipment to Inclusive Environments, AAATE. Assistive Technology Research Series*, IOS Press, Amsterdam, vol. 25, pp. 185–189, 2009.

Medical Applications of BCIs for Patient Communication

3.1. Introduction

Communicating is a daily challenge for many people who have lost the ability to speak and who only possess a limited range of gestures: patients with brain damage or suffering from cerebral palsy, multiple sclerosis, amyotrophic lateral sclerosis (ALS), locked-in syndrome (LIS) and patients in intensive care who are conscious but fully paralyzed (Guillain–Barré syndrome, critical illness neuropathies, etc.). Even though in most cases family and human contact remain the most effective form of assistance for communication, there is an increasing need for relevant technical assistance systems to help patients to communicate.

In fact, persons with disabilities (PWD) have often been at the forefront of new technologies designed to compensate for deficiencies and restore family and social relationships [BIG 07]. There is no doubt that information and communication technologies and their applications have the potential to considerably improve the integration, independence and safety of PWD in many aspects of their daily lives. Because of this, research into BCIs has long benefited from public financing to aim at rebuilding control and communication for PWD.

Chapter written by François CABESTAING and Louis MAYAUD.

Unfortunately, more than 40 years after the first Brain–Computer interface (BCI) experiments performed by Vidal *et al.* [VID 73], this promise has only been partially fulfilled. Still, important progress in the domains of supervised learning and electroencephalography (EEG) data collection together with a significant decrease in the cost of these kinds of system suggest that there may yet be a positive outcome for bedside applications of this technology. We will present the rich body of recent works in this area, with a special focus on a few teams in various parts of the world who achieved standards of performance that would allow these systems to truly benefit patients in the context of cross-disciplinary care.

3.1.1. *Augmentative and alternative communication*

The goal of techniques of augmentative and alternative communication (AAC) is to complement verbal communication – if it is present but deficient – or to replace it if it is absent [BEU 98]. We will focus on the very specific case of users whose disability is sufficiently severe so as to prevent all communication without assistance from an AAC system, whether verbal or non-verbal. AAC methods are generally categorized according to whether they require the use of physical equipment or a technical assistance system.

In approaches without technical assistance systems, communication is established with a partner – medical staff member, caregiver or family member – who is perfectly acquainted with the patient. The partner provides prompts – words, syllables or individual letters – that the patient can select to add to the message. The patient must therefore possess some residual motor capacity in order to select one of the options, for example the ability to blink or move the eyes for patients with LIS. The effectiveness of this AAC method depends both on the capacity of the patient to select his/her choice reliably and the strategy chosen by the partner to provide a limited but exhaustive list of relevant options at each step. In general, this strategy is defined by collaborating with the patient, depending on the context of the dialogue.

Within the category of AAC approaches that use technical assistance systems, a further distinction is made between two subcategories depending on the technicality of the equipment required as a platform for communication. "Low-tech" techniques are based on simple props – paper/pencil, image thumbnails, alphabet cards, etc. – that are used to present options to the patient non-verbally. The patient might also have access to a simple device – switch, laser pointer, etc. – that can be used to indicate the option that he/she wishes to select. The "high-tech" category generally includes assistance systems that no longer necessarily require the presence of a partner. The system must both suggest choices and analyze the selection made by the patient with LIS.

The most common type of "high-tech" AAC system is the virtual scrolling keyboard. The options are displayed on a screen, in a layout that is either predefined or that adapts predictively based on the message entered so far. Patients usually select just one of the options, for example using a button based on some type of residual movement. More recently, systems that select options by analyzing the direction the patient is looking have been introduced, which improves the efficiency of communication, as the options are no longer required to be presented and selected sequentially. Despite all of this, there is a major obstacle with these devices inherent to the technique, described as the "Midas touch": a change in the direction the user is looking does not necessarily indicate that he or she wishes to select an option, but might simply be to read another part of the screen, or look at something else nearby.

3.1.2. *Logical and semantic control*

To implement a "high-tech" AAC technique, a "low-level" channel of communication must first be established between the user and the assistance system. Signals passed through this channel can be generated from devices directly controlled by the user – mechanical switches, joysticks, etc. – or result from the processing of measurements obtained from sensors observing the patient. These signals provide a *logical* control of the system, equivalent to that of a healthy user achieved via direct mechanical interaction. In patients with LIS, it is very difficult to establish a control signal at a logical level that is both reliable, robust and sufficiently dynamic. Because of this, the effectiveness of the communication process remains relatively low, in particular for dialogues with a partner via an AAC system.

One way to improve the effectiveness and usability of the AAC system is to add one or more postprocessing modules between the logical control level and the system responsible for creating the message to be communicated. This processing can take one of three possible forms [THO 13], either increasing the effective rate of transmission of symbols by encoding or prediction, correcting errors in the selection process, or simply toggling the AAC system on/off. When one or more of these kinds of postprocessing modules are implemented, the user is said to have *semantic* control over the AAC system [GAR 06].

When a patient with LIS dialogues with a partner, this partner is using his or her knowledge of spelling and syntax as well as the semantic and pragmatic context of the conversation to suggest appropriate options for communication. Currently, the efficiency of predictions proposed by human partners has not been equaled in terms of performance, because humans are capable of understanding the full context of the dialogue and correspondingly improving the ratio of performance to fatigue by correctly anticipating most choices. In concrete terms, prediction techniques must achieve a compromise between two opposing performance criteria: exhaustiveness of the options suggested to the user on the one hand, and communication fluidity on the other hand [GAR 06].

When patients use an AAC system for communicating with their partner, we must also be careful to ensure that mechanisms of semantic control do not excessively increase the cognitive burden. Fatigue induced by an overly restrictive paradigm decreases the short-term performance, and in the long-term performance, it can also lead to the patient rejecting the AAC system. The benefit of allowing the patient to personally configure the compromise between the efficiency of the AAC system and the level of cognitive burden has been shown by analyzing user behavior "offline", i.e. when messages are composed without a partner present. In this mode, patients often choose to deactivate semantic improvement features to regain control at a logical level [BIR 00].

3.1.3. *BCIs dedicated to AAC*

BCIs designed for purposes of augmentative and alternative communication are of course classed as "high-tech". They allow a channel of communication between the patient and the machine to be established, even for patients with complete LIS (cLIS). Command signals operating at a logical level are constructed by directly analyzing brain activity, meaning that users do not require any residual motor capacity. In some cases, logical control can be implemented by a "mental switch" that allows an option to be selected. In other cases, the design is more complex, simultaneously exploiting one or more analog or multivalued signals. It is important to note, as was heavily emphasized in the seminar on "Augmentative and Alternative Communication for BCI" at the 5th international workshop on BCIs [HUG 14a], how crucial it is that AAC systems with BCIs are hybrid in nature, i.e. that they exploit as fully as possible any residual means of communication available to each given patient.

The state-of-the-art generally divides BCIs into two categories, corresponding to either the continuous monitoring of a process, or the detection of an intention at specific moments in time. In most of the AAC systems described in the scientific literature, with the occasional exception, the second approach seems to have been preferred by system designers [WOL 02]. Moreover, many authors claim that the BCI systems developed by them are suitable to be implemented for AAC with patients with severe disabilities. In practice, a careful review of the literature showed that very few concrete results have been obtained in this area outside of a laboratory setting, and in particular without requiring the continuous involvement of an expert [LEE 13, MOG 13]. It can also be observed that there is currently very little real proof of the long-term effectiveness of integrating BCIs into AAC techniques for patients with ALS [MAR 15].

3.1.4. *Estimating the performance of BCIs dedicated to AAC*

The effective implementation of a BCI requires the user to acquire – and maintain over time – the specific ability to control one or more electrophysiological markers (see Chapter 4 of Volume 1 [CLE 16]). In order to remain effective, the automatic marker recognition system must also be able to adapt to any drift in the characteristics of these markers that might occur over time. The question of evaluating the effectiveness of an AAC system can be considered on two different levels [THO 13]. First, we can analyze the performance at the logical level by evaluating the section of the processing chain from the user input to the system responsible for detecting mental states, i.e. the classifier. But we can also analyze the performance at the semantic level by considering the benefits of any systems in place that improve the process of message composition, supplying predictions from a dictionary, eliminating selection errors, etc.

Many different performance metrics have been suggested in the literature for the logical level, but an in-depth literature review performed by Thompson *et al.* [THO 13] shows that the two most commonly used criteria are the classifier accuracy and the information transfer rate [THO 13]. In line with the majority of authors, we will denote by *trial* a sequence of steps corresponding to one of option suggestion, response analysis and/or selection that allows an elementary symbol to be appended to communicated message. The classifier accuracy is a parameter P taking values between 0 and 1 that statistically measures the probability that the symbol selected by the BCI after each trial correctly corresponds to the user's intentions. This metric takes into account both the capacity of the user to operate the BCI, and the effective ability of the BCI to correctly identify the selection. However, it does not take into account the effective rate at which the symbols are communicated, i.e. the speed of communication. The information transfer rate, or *bitrate*, is a metric introduced by Wolpaw *et al.* to integrate the additional factor of time [WOL 02]. It considers both the number N of options that may be selected in each trial, the accuracy P of the classifier – considering all options to be equally likely – and the duration d of each trial. The transfer rate is given by the expression $B = (\log_2 N + P \log_2 P + (1 - P) \log_2[(1 - P)/(N - 1)])/d$.

The semantic performance metrics that have been suggested in the literature are for the most part extensions to logical metrics obtained by considering the added value of prediction or error correction systems [THO 13]. But metrics that specifically evaluate the performance of prediction or error correction modules have also been suggested, in particular the *utility metric* introduced by Dal Seno *et al.*, which is given by the ratio of the expected benefit per selection and the effective time required for each selection [SEN 10]. Depending on the postprocessing modules added to the end of the chain, the expected benefit per selection can be greater than 1 (for prediction systems), equal to 1 (no postprocessing) or less than 1, for example if the user is asked to give final confirmation.

Taking a step back from these theoretical performance metrics, we must also consider the high variability in performance originating from the users themselves. There are many factors that can influence performance: fatigue, user investment in the communication task, motivation, etc. It is important for users to be able to adjust performance levels themselves, either directly by configuring the interface, or indirectly, by allowing the level of concentration or investment in the task to vary. Indeed, it is not always necessary for users to maintain high levels of concentration when working on an offline document, which rapidly results in cognitive fatigue, whereas doing so may be desirable when using the BCI for dialogue [RIC 12]. Instead, in order to learn to improve their personal performance, users must, for example, be able to decide to toggle off error correction and prediction modules [BIR 00].

3.2. Reactive interfaces for communication

Since the work performed by Farwell in the late 1980s [FAR 88], reactive interfaces have occupied a decisive role in the evolution and popularity of BCIs. This interface is sometimes described as the "P300 Speller" after the P300 potential on which it is based (as described in Chapter 4 section 4.3.2 of Volume 1 [CLE 16]), this is a positive electrical potential that arises on average 300 ms after an "infrequent" stimulus. Over the years, this work has been complemented by the introduction of interfaces exploiting increasingly diverse and early-arising types of evoked potentials (EPs). Similarly, every kind of stimulus imaginable has been suggested, with greater or lesser degrees of success. Today, visual interfaces remain a major focus of this field of research and medical applications of BCIs for purposes of communication.

3.2.1. *Visual interfaces*

Almost 90% of BCIs used for communicating with patients are visual interfaces [MAR 15]. The visual EPs used by these interfaces can be roughly divided into two categories, which we will discuss separately: endogenous potentials whose characteristics (amplitude, latency) depend on the subject's internal state (concentration, fatigue) and exogenous potentials that are primarily determined by the type of stimulus (frequency, amplitude).

3.2.1.1. *Endogenous interfaces*

The reason that the P300 was chosen in the original paradigm of the first "mental typewriter" may have been neurophysiological: it is *a priori* the EP with the largest amplitude, which suggests that it might provide the highest detection rate. In this paradigm, the letters are laid out on a square grid whose lines and columns are randomly illuminated. The subject focuses attention on the letter that he or she wishes to select, causing a "surprise" potential, the P300, to be generated by the subject and subsequently identified in the multivariate time series given by the EEG. This is by far the most popular interface for communication, and its design has remained unchanged until very recently. These interfaces have been extensively tested on healthy subjects, but the performance in groups of patients is less unambiguous [SEL 13]. Furthermore, the few studies that examine this discrepancy appear to struggle to reach a consensus, which is first and foremost indicative of heterogeneous patient groups and small sample sizes [MAR 15].

For example, a comparison of three ALS patients with three non-ALS subjects revealed equivalent performance for at least two of the ALS subjects with a simple communication protocol (four choices) repeated in 10 sessions over the course of 6 weeks. Similarly, a comparison between $n = 10$ healthy subjects and $n = 10$ patients suffering from various neurological disorders in a single session of "P300 speller" did not reveal any significant difference in performance in connection with the etiology of the disorder [MAY 13]. Again, a 3-year longitudinal study of $n = 25$ patients with ALS did not find any correlation between performance and the progression of the disease [SIL 13], which was confirmed in another group of equivalent size ($n = 15$) [COR 14]. But on the other hand, some studies observe lower performance in patients than in healthy subjects [PIC 06]. One interesting explanation was recently proposed in a meta-analysis of the data of $n = 35$ patients suffering from severe neurological disorders, suggesting that this heterogeneity could possibly be explained by underperformance on the part of the subgroup of patients in most severe condition, namely the patients that had reached the stage of cLIS [KÜB 09]. This opinion seems to have been widely accepted by the scientific community [LUL 13, SEL 13, MAR 15]. It is possible that the learning capacity of these patients is severely limited, which would explain the discrepancy [BIR 07], and it remains to be determined whether learning could be effective if introduced before patients reach the cLIS stage [KÜB 09].

The analysis of the data of $n = 25$ ALS patients suggests that the extent of visual deficiency alone may be sufficient to explain the variations in the observed results [MCC 14], which rekindles the debate on the importance of the capacity to control the eyes in visual BCI paradigms based on the P300 [SEL 13]. One interesting way to circumvent this pathological limitation is to implement a non-dependent interface, i.e. an interface that does not require control over the direction the eyes are facing. For example, in rapid serial visual presentation systems, each symbol in the alphabet is presented one after the other, in rapid succession, on a single region of the screen [ORH 14].

After all, a significant proportion (between 10% and 30%) of subjects is incapable of controlling a visual interface based on the P300 [LUL 13, MAY 13, COR 14]. This "illiteracy" could possibly be due to anatomical differences (shape and orientation of cortical electrical dipoles) in the functional regions involved in the generation of EPs. Distinguishing the effect of neuroanatomical differences from the effect of functional differences (pathologies) on the performance of visual BCIs based on the P300 could represent an interesting challenge for the scientific community in the upcoming years [MAR 15].

In general, and probably for historical reasons, medical studies have primarily concentrated their efforts on groups of patients with ALS [PIC 06, KÜB 09, BIR 07, MAR 15]. But as the performance and user-friendliness of BCIs improve, the benefits they provide become relevant to other patient groups [SEL 13]. For example, one study with $n = 15$ tetraplegic patients admitted to an intensive care unit showed that the majority (66%) was in a position to benefit from the technology, in particular patients with Guillain–Barré syndrome or other critical illness neuropathies [MAY 13], and that these benefits were independent of sedation and mechanical ventilation. Similarly, Lulé et al. [LUL 13] showed that some patients suffering from disorders of consciousness ($n = 18$) might be capable of using an auditory interface. More recently, in a pilot study in $n = 1$ patient with damage to the brainstem following a stroke, Sellers et al. showed that BCIs had a positive impact over 62 sessions; they managed to communicate with the patient in 40 (64%) of these sessions [SEL 14].

The recent benefits of these techniques for groups of patients with potentially less severe conditions might be the result of a significant increase in performance. The use of techniques based on Riemannian geometry have in particular strongly contributed to this, providing systems that are more robust and that require less calibration data (or even none) [BAR 14]. Other simpler improvements can also have a positive hand in characterizing these systems. For example, replacing the regular intervals between two consecutive stimuli with intervals of random duration (drawn from an exponential distribution) both relieves the visual cortex from a fatigue-inducing stimulus applied at an unnatural frequency and optimizes the "surprise" factor of the stimulus [MAY 13]. Another equally simple example is the departure from the "row-column" paradigm by using groups of pseudo-random characters, which both reduces side-effects and improves user-friendliness. This kind of progress is key in technology that is geared toward patients for whom the ability to focus is often detrimental to the exercise [SEL 06, MAY 13].

3.2.1.2. *Exogenous interfaces*

Except for the category of BCIs based on the P300 wave, whose significance is historic in the context of BCIs, the most frequently used category of reactive visual BCIs is based on steady-state visual evoked potentials. The idea behind communicating with these interfaces is to flash certain targets on the interface (letters or groups of letters) at a given frequency then, in real time, to identify activity with the same frequency in the occipital cortex, located at the back of the head, responsible for processing visual nervous input. At first glance, there is less variation between subjects with these signals compared to slow EPs such as the P300, whose shape can differ significantly from person to person [LUL 13]. These interfaces generally support a lower number of choices than P300 systems, but they can attain equivalent information transfer rates [CHE 02, DON 00]. However, this performance is strongly reliant on the presence of ocular control, likely more so than the situations discussed earlier [WAN 08].

Unfortunately, there are little data available for assessing the effect of this phenomenon on the performance of the patients for whom these systems were specifically designed. A comparison of the performance of 16 healthy volunteers with the data of 11 patients with tetraplegia originating from – spinal cord – trauma (C4–C7) shows that the information transfer rate in the group of patients was roughly half that of the healthy subjects [WAN 06]. To circumvent this problem, Lim *et al.* suggest an "eyes-closed" binary decision system tested by a patient with ALS that achieved an accuracy rate of 80% [LIM 13]. The low level of validation in target groups and the low information rates seem to suggest that applying these systems in a clinical context is an unlikely prospect. Only one-tenth of systems based on visual EPs presented in the scientific literature ever reach the stage of working prototype for communication [WAN 08].

In future, exploiting clever paradigms such as those based on m-codes could open promising new horizons for this category of interface. Indeed, despite the low interest in these systems, they appear to provide impressive levels of performance (almost twice as fast as existing BCIs) [BIN 11] and have long been used in applications with patients [SUT 92].

3.2.2. *Auditory stimulation*

Auditory interfaces have also been studied in BCI target groups to compensate for loss of vision [MCC 14]. These interfaces have a limited number of simple commands (for example "yes", "no", "end", "pass"), either recited consecutively or selected by using the subject's ability to locate sounds in space by emitting stimuli from speakers arranged in a circle around the subject. More classically, letters can be arranged on a grid with numbered rows and columns. Clearly, these interfaces require a more advanced level of cognitive function, starting with working memory and the capacity for sustained concentration, which patients sometimes lack [KÜB 09].

The performance and accuracy of these interfaces is inferior by far to user needs, but they have at least been shown to work. 9 out of 13 (69%) healthy volunteers were able to control an interface of this type [FUR 09], and the EPs observed during sessions had lower amplitudes and higher latency than equivalent data gathered while the same subjects operated visual interfaces. In four patients, a similar comparison found a significant decrease in performance [KÜB 09] associated with difficulties in concentrating. A more recent study with healthy subjects ($n = 20$) confirmed these observations, finding that indicators of motivation were linked to higher P300 amplitudes, and that using the auditory system resulted in a greater mental burden [KÄT 13]. Today, auditory interfaces nonetheless remain a serious alternative for certain categories of patient such as minimally conscious patients for whom this kind of system could also improve the diagnostic process.

3.3. Active interfaces for communication

The communication paradigms used in active interfaces are quite different from those described in the last few sections. Even though active BCIs generally send specific instructions to the user at specific moments in time, these instructions are not strictly speaking stimuli to which the user spontaneously reacts. Thus, it is no longer a direct response to a stimulus that is analyzed, but rather the spatiotemporal variations of one or more physiological signals that are modulated when the user performs a specific mental task, which may or may not be in response to the instruction. These paradigms are sometimes described as asynchronous because of the lack of synchronization between the moments at which the physiological signals vary and the moments at which the instructions are emitted.

The BCI detects certain physiological markers (see Chapter 4 of Volume 1 [CLE 16]) in order to construct one or more control signals. These signals can be analog, multivalued or binary, depending on whether the variational analysis includes thresholds or classifications. Analog signals allow the context of the communication to be modified progressively and continuously, for example by guiding a cursor toward an option. Multivalued signals allow direct selection or preselection of one item from a set of options. Binary signals can be used to validate a previous selection. In this context, the process of selecting a symbol to be added to the communicated message can require multiple steps, each of which is logically equivalent to a *trial* as defined in section 3.1.4. Each step ends with the selection of one option from a limited number of options, and each choice influences the options that are presented in future steps.

In practice, this method of selection in successive steps amounts to choosing a path in a tree from the root to the end node. The end-points – or leaves – of the tree are the symbols that can be added by the user to the communicated message. For example, in the spelling system operated via the adaptive brain interface (ABI) developed by Millán *et al.* [DEL 03], the user can select one of 27 terminal elements, namely the letters of the Latin alphabet plus a space symbol. The ABI constructs a single control signal with three possible states, each of which corresponds to a mental task that can be reliably detected for the user operating the interface: motor imagery, mental calculation, visualization of 3D motion of an object, imagination of a musical tune, etc. In each trial, the user performs one of the three mental tasks for a fixed amount of time, after which the selection is made. Each node of the tree has three branches or leaves, so three successive step are necessary to select one specific symbol from the 27 available options.

In practice, control signals are imperfect and noisy, which results in unwanted selections in the iterative process. Regardless of the method used to allow the user to correct these errors, the act of correction can be viewed as adding additional edges to the tree of choices, allowing the user to travel backwards, i.e. toward a previous node, or the root. The tree therefore becomes a directed graph with special nodes, one of which is the origin and multiple others of which are final destinations. With this configuration, there is no longer an *a priori* fixed value for the number of stages necessary to select a symbol at one of the end nodes.

In the next part of this section, we will only describe the main paradigms of communication via active BCI that have been studied in a clinical setting in patients with motor disabilities. First, we present the "thought translation device" (TTD), which is a BCI that uses variations in the average cortical potential as a marker (see Chapter 4, section 4.2.1.1 of Volume 1 [CLE 16]), allowing either a spelling system or an internet browser to be operated. Second, we present an example from the category of BCIs that analyze variations in the sensorimotor rhythms (SMR, see Chapter 4, section 4.2.1 of Volume 1 [CLE 16]) when motor imagery tasks are executed: the BrainTree interface [LEE 13].

3.3.1. *Thought translation device*

Birbaumer *et al.* were the first to use an operant conditioning approach in a system that they called a TTD [BIR 00]. Simple visual feedback allows the user to learn to reliably control very low-frequency variations in the average electrical potential in the cortex (slow cortical potential (SCP)). In the system originally described by the research team, one single electrode recorded the EEG at the vertex – at position Cz in the 10–20 system – and a simple preprocessing procedure for eliminating artifacts caused by eye movements was used. The visual feedback on which learning is based takes the form of a round cursor whose vertical position is controlled by the average level of the EEG signal, calculated over a sliding window of 500 ms.

Learning requires a very high number of sessions, sometimes hundreds, each composed of 70–100 trials. In each trial, the user receives the instruction to either increase or reduce his or her SCP. Next, a high-pitched sound indicates the start of the 2-s period during which the BCI determines the EEG baseline. A low-pitched sound indicates the start of the 2- to 4-s period during which the SCP must be modified as specified by the instruction. Visual feedback is presented to the user during this final period. Finally, if the instruction is successfully executed, the cursor changes into a "smiley" until the start of the next trial. Users progressively make the transition from learning mode to real applications in which variations trigger actions [HIN 04].

In the spelling system described in [BIR 00], the successive selections controlled by varying the SCP define a path in a binary graph. For each trial, an increase in the SCP is considered to represent validation, and a decrease to represent cancellation. Making a step toward an end node requires either a single validation, to take the path leading to the set of most likely symbols from the current node, or a cancellation followed by a validation to take the path leading to the set of less likely symbols. Canceling twice allows the user to return to the root node of the graph, except if the user is already there, in which case canceling twice allows the user to delete the previously selected symbol, similar to the "backspace" key on a standard keyboard.

Validating and canceling by increasing and decreasing the SCP have also been used to operate an adapted version of the Mozilla web browser – baptized Nessi[1] [BEN 07]. Three principal adaptations were established; first, a specific way to display links in the browser window was added; second, a binary graph was defined allowing these links to be selected; and third, the browser was modified so that it could be controlled by the binary signal generated by the logical unit of the BCI. Whenever required, the user can open a virtual keyboard in the interface, for example to enter text into a questionnaire. This keyboard is operated in the same way as the spelling interface described above. The Nessi interface also has an integrated application for reading and writing e-mails.

An initial study was performed in 1999 by the designers of the TTD with three ALS patients who had reached the phase of full motor paralysis [BIR 00]. The patients used an autonomous home system that had been entrusted to them by the researchers. All three patients acquired the ability to operate the TTD after several months of learning, and two patient achieved an average accuracy rate of 70 and 80%. In 2003, the same team published a summary of the progress of this study, describing the experiments performed with 11 ALS patients, nine of which were in a state of full motor paralysis, over periods ranging from 6 months to 6 years [BIR 03]. One of these patients agreed to contribute to the research performed by the team by

---

1 Open-source software available from *http://nessi.mozdev.org/*.

testing different methods of EEG signal classification so that they could be compared [HIN 03].

These studies show that it is essential that the process of learning to regulate the SCP begins very early in the progression of the disease, and if possible before complete motor paralysis sets in. Indeed, the average slope of the learning curves – representing the change in the accuracy rate as a function of the number of training sessions – correlates with the patient's level of residual motor capacity [BIR 03]. Regression analysis of the learning curve over the first 30 sessions was also used to accurately predict the ultimate effectiveness of the spelling system in five of the patients. Finally, the results suggest that patients who acquire the ability to control their SCP have a good chance of being able to reliably operate AAC systems based on the TTD.

Since 2003, there do not seem to have been any clinical studies that evaluate the performance of this AAC approach in patients suffering from complete motor paralysis, as noted by the meta-analysis performed by Marchetti and Priftis [MAR 15]. However, the ability to control the SCP was used to evaluate the cognitive state and short-term memory of patients in the terminal stage of ALS [IVE 08].

3.3.2. *BrainTree interface*

Another approach that has been explored in depth for constructing logical control signals involves analyzing spatiotemporal variations in the SMR (see Chapter 4, section 4.2.1 of Volume 1 [CLE 16]). These variations arise as the result of performing a mental motor imagery task; the capacity to modulate these rhythms can be either innate, or acquired by learning with operant conditioning techniques. In the latter case, the ability to operate a BCI dedicated to AAC is an acquired skill, which is generally retained in the long term by the user [WOL 02].

Wolpaw *et al.* were the first to suggest a paradigm allowing users to learn to control the movement of a cursor by modulating the amplitude of their SMR, more precisely their mu rhythm [WOL 91]. Several research teams subsequently developed similar techniques for constructing two or three logical control signals, and validated their approaches by performing tests with healthy subjects. However, as is common for BCIs dedicated to AAC in the literature, there are relatively few studies describing complete AAC systems – i.e. with an integrated paradigm for composing messages – that have been tested and validated in sufficiently large groups of patients with LIS and/or ALS [MAR 15].

Leeb *et al.* developed a BCI that analyzes the modulations of the SMR as the user performs two specific motor imagery tasks chosen from a set of three tasks defined *a priori*: moving the left or right hands and moving the feet. The EEG signals are recorded by 16 electrodes placed directly above the sensorimotor cortex. During an initial evaluation session, new users perform the three motor imagery tasks, and the system determines the two tasks that can be most effectively discriminated. Users must then learn to modulate their SMR more specifically over the course of up to 10 training sessions, performed in a clinical setting or at home. If the results are not significant after 10 sessions, the training process is terminated and the user ceases to participate in the experiment.

If, on the other hand, the user manages to reliably operate the BCI after the training process is complete, he or she is offered a choice of two particular applications. The first is to control a telepresence robot, and the second is to compose text messages via an AAC system. This system was given the name of BrainTree, as it allows symbols to be selected by navigating through a tree in a similar manner to the system described in section 3.3.1. The user interface for spelling out messages is shown in Figure 3.1. The major benefit of the proposed approach is that semantic selection techniques are directly integrated into the interface. The logical control signal determines the horizontal position of a cursor that moves continuously. If this signal passes below the lower threshold, it prompts a second cursor to move one step to the left, which allows a character to be preselected. Similarly, if the control signal passes above the upper threshold, this cursor moves one step to the right.

To demonstrate the value of this approach, an experiment was performed with 24 patients with severe motor deficits due to neuropathy conditions, a lesion on the spinal cord, cerebellar ataxia and advanced multiple sclerosis [LEE 13]. None of these patients, however, had any form of cognitive deficit. Only 10 patients achieved sufficiently high performance to continue the experiment after 10 training sessions, six of which were presented with the opportunity to use the BrainTree spelling system. These six patients managed to perfectly master the system; one patient did not make a single mistake when asked to recopy a text for one of the validation tasks.

The highest performance achieved in terms of transfer rate was two characters per minute.

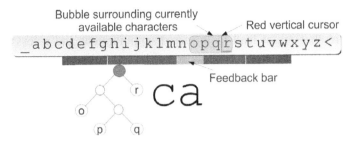

Figure 3.1. *Graphical spelling interface of the BrainTree system (reproduced from [LEE 13] with the authors' permission)*

3.4. Conclusions

Although more than 90% of resources have been allocated to the search for new algorithms and paradigms [SEL 13] for BCIs, and despite a strong acceleration in the research performed in this field [HUG 14b], it seems that medical interfaces for patients' communication have benefited little or not at all from these efforts [MAR 15]; consequently, today, their medical impact remains limited. This undoubtedly stands in contrast with the ambitions of the vast majority of scientific publications in the field. Ethical aspects of the application of BCI systems are often neglected [HUG 14b]. The principal risk probably lies in the relationship between the interface and the patient and his/her close friends and family. In the context of experimental protocols, given the latent imperfections of the technology and the numerous practical difficulties in using these kinds of system (signal quality, programming errors, explanation of instructions), it seems important to manage the expectations of patients and their loved ones. This might mean being careful not to present the system as an interface for communication before ensuring that there is a real chance that the patient's brain signals can be correctly interpreted. Experience shows that patients and their loved ones are quick to blame themselves for failures that are the result of an imperfect technical solution. The importance of this is highlighted by the fact that even in the literature on healthy subjects it has not always been possible to detect the EEG markers in the brain activity on which most BCI systems rely, and even fewer subjects have managed to successfully operate these systems. In this context, special care is necessary when presenting a potential experimental protocol to patients who are sadly all too familiar with disappointment. Discussions with the general public and the media must also be conducted honestly, so as not to generate artificial expectations that might lead to further disappointment and a loss of public interest, with the long-term consequence of loss of public funding.

The performance of medical communication BCIs has been proven in a number of clinical trials with patients. These studies have exhibited a large variety of techniques and interfaces, with a strong preference for visual interfaces and in particular interfaces based on the P300 wave. A small number of minor paradigm adjustments have the potential to greatly improve the user-friendliness of these systems; this potential needs to be exploited for more than just its scientific value. This is indicative of the fact that medical communication BCIs have achieved a certain level of technological maturity, and need to be slowly released from the research laboratory into the hands of engineers to benefit from their expertise in product development. Unfortunately, there may well be a lack of interest from the medical industry due to low patient volumes, meaning that the public authorities and major organizations must take the initiative to provide the key players with the resources necessary to properly accomplish this task.

3.5. Bibliography

[BAR 14] BARACHANT A., CONGEDO M., *A Plug&Play P300 BCI Using Information Geometry*, available at http://arxiv.org/abs/1409.0107, 2014.

[BEN 07] BENSCH M., KARIM A.A., MELLINGER J. *et al.*, "Nessi: an EEG-controlled web browser for severely paralyzed patients", *Computational Intelligence and Neuroscience*, vol. 2007, pp. 1–5, 2007.

[BEU 98] BEUKELMAN D.R., MIRENDA P., *Augmentative and Alternative Communication: Management of Severe Communication Disorders in Children and Adults*, Brookes Publishing Company, 1998.

[BIN 11] BIN G., GAO X., WANG Y. *et al.*, "A high-speed BCI based on code modulation VEP", *Journal of Neural Engineering*, vol. 8, no. 2, 2011.

[BIG 07] BIGOT R., CROUTTE P., *La diffusion des technologies de l'information dans la société française*, Credoc, 2007.

[BIR 00] BIRBAUMER N., KÜBLER A., GHANAYIM N. *et al.*, "The thought translation device (TTD) for completely paralyzed patients", *IEEE Transactions on Rehabilitation Engineering*, vol. 8, no. 2, pp. 190–193, 2000.

[BIR 03] BIRBAUMER N., HINTERBERGER T., KÜBLER A. *et al.*, "The thought-translation device (TTD): neurobehavioral mechanisms and clinical outcome", *IEEE Transactions on Neural Systems and Rehabilitation Engineering*, vol. 11, no. 2, pp. 120–123, 2003.

[BIR 07] BIRBAUMER N., COHEN L.G., "Brain–Computer interfaces: communication and restoration of movement in paralysis", *The Journal of Physiology*, vol. 579, no. 3, pp. 621–636, 2007.

[CHE 02] CHENG M., GAO X., GAO S. *et al.*, "Design and implementation of a brain-computer interface with high transfer rates", *IEEE Transactions on Biomedical Engineering*, vol. 49, no. 10, pp. 1181–1186, 2002.

[CLE 16] CLERC M., BOUGRAIN L., LOTTE F., (eds), *Brain–Computer Interface 1*, ISTE, London and John Wiley & Sons, New York, 2016.

[COR 14] CORRALEJO R., NICOLÁS-ALONSO L.F., ÁLVAREZ D. *et al.*, "A P300-based Brain–Computer interface aimed at operating electronic devices at home for severely disabled people", *Medical & Biological Engineering & Computing*, vol. 52, no. 10, pp. 861–872, 2014.

[DEL 03] DEL R. MILLÁN J., NO J.M., "Asynchronous BCI and local neural classifiers: an overview of the adaptive brain interface project", *IEEE Transactions on Neural Systems and Rehabilitation Engineering*, vol. 11, no. 2, pp. 159–161, 2003.

[DON 00] DONCHIN E., SPENCER K.M., WIJESINGHE R., "The mental prosthesis: assessing the speed of a P300-based brain-computer interface", *IEEE Transactions on Rehabilitation Engineering*, vol. 8, no. 2, pp. 174–179, 2000.

[FAR 88] FARWELL L.A., DONCHIN E., "Talking off the top of your head: toward a mental prosthesis utilizing event-related brain potentials", *Electroencephalography and Clinical Neurophysiology*, vol. 70, no. 6, pp. 510–523, 1988.

[FUR 09] FURDEA A., HALDER S., KRUSIENSKI D. *et al.*, "An auditory oddball (P300) spelling system for brain-computer interfaces", *Psychophysiology*, vol. 46, no. 3, pp. 617–625, 2009.

[GAR 06] GARAY-VITORIA N., ABASCAL J., "Text prediction systems: a survey", *Universal Access in the Information Society*, vol. 4, no. 3, pp. 188-203, 2006.

[HIN 03] HINTERBERGER T., KÜBLER A., KAISER J. *et al.*, "A brain-computer interface (BCI) for the locked-in: comparison of different EEG classifications for the thought translation device", *Clinical Neurophysiology*, vol. 114, no. 3, pp. 416-425, 2003.

[HIN 04] HINTERBERGER T., SCHMIDT S., NEUMANN N. *et al.*, "Brain-computer communication and slow cortical potentials", *IEEE Transactions on Biomedical Engineering*, vol. 51, no. 6, pp. 1011–1018, 2004.

[HUG 14a] HUGGINS J.E., GUGER C., ALLISON B. *et al.*, "Workshops of the fifth international brain-computer interface meeting: defining the future", *Brain-Computer Interfaces*, vol. 1, no. 1, pp. 27–49, 2014.

[HUG 14b] HUGGINS J.E., WOLPAW J.R., "Papers from the fifth international Brain–Computer interface meeting", *Journal of Neural Engineering*, vol. 11, no. 3, 2014.

[IVE 08] IVERSEN I., GHANAYIM N., KÜBLER A. *et al.*, "A brain-computer interface tool to assess cognitive functions in completely paralyzed patients with amyotrophic lateral sclerosis", *Clinical Neurophysiology*, vol. 119, no. 10, pp. 2214–2223, 2008.

[KÄT 13] KÄTHNER I., RUF C.A., PASQUALOTTO E. *et al.*, "A portable auditory P300 Brain–Computer interface with directional cues", *Clinical Neurophysiology*, vol. 124, no. 2, pp. 327–338, 2013.

[KÜB 09] KÜBLER A., FURDEA A., HALDER S. *et al.*, "A Brain–Computer interface controlled auditory event-related potential (P300) spelling system for locked-in patients", *Annals of the New York Academy of Sciences*, vol. 1157, no. 1, pp. 90–100, 2009.

[LEE 13] LEEB R., PERDIKIS S., TONIN L. *et al.*, "Transferring brain-computer interfaces beyond the laboratory: successful application control for motor-disabled users", *Artificial Intelligence in Medicine*, vol. 59, no. 2, pp. 121–132, 2013.

[LIM 13] LIM J.-H., HWANG H.-J., HAN C.-H. *et al.*, "Classification of binary intentions for individuals with impaired oculomotor function:'eyes-closed' SSVEP-based Brain–Computer interface (BCI)", *Journal of Neural Engineering*, vol. 10, no. 2, 2013.

[LUL 13] LULÉ D., NOIRHOMME Q., KLEIH S.C. *et al.*, "Probing command following in patients with disorders of consciousness using a Brain–Computer interface", *Clinical Neurophysiology*, vol. 124, no. 1, pp. 101–106, 2013.

[MAR 15] MARCHETTI M., PRIFTIS K., "Brain-computer interfaces in amyotrophic lateral sclerosis: a metanalysis", *Clinical Neurophysiology*, vol. 126, no. 6, pp. 1255–1263, June 2015.

[MAY 13] MAYAUD L., FILIPE S., PÉTÉGNIEF L. *et al.*, "Robust brain-computer interface for virtual keyboard (RoBIK): project results", *IRBM*, vol. 34, no. 2, pp. 131–138, 2013.

[MCC 14] MCCANE L.M., SELLERS E.W., MCFARLAND D.J. *et al.*, "Brain-computer interface (BCI) evaluation in people with amyotrophic lateral sclerosis", *Amyotrophic Lateral Sclerosis and Frontotemporal Degeneration*, vol. 15, no. 3–4, pp. 207–215, 2014.

[MOG 13] MOGHIMI S., KUSHKI A., GUERGUERIAN A.-M. *et al.*, "A review of EEG-based brain–computer interfaces and access pathways for individuals with severe disabilities", *Assistive Technology: The Official Journal of RESNA*, vol. 25, no. 2, pp. 99–110, 2013.

[ORH 14] ORHAN U., "RSVP keyboard: an EEG based BCI typing system with context information fusion", available at https://repository.library.northeastern.edu/files/neu:1429, 2014.

[PIC 06] PICCIONE F., GIORGI F., TONIN P. *et al.*, "P300-based brain computer interface: reliability and performance in healthy and paralysed participants", *Clinical Neurophysiology*, vol. 117, no. 3, pp. 531–537, 2006.

[RIC 12] RICCIO A., MATTIA D., SIMIONE L., OLIVETTI M. *et al.*, "Eye-gaze independent EEG-based brain-computer interfaces for communication", *Journal of Neural Engineering*, vol. 9, pp. 1–15, 2012.

[SEL 06] SELLERS E.W., DONCHIN E., "A P300-based Brain–Computer interface: initial tests by ALS patients", *Clinical Neurophysiology*, vol. 117, no. 3, pp. 538–548, 2006.

[SEL 13] SELLERS E.W., "New horizons in brain-computer interface research", *Clinical Neurophysiology: Official Journal of the International Federation of Clinical Neurophysiology*, vol. 124, no. 1, p. 2, 2013.

[SEL 14] SELLERS E.W., RYAN D.B., HAUSER C.K., "Noninvasive Brain–Computer interface enables communication after brainstem stroke", *Science Translational Medicine*, available at http://stm.sciencemag.org/content/6/257/257re7, vol. 6, no. 257, pp. 257re7, 2014.

[SEN 10] SENO B.D., MATTEUCCI M., MAINARDI L.T., "The utility metric: a novel method to assess the overall performance of discrete brain-computer interfaces", *IEEE Transactions on Neural Systems and Rehabilitation Engineering*, vol. 18, no. 1, pp. 20–29, 2010.

[SIL 13] SILVONI S., CAVINATO M., VOLPATO C. *et al.*, "Amyotrophic lateral sclerosis progression and stability of brain-computer interface communication", *Amyotrophic Lateral Sclerosis and Frontotemporal Degeneration*, vol. 14, no. 5–6, pp. 390–396, 2013.

[SUT 92] SUTTER E.E., "The brain response interface: communication through visually-induced electrical brain responses", *Journal of Microcomputer Applications*, vol. 15, no. 1, pp. 31–45, 1992.

[THO 13] THOMPSON D.E., BLAIN-MORAES S., HUGGINS J.E., "Performance assessment in brain-computer interface-based augmentative and alternative communication", *Biomedical Engineering Online*, vol. 12, no. 43, pp. 1–23, 2013.

[VID 73] VIDAL J.-J., "Toward direct brain-computer communication", *Annual Review of Biophysics and Bioengineering*, vol. 2, no. 1, pp. 157–180, 1973.

[WAN 06] WANG Y., WANG R., GAO X. *et al.*, "A practical VEP-based brain-computer interface", *IEEE Transactions on Neural Systems and Rehabilitation Engineering*, vol. 14, no. 2, pp. 234–240, 2006.

[WAN 08] WANG Y., GAO X., HONG B. *et al.*, "Brain-computer interfaces based on visual evoked potentials", *Engineering in Medicine and Biology Magazine,* vol. 27, no. 5, pp. 64–71, 2008.

[WOL 91] WOLPAW J.R., MCFARLAND D.J. *et al.*, "An EEG-based brain-computer interface for cursor control", *Electroencephalography and Clinical Neurophysiology*, vol. 78, no. 3, pp. 252–259, 1991.

[WOL 02] WOLPAW J.R., BIRBAUMER N., MCFARLAND D.J. *et al.*, "Brain-computer interfaces for communication and control", *Clinical Neurophysiology*, vol. 113, no. 6, pp. 767–791, 2002.

BrainTV: Revealing the Neural Bases of Human Cognition in Real Time

4.1. Introduction and motivation

After the neuroimaging boom of the 1990s, brain activity measurement tools have continued to improve, providing increasingly accurate access to the human brain at both the anatomical and the functional levels. Somewhat provocatively, we could say that the new challenge is now to give meaning to all these data, that is to establish the connection between these measurements and our conscious experience of everyday life. For example, to find out how my brain will react at the precise moment when I will raise my eyes to look at the face of my neighbor who has just turned to me. In order to best predict this reaction, I could, like any neuroscientist, rely on an entire experimental dataset collected from healthy volunteers or patients during an experiment that required from them to look patiently at a hundred faces on a computer screen being displayed one after the other in a dark laboratory room. I would patiently reread the findings of advanced statistical analyses, more or less amounting to an averaging of the signals – electroencephalograms (EEG), magnetoencephalography (MEG), functional magnetic resonance imaging (fMRI) or positron emission tomography (PET) – captured during this whole experiment. These average values, represented in the form of brain maps or curves, would then constitute the best possible prediction of the activity of my

Chapter written by Jean-Philippe LACHAUX.

brain at the moment I look at the face of the person in front of me. Unfortunately, the only thing that I can predict with certainty is that this prediction will be wrong.

Naturally, it will not be entirely wrong: by recording 100 times the hemodynamic response of my brain confronted with faces, I would obtain a nice looking activation map highlighting one of the areas of my temporal lobe called the "fusiform face area" (FFA) [KAN 97]. Furthermore, a similar analysis of the 100 corresponding measurements of my EEG would reveal an elegant potential curve showing a negative peak 170 ms after a face has appeared, the "N170" [BEN 96]. These analyses would allow me to predict that when perceiving my neighbor's face, my FFA will be activated with a delay of about two-tenths of a second to identify this person. This is a good start, but once again is only a rough approximation of what is really happening in my brain at that time.

A detailed examination of 100 responses, electrophysiological or hemodynamic, at each of the 100 images of faces flashed on the screen before me would reveal a great variability of the brain activity from one image to another: a slightly stronger response than the average for image 46, a slightly longer response for image 48, etc., with no apparent reason. Any researcher in cognitive neuroscience will confirm this: the human brain never reacts twice in the same way, even if the stimulation conditions are absolutely identical, and this is why I cannot predict how my brain will react to my neighbor, or even how it would react if I was shown, in the dark laboratory room, a hundred and first face.

4.2. Toward first person data accounting

For an experimenter, the human brain is a noisy system and this noise is the enemy of the researcher in cognitive neuroscience. It is clear that the final objective of this researcher is to be able to correlate in an accurate manner the recordings of cognitive processes (or perceptual, motor, emotional, etc.). This is the reason why all experiments in this field strive to control as specifically as possible what the recorded brain is doing. The face will be presented in a very controlled manner, in an environment where the brightness and the sound ambience are precisely defined, by ensuring that the participant always gazes in the same direction; all this to maximally reduce any source of variability of brain activity that is not easily attributable to the parameters of the experiment. The reason why everything is so thoroughly controlled is because we do not acknowledge any way of *knowing* what a human brain does other than by *compelling* it to act in a certain fashion. Any source of variability in its activity, apart from that explicitly manipulated by the experience (presenting images of faces or cars) must be eliminated because of the risk that it may render the data uninterpretable, since interpreting the data consists of precisely explaining this variability of the brain activity according to the variability that the experimenter has himself imposed in his protocol. Unfortunately, the main source of variability comes from cognitive processes that the participant brings into play, which imposes, following the logic of neuroimaging, also that these processes be controlled to obtain information about them (what was the participant really doing?). This control is achieved by imposing a task to the participant, and ideally hoping that this task will impose a fixed sequence of cognitive processes in his brain. In this manner, it is possible that certain brain activities be associated for instance with the encoding phase of a stimulus in the memory, or to the recalling phase, or to the recognition phase of a face or of a facial expression. Unfortunately, any attempt to control human cognitive activity invariably ends up with failure, and that is what the variability of the observed responses reveals through identical stimulus situations. It is simply impossible to prevent a participant from seeing the form of a face in an image of a car, seen frontally, just because the headlights make him think about eyes, and thus to activate his FFA, *from time to time*. It is not possible to force someone to see cars as cars only, or to not think about the last dinner with one of his friends when confronted with the image of a face that looks like him.

It is easy to understand, therefore, that the unexplained variability of the brain activity from one trial to another is a nightmare for the experimenter. The activity has changed between the trial N and N + 1 without being possible to say why, because all the parameters controlled by the experiment have remained the same. Has the participant thought about his friend? Has he focused his attention on the left nostril of the face which seemed strange to him? To work around this problem, the conventional approach in brain imaging consists of averaging the brain activities collected in response to the many presentations of the stimulus and to show only this average activity, stripped of intertrial variability. This variability is therefore considered as an uninterpretable noise, and disgarded in the same way as the measurement noise originating from the devices. On the other hand, this noise of neuronal origin is of a different nature, because it actually corresponds to the spontaneous life of the brain that simply cannot be matched to the parameters controlled by the experiment. It is therefore impossible for the experimenter to make sense of it.

This observation is by no means satisfactory. As long as neuroimaging experiments continue, this variability will be there to remind us how limited is our understanding of the human brain, even for processes as simple as face recognition. Naturally, several studies have focused on this variability by trying to further improve its understanding, by showing, for example, that the amplitude of the neuronal response to a sensory stimulus depends to a certain extent on the neuronal activity prior to this stimulus [WYA 09]. This type of study shows that variability should not be reduced to simple noise with no functional nor cognitive correlate. Variability more likely concerns variations in attention, in alertness or even in cognitive strategy such as those that we clearly feel every day in our daily lives. Moreover, any person having undergone a long laboratory experiment could testify that, faced with the succession of images or of sounds presented during the experience, attention and alertness spontaneously fluctuate, and that it is not uncommon to engage in brief mind-wandering. It should not be surprising that the brain does not responds in the same way each time because its state keeps on changing.

It is therefore not unreasonable to assume that these spontaneous fluctuations in mental activity, that we can all experience, participate in a certain manner to the variability of the observed brain activity. Unfortunately, once the experiment is complete, the experimenter does not have any *first person* information on these fluctuations experienced by the participant because they were not recorded. However, there must exist some correspondence between the variability measured through testing in brain activity, and the variability felt by the participant, in the experience of being the living and thinking subject of this protocol. However, this correspondence cannot be investigated unless the participants share this experience in a scientifically readable form. Without these first-person data, there is nothing to which the neuronal variability can be connected and the latter is doomed to remain a noise without any meaning.

4.3. Bringing subjective and objective data into the same space: conscious experience of the subject

During a simple visual perception experiment, Lutz *et al.* [LUT 02] asked participants to annotate each episode – the presentation of an image and the motor response to this image – according to a system of categories corresponding to different attentional states. This classification resulted in several groups of trials, called phenomenological clusters, fully related to what the subject felt ("highly concentrated on the screen" or "an open attention field taking the whole room into account", etc.). Within each cluster, the variability of the measured responses in EEG was much smaller than if the responses were considered together. This fact thus demonstrated that the subjective experience of the patients was an explanatory factor of the variability of EEG activity, which would be totally missed by the experimenter in a conventional experimental approach.

This first study was interesting, but enabled one variability factor to be addressed: the attention mode of the subject. However, numerous components of mental life may influence the measured signals, and if they are not addressed by the experiment, they remain invisible. Another way to proceed consists of adopting an opposite approach, and not to start from a particular mental component, but from the brain signal itself. As a matter of fact, if the participant receives some feedback, in graphical form or otherwise, of his brain activity as it has just been recorded, and for example by comparing it to the previous activities or to the average activity measured so far, then he has the possibility to link the feedback he receives with something that he knows he has done, or experienced, at that moment. The question asked to the participant is then: what have you done or felt, which is specific to this last episode and that could correspond to this component of the signal which seems specific to it? The basic principle of this approach is that it is necessary to establish a correlation between events in the first-person, specific to the experience of the patient, and events in the third-person, that is to say observable by a third party (the fluctuations of the cerebral signal) *in order to present them in the same space so that they are confronted therein*. The conscious experience of the subject appears as the most natural space given the difficulty in projecting the intimate contents of his mental life in another way (it may be considered in the form of verbal reports, of classifications, etc., but this projection is unavoidably a degraded version of the initial experience).

At the same time, it should be noted that such a device, which would immediately represent the brain activity of the participant, also allows the experimenter to interpret its variations according to events that he may himself observe. If, for example, and despite the precautions being taken, a voice is heard in the distance during the experiment, as is sometimes the case, the experimenter could potentially observe the effect of a sudden redirection of the subject's attention in the measured signal, and could deliberately repeat this type of distraction to verify the casual relationship envisaged.

The constraints upon any researcher in cognitive neuroscience deeply concerned with making sense of the brain signals recorded, notably through an interpretation of the unexplained variability by the experimental protocol, point toward the development of a system allowing the visualization or the sonification of the brain activity of the subject in order to represent it, to himself and to the experimenter throughout the experience. This is precisely what the device called BrainTV is capable of, which forms the topic of this chapter. BrainTV aims to overcome certain current limits of cognitive neuroscience, and to actually take into account the subject; the objective concerns real-time neuroimaging directly related to the most active field of research in this area: that of brain–computer interfaces. On the other hand, unlike BCIs, the aim is not to produce devices that enable a subject to physically act and to communicate without using his members; the objective is to better understand the human brain and to give meaning to its spontaneous activity. It is also significantly different from neurofeedback techniques, whose goal consists of bringing the subject, by closing the loop connecting him to neuroimaging, to better control her brain activity and consider states deemed as desirable.

4.4. Technical aspects: the contribution of brain–computer interfaces

In order for such a system to be operational and genuinely useful, it is therefore necessary for it to operate in real time, with an adequate temporal resolution adapted to the speed of transient internal mental processes such as thoughts, emotions or slight attention instabilities. It should also be rather accurate, spatially, to measure the activity of relatively homogeneous brain regions at the functional level; that is to say that whose measured activity is not the average of processes of a totally different nature. Due to the anatomical and functional organization of the brain, functional accuracy is known to be closely related to anatomical accuracy: such a system is expected to distinguish, for example, the activity of a region specialized in the analysis of a musical acoustic signal, from that of a neighboring region specialized in the perception of speech. Moreover, we know that a few millimeters barely separate these two regions [LAC 07], and this order of magnitude is similar when considering other functions. These "few millimeters" therefore specify the level of spatial accuracy required here. With regard to the temporal resolution, considering that the mental recollection of an image, the face of a friend, for example, requires barely a few hundred milliseconds [BEN 96]; this gives an idea of the required resolution. Finally, for this kind of approach it is of course essential that the neuronal activity corresponding to the cognitive process of interest can be directly observed, without any averaging, which still requires an additional constraint regarding the quality of the recorded signal: the measurement "noise" must be very low.

These constraints preclude from the start all the techniques used to measure the brain activity in a conventional and non-invasive manner. Electroencephalography and magnetoencephalography are far from having the necessary spatial resolution and signal-to-noise ratio for such an endeavor. Even combined with the most modern source reconstruction techniques and imaging methods relying on metabolic measurements, such as fMRI or PET, they suffer from an inadequate temporal resolution. Regarding MRI, some attempts should however be mentioned whose aim was similar to the one exposed here. A program such as turbo BrainVoyager [CAR 07], for example, provides the subject with the possibility of controlling the metabolic activity of her brain (in this case, the quantity of oxygen locally consumed by a specific area of the cortex) by means of feedback. The system works as soon as the participant is able to stand in a relatively stationary cognitive state, over several seconds typically, in which case the low temporal resolution of the fMRI is no longer a limitation. On the other hand, the feedback is too slow to be able to associate the measured variations of the brain activity to brief events, such as reactions to sudden sounds or sudden redirections of the attention for instance. Nevertheless, Christopher DeCharms's team [DEC 05] have been able to show that it was possible to train a subject to selectively manipulate the activity of her anterior cingulate gyrus to regulate her sensitivity to pain. The mere possibility of this type of manipulation, which very clearly and unequivocally combines the activity of a particular brain region with a cognitive strategy (what the subject "is doing" to modulate the activity), provides an extremely interesting hint to go deeper into the functional mapping of the human brain.

Naturally, this type of experiment recalls immediately the long history of EEG biofeedback, initiated in particular by Rémond at the LENA laboratory at the Hôpital de la Salpêtrière in Paris [REM 94]. As soon as the demonstration was made that subjects could sometimes recognize in their conscious experience (sensation of decline in vigilance, of transitional disconnection with the immediate sensory environment, etc.) correlates with the level of alpha activity recorded in their EEG signal (rhythmic activity around 10 Hz), electrophysiologists have attempted, with success, to train these same subjects to control their alpha activity through a feedback of this activity in real time (neurofeedback principle, see Chapter 13 of Volume 1 [CLE 16]). However, in this form, this technique only resembles the system discussed in the context of this chapter. In practice, the activities detected by EEG are the sum of numerous contributions originating from brain regions having completely different functions, so that the real-time EEG does not allow, because of its clearly insufficient spatial resolution (of at least one order of magnitude, if not two) redirecting to the subject a faithful reflection of the activity of homogeneous neuronal populations at the functional level. It is therefore impossible for the subject to give a precise meaning to the activity that is sent to her, except as in the form of rather global changes in cognitive states (reduced vigilance, see above). Unfortunately, due to the physics of the EEG (and to a lesser extent MEG) signal, this limitation also applies to other brain rhythms that can be measured from the surface of the scalp (theta, beta, gamma, etc.). In practice, the only measurements that are really adapted to the project introduced in this chapter are those invasively performed in the brain, in patients suffering from neurological diseases and "implanted" for therapeutic reasons. Several pathologies justify this type of recordings, but among these, epilepsy offers a particularly interesting framework. Indeed, the surgical treatment of epilepsy sometimes imposes a planning phase (to identify the target brain areas for surgery), which involves the placement of intracerebral electrodes in distributed areas of the cortex, unlike other pathologies, such as Parkinson's disease whose treatment targets a stereotypical region (here, basal ganglia or the subthalamic nucleus). In the case of epilepsy, the brain activity is recorded in multiple cortical sites (several hundred, sometimes) that vary from one patient to another, depending on the precise organization of the epileptogenic network. In the context of these intracerebral recordings, which may take place continuously for 2 or even 3 weeks, it is therefore possible to present to the patient, according to the neurofeedback principle, the activity of each of the recorded cortical sites, with a temporal resolution in the order of the millisecond (depending on the sampling frequency of the acquisition chain) and a spatial accuracy of a few cubic millimeters (corresponding to homogeneous neuronal populations on the functional level). The recorded signal is an electrophysiological signal of the same nature as the EEG signal, but exhibiting a much higher signal-to-noise ratio, sufficient for detecting the elaboration of a cognitive process without any averaging. This signal is called intracerebral EEG (iEEG), or sometimes electrocorticogram or stereoelectroencephalogram, according to the type of intracranial electrodes used. The iEEG is therefore the ideal signal for observing the neural correlates of human cognitive activity "in real time" and to collect the opinion of the subject thereupon. Naturally, certain precautions are required if one wishes to generalize the obtained findings to the human species in general, as claimed by most brain imaging studies. It is mainly necessary to ensure that the recorded signal is not affected by the epileptic activity of the patient and that her brain has not suffered significant reorganizations due to the disease. It is also important to take into consideration the medications that the patient may be taking, and their possible impact on iEEG activity. These difficulties have been discussed in several journals on the use of the iEEG for cognitive research (e.g. [LAC 12]). The most common precautions consist of evaluating the signal recorded by a neurologist for the presence or the absence of epileptiform activities, to ensure that the site of interest is not part of the epileptogenic network, to reproduce the same observations in patients showing various forms of epilepsy and, of course, to ensure the normality of the zone under study on the purely anatomical level (MRI).

These precautions having been taken, it should then be decided which components of the iEEG signal should be presented to the patient in the form of feedback. The raw iEEG signal, like the EEG, does not have a great significance. It is composed of multiple components, often associated with specific frequencies (theta, alpha, beta, gamma, etc., from 4 to 150 Hz, beyond, below and above), which vary in a differentiated manner according to the current cognitive activity: they do not constitute the "signatures" of the same neural processes. An overall visualization of all these components at the same time would therefore be bound to fail. It was necessary to wait until the end of the 1990s and early 2000s for the "good" component to be identified. During the same period, in Paris (in the visual system, [LAC 00]) and in Baltimore (in the motor system, [CRO 98]), two teams showed that the components of the iEEG signal above 40 Hz, in the frequency band known as "gamma", reproduced in an extremely faithful and reliable manner, at the time, the engagement of neuron populations recorded in the motor or in the perceptual processes brought into play by the experience. Nathan Crone, for example, showed that it was possible to reconstruct the motor homunculus from measurements of the gamma activity registered in iEEG in the motor cortex, while asking the patient to perform movements of the different parts of the body. During motion, the gamma activity specifically increased in the cortical area associated with the part of the body concerned an (association previously revealed during direct electrical stimulation of the cortex). Lower frequency activities were also modulated by the gesture made, but in a less specific way (with decreased activity in the alpha and beta bands, between 8 and 30 Hz, and a less precise relationship between the cortical area and performed motion). These observations have been reproduced many times since (see [LAC 12] for a review) to now bring the community of experts of the iEEG signal to consider the "broadband" gamma activity (between approximately 50 and 150 Hz) as the most accurate index of the participation of a neuronal population in the sensory, motor or cognitive process in progress. The final task was to demonstrate that these modulations of the gamma activity, now called high-frequency activity (HFA) (50–150 Hz) could be detected without applying the averaging techniques commonly in use in electrophysiology, "through several trials". The evidence was achieved as of 2005 (study published in 2007, [LAC 07]) by means of the first system allowing the real-time visualization of the HFA (50–150 Hz) in a patient busy with daily chores, and spontaneously interacting with her immediate environment. This system was christened BrainTV, in reference to the possibility for the patient to select herself the site whose activity she wishes to observe, in the same way that one would change channels on a TV.

From a technical point of view, the procedure applied to the iEEG signal within the BrainTV system is extremely simple. The signal is filtered (bandpass filter) to retrieve the oscillatory components of 10 consecutive frequency bands (50–60 Hz) to (140–150 Hz), to which a Hilbert transform is applied to retrieve the envelope of each component; that is a continuous signal coinciding with the oscillatory signal at each of its maxima. Each envelope is then normalized by dividing at each sampling point, the value obtained by the average value measured during the last 10 s registered and by multiplying the result obtained by 100. In other words, after this transformation, a value of 150 indicates that at this sample point, the envelope has reached a value one and a half times (150%) greater than the measured value during the previous 10 s. The last step of calculation consists of averaging all together the 10 standard envelopes corresponding to each of the 10 frequency bands. This technique has several advantages: (1) it is simple, (2) it is robust to possible changes in the precise frequency range of the iEEG activity (if the activation of the group of neurons translates once by an increase in energy between 60 and 90 Hz and the second time between 70 and 110 Hz, the effect on the signal is similar), (3) it sums the effects measured in 10 frequency bands, consequently increasing the signal-to-noise ratio, (4) it compensates for the natural decrease in amplitude of the iEEG signal with frequency (higher frequency components have a lower amplitude than the lowest frequency components, according to a "1/f" law), (5) it presents the relative changes in the HFA activity compared with the recent past: in a real-time interface of this type, the absolute value of the signal is less interesting than the relative variations induced by the activity of the participant; it is therefore helpful to normalize the signal with respect to the period that has just elapsed. Numerous variants are possible to extract the HFA in real time (average wavelet coefficients, short-term Fourier transform) but we should be pragmatic: in the end, all that matters is the possibility for the patient to relate this signal to what she does or to what she feels. If this relationship is possible, it is proof that the analysis technique of the signal is a right one.

4.5. The BrainTV system and its applications

The principle that has just been described is implemented in the original BrainTV system (Figure 4.1) developed at the Centre Hospitalo-Universitaire de Grenoble and which, except for some details, corresponds to the systems that have recovered this approach in other centers [RAM 06, MIL 10]. One of the major points of interest of BrainTV is its ability to formulate and to test in a very short time several hypotheses concerning the functional role of a region of the brain: a dozen hypotheses can be invalidated in a few minutes to further focus reasoning on the only really valid avenues. In order to reach the same findings with conventional experimental protocols, it would be necessary to design and to test scores of cognitive paradigms, exceeding by far the time that may be reasonably available with the patient. This possibility is both clinically (to map the brain of the patient) and fundamentally significant (to understand the structure/function relationships of the human brain).

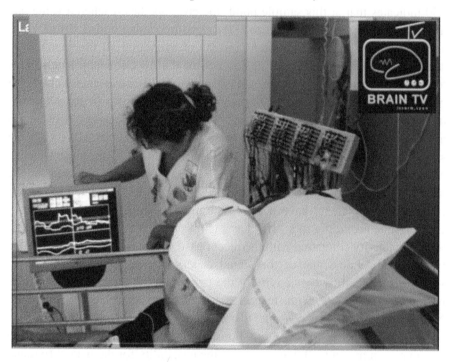

Figure 4.1. *The in situ BrainTV system. Here, the patient observes the high-frequency activity (50–150 Hz) (in orange) as well as the low-frequency activity (8–24 Hz) measured during the last 10 s (and updated four times per second) at four sites in his brain that he can change at will*

4.5.1. Application of BrainTV in fundamental research

In an application of BrainTV published in 2012 [HAM 12], the patient was recorded in the inferior temporal gyrus (Figure 4.2). A conventional experimental protocol had shown that the gamma activity of this region increased systematically as soon as she had to keep an image in memory (that of a 4 × 4 grid where some boxes were grayed out). The question posed by the experimenter and clinicians was whether this activity (and the region) was specific to retention in visual memory, or related to any form of retention in memory (including in a verbalized form) or to the stabilization of a mental image, whether previously presented or simply imagined by the patient. In effect, a few seconds of introspection suffice to realize that the retention of an image in memory, in a visual form, is accompanied by a mental image similar to that which could be generated to prepare a drawing, for example. In the BrainTV session that followed, the patient was simply encouraged to stare at a sheet of white paper, imagining that letters were drawn on this sheet. Immediately, the gamma activity of the inferior temporal gyrus increased prior to oscillation between rising and descending phases throughout the whole duration of the concentration effort of the patient. However, was the rise of the activity due to the simple act of staring? By asking the patient to stare at the sheet, without projecting upon it any mental image, the gamma activity remained low. The participant was then encouraged to generate other mental images, without necessarily staring at the sheet and each time, the gamma activity increased accordingly to the involvement of the patient. The cause and effect relationship between the gamma activity of the inferior temporal gyrus and imagination could be deduced from the observation of the curve fluctuations on the screen according to the instructions provided to the patient, but what was she thinking about? By regularly observing the effect of her mental activity on the screen representation, the patient confirmed that she could control the curve. By increasing the vivacity of her mental image, proof was thus provided about the usefulness of combining first-person and third-person data since the mental images are inherently a purely subjective phenomenon invisible to an experimenter. In passing, two features of the BrainTV system should be noted: the on-screen display of the last 10 s of brain activity and the possibility of "covering the tracks" by feeding back to the participant not the last data acquired, but older data, recorded 1 min earlier for example. By displaying the last 10 s, and not only the instantaneous value of the cerebral signal, the participant may attempt to apply a cognitive strategy incompatible with the tracking of the curve (for example picture a mental image with eyes closed), and then observe the effect of this strategy on the immediate past. This trick avoids confronting the subject with a situation of shared attention since she can alternate between her main activity and the observation of the curve. The selected time, 10 s, corresponds to the time window during which the participant still maintains a clear memory of what she has done. The second characteristic, to confuse things, allows the detection of situations during which the patient has the impression of controlling the curve on the screen, or that she is able to relate it to mental phenomena, even if it is not necessarily the case. In this case, this latter will not realize if the data projected on the screen are not the latest recorded.

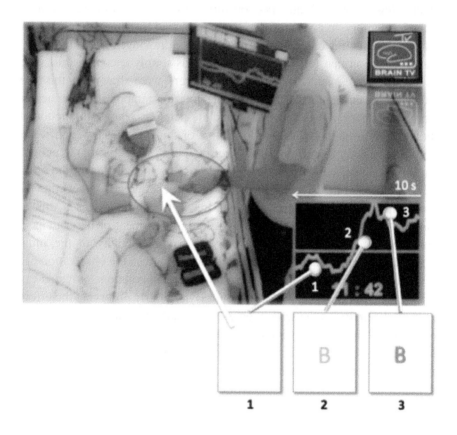

Figure 4.2. *BrainTV session example. The experimenter asks the patient to imagine that a letter is drawn on the white sheet which he presents her with. The evolution in real time of the high-frequency activity (50–150 Hz) measured in the lower temporal gyrus (bottom-right view) reveals the progressive implementation (stages "1", "2" and "3") of the mental image. The letter B drawn under the image illustrates an estimate of the mental image at each of its steps (session exposed in [HAM 12])*

This example properly illustrates several fundamental characteristics of the BrainTV approach and its derivatives. First, this approach is based on a principle of hypotheses formulation and their rapid testing. Although in the conventional cognitive neuroscience approach the experimenter formulates a hypothesis and devises an experiment to test it within a long-term research project, here, the hypothesis is immediately formulated during the interaction with the patient ("what if this activity was related to the mental imaging component of memory?"). As a matter of fact, it is also one of the difficulties of this approach because it requires a significant responsiveness and creativity from the experimenter, on the site of the experiment. It is then possible to distinguish between several equiprobable functional interpretations on the basis of the experiments previously performed. Effectively, it is common that the results of an experiment be compatible with several possible interpretations: BrainTV allows for quickly testing each one of them and establishing that most be eliminated. In the previous example, the region of the inferior temporal gyrus, which was targeted in this patient, was activated during the retention phase of a conventional protocol of visuospatial working memory, which could suggest that it was specific to working memory retention. The BrainTV session that followed has shown that this was not the case, since it was active in any situation demanding the generation of mental images, including to picture the future.

Another advantage of the BrainTV system is that it allows discoveries to be made "by accident", as was the discovery of the mirror neurons in the monkey in Parma [GAL 96]. The principle of monitoring in real time the responsiveness of a particular area of the brain makes it possible to notice a specific selectivity to certain events that would have been difficult, if not impossible, to design in a purely theoretical way. This is how we were able to discover by accident in the auditory cortex, a region selectively activated by the changes in speakers, during a conversation involving several of them [LAC 07]. This selectivity was observed during a debate between two interlocutors in the patient's room, on the function of this particular population of neurons.

Finally, it is important to note that BrainTV has also contributed to research on BCI by proposing new forms of brain activity that can be controlled at will by a subject. It should be noted that a BCI system depends on an effective association between an electrophysiological marker and a cognitive strategy that allows the subject to deliberately cause this marker to vary. BrainTV regularly provides associations of this type, as illustrated by the example that has just been detailed: the HFA activity in the inferior-temporal gyrus can be voluntarily controlled by an effort of mental imaging. It can therefore provide a basis for a BCI system easily controllable by the participant.

4.5.2. BrainTV clinical applications

The BrainTV system also has direct clinical applications, since it allows the identification of the function supported by the brain regions recorded in the patient during the prechirurgical tracking phase. It should be borne in mind that the purpose of this tracking is not only to target ill areas that will have to be removed, but also to identify the healthy areas essential to proper cognitive functioning and that it is essential to preserve. By giving the clinical team the opportunity to observe in real time the responsiveness of the recorded areas, BrainTV makes it possible to specify their function and eventually exclude them from the surgical strategy if their eloquence is proven.

In particular, BrainTV complements the phase of brain electrical stimulation performed in the usual framework of the presurgical exploration. In this procedure, the clinician electrically stimulates each of the sites for recording one after the other to induce cognitive and motor deficits or notable impressions for the patient (appearance of light flashes, strange auditory sensations, itching, etc.). These stimulations provide insight into the clinician about the function of the cortical territories being explored, but they are not well suited to the high-level cognitive functions: for example, the stimulation of a region involved in mental imaging leads to significant consequences only if the patient is in the process of forming a picture at the time of stimulation. This explains why most of the brain electrical stimulations are not accompanied of any visible manifestation, all the more that they cannot be extended for longer than a few seconds because of their invasive character. BrainTV allows the upstream identification of the function of the recorded sites and makes it possible to propose to the clinician the optimal manner to test the effect of the stimulations (for instance by requiring the patient to maintain a mental picture during stimulation). Note also that the effect of the stimulation (and the precise function of the recorded area) cannot be deduced from the simple localization of the electrode obtained by neuronavigation due to the significant variability of the structure/function correspondence from one person to another. Neuronavigators are thus helpful to the neurosurgeon, but not for identifying the function of the populations of neurons recorded.

Finally, it should be noted that the role of the patient changes radically: from passive subject, she becomes a key player in the research process. She actively participates in the scientific study by providing researchers with the information available to her, on her own mental activity, and which are invisible to researchers or to clinicians. We thus make use of the fact that the participant is an expert of her own brain.

4.6. BrainTV limitations

Apart from the obvious technical limitations of BrainTV (the need for invasive recordings), it should be noted that the results deduced from BrainTV concern most often unique cases, since each session is conducted with a single participant. It is naturally possible to try to reproduce the same observations in other patients, but then the fact that the electrodes are never exactly placed at the same location from one patient to another should be taken into consideration. It is therefore common to obtain a very dramatic effect in a patient and a less pronounced one in another, without knowing whether this difference is due to a distinct brain functioning or to a slightly different position of the electrode.

Moreover, the limitations of BrainTV depend on the ability of the participant to consciously experience the mental phenomena associated with brain activity that she observes. BrainTV is therefore most effective in patients with the finest introspection. BrainTV is also more suited to brain regions supporting cognitive processes the patient is aware of, which recalls the broad and unresolved issue of the neural correlates of consciousness: are we more aware of the activity of certain brain regions than others? Is it necessary that the activity triggers reaction in a large network to be consciously perceived? For example, few epilepsy patients note a change in their perception of the world and themselves at the time of an epileptic spike, although it concerns a very prominent electrophysiological activity, which suggests that we are not sensitive to the slightest change in activity in our brain. BrainTV enquires this boundary between neuronal activities accessible and inaccessible to consciousness and the impact of the capacity of introspection over this limit.

Moreover, regardless of the patient's ability for introspection, BrainTV allows also the experimenter to associate changes in brain activity with perceptible events (sudden noise, patient's movement, change in TV channel, etc.) and these associations also contribute to better understanding the function of the areas being studied when these do not relate to purely endogenous cognitive processes.

4.7. Extension to other types of recordings

The BrainTV system can be applied to any situation producing recordings of the human brain with very high spatial and temporal accuracy of the human brain. For example: the initial tests have been conducted during a feasibility study using local field potential recordings of the subthalamic nucleus in the Parkinsonian patient. This type of application may prove to be useful in distinguishing within this cerebral microstructure the subregions which are more specialized in motor behavior or in cognition. On the other hand, it is still difficult to think of an extension of BrainTV to non-invasive recordings because of the limitation of spatial accuracy that has already been mentioned. In addition, the most informative components of the EEG signal for BrainTV are within a frequency range (HFA, between 50 and 150 Hz) very vulnerable to artifacts of electromyographic origin. This is not a problem for intracerebral EEG, which is relatively immune to such artifacts from this contamination by muscle activity, but the EEG recorded on the surface of the scalp is very sensitive to this.

The best option at the moment is to use magnetoencephalography, as some studies show that it can record the induced HFA activity supporting cognitive processes [DAL 09]. A field of methodological research has been developed to reconstruct the source of these high-frequency activities with a spatial accuracy sometimes presented as equivalent to that of intracerebral EEG. This line of research should be followed with interest since it could allow all BrainTV applications to healthy subjects.

4.8. Conclusions

The BrainTV system, and its variants in other laboratories, therefore provide a new component to neuroimaging, rather oriented toward the individuality of the subject, toward the unique moment and toward life realistic situations. This is in sharp apparent contradiction with the conventional approach of neuroimaging, where the basic rule implies a control over experimental parameters and averaging over multiple trials or subjects in order to eliminate as for as possible any source of unexplained variability. It would be ridiculous to proclaim the superiority of one approach over the other, since they are naturally complementary. Moreover, we should not expect that the BrainTV approach will become as popular as the conventional approach, because of the very strict clinical framework that it implies. On the other hand, the hospitals where this technique is possible are nonetheless numerous (several dozens throughout the world), and it is expected that this approach and the associated research grow further in 10 to 20 years as collaborations are established between researchers and clinicians increasingly more interested in the opportunity to functionally explore the living brain of their patient. The relative technical simplicity of the necessary systems, and the collaboration with the industry providing iEEG data acquisition devices should facilitate this expansion. A collaboration of this type is already underway to integrate BrainTV into one of the most common systems of iEEG recordings in Europe, and regarding the other acquisition systems, it is not difficult to consider an implementation of BrainTV within free software for real-time EEG signal analysis such as BCI2000 or OpenVIBE (BrainTV is currently programmed within Matlab, in a form that is not distributed). With these developments, we should soon witness a wealth of discoveries regarding the activity of the human brain in real-life situations, in relation to its most intimate and internal dimension, when it will be allowed to roam freely. Only time will tell.

4.9. Bibliography

[BEN 96] BENTIN S., ALLISON T., PUCE A. et al., "Electrophysiological studies of face perception in humans", Journal of Cognitive Neuroscience, vol. 8, no. 6, pp. 551–565, 1996.

[KAN 97] KANWISHER N., MCDERMOTT J., CHUN M.M., "The fusiform face area: a module in human extrastriate cortex specialized for face perception", Journal of Neuroscience, vol. 17, no. 11, pp. 4302–4311, 1997.

[CAR 07] CARIA A., VEIT R., SITARAM R. et al., "Regulation of anterior insular cortex activity using real-time fMRI", Neuroimage, vol. 35, no. 3, pp. 1238–1246, 2007.

[CLE 16] CLERC M., BOUGRAIN L, LOTTE F. (eds), Brain–Computer Interfaces 1, ISTE, London and John Wiley & Sons, New York, 2016.

[CRO 98] CRONE, N.E., MIGLIORETTI, D.L., GORDON B. et al., "Functional mapping of human sensorimotor cortex with electrocorticographic spectral analysis. II. Event-related synchronization in the gamma band", Brain, vol. 121, no. 12, pp. 2301–2315, 1998.

[DAL 09] DALAL S.S., BAILLET S., ADAM C. *et al.*, "Simultaneous MEG and intracranial EEG recordings during attentive reading", *Neuroimage*, vol. 45, no. 4, pp. 1289–1304, 2009.

[DEC 05] DECHARMS C.R., MAEDA F., GLOVER G.H. *et al.*, "Control over brain activation and pain learned by using real-time functional MRI", *Proceedings of the National Academy of Sciences*, vol. 102, no. 51, pp. 18626–18631, 2005.

[GAL 96] GALLESE V., FADIGA L., FOGASSI L. *et al.*, "Action recognition in the premotor cortex", *Brain*, vol. 119, no. 2, pp. 593–610, 1996.

[HAM 12] HAMAMÉ C.M., VIDAL J.R., OSSANDÓN, T. *et al.*, "Reading the mind's eye: online detection of visuo-spatial working memory and visual imagery in the inferior temporal lobe", *Neuroimage*, vol. 59, no. 1, pp. 872–879, 2012.

[LAC 00] LACHAUX J.P., RODRIGUEZ E., MARTINERIE J. *et al.*, "A quantitative study of gamma-band activity in human intracranial recordings triggered by visual stimuli", *European Journal of Neuroscience*, vol. 12, no. 7, pp. 2608–2622, 2000.

[LAC 07] LACHAUX J.P., JERBI K., BERTRAND O. *et al.*, "A blueprint for real-time functional mapping via human intracranial recordings", *PLoS One*, vol. 2, no. 10, e1094, 2007.

[LUT 02] LUTZ A. *et al.*, "Guiding the study of brain dynamics by using first-person data: synchrony patterns correlate with ongoing conscious states during a simple visual task", *Proceedings of the National Academy of Sciences*, vol. 99.3, pp. 1586–1591, 2002.

[LUT 12] LUTZ A., LACHAUX J.P., MARTINERIE J. *et al.*, "High-frequency neural activity and human cognition: past, present and possible future of intracranial EEG research", *Progress in Neurobiology*, vol. 98, no. 3, pp. 279–301, 2012.

[MIL 10] MILLER K.J., SCHALK G., FETZ E.E. *et al.* "Cortical activity during motor execution, motor imagery, and imagery-based online feedback", *Proceedings of the National Academy*, vol. 107, no. 9, pp. 4430–4435, 2010.

[RAM 06] RAMSEY N., SCHALK G., FETZ E.E. *et al.*, "Towards human BCI applications based on cognitive brain systems: an investigation of neural signals recorded from the dorsolateral prefrontal cortex", *IEEE Transactions on Neural Systems and Rehabilitation Engineering*, vol. 14, no. 2, pp. 214–217, 2006.

[REM 94] REMOND A., *Biofeedback: Principes et Applications*, Masson, Paris, 1994.

[WYA 09] WYART V. TALLON-BAUDRY C., "How ongoing fluctuations in human visual cortex predict perceptual awareness: baseline shift versus decision bias", *The Journal of Neuroscience*, vol. 29, no. 27, pp. 8715–8725, 2009.

BCIs and Video Games: State of the Art with the OpenViBE2 Project

Video games are often cited as a very promising field of application for brain–computer interfaces (BCIs). In this chapter, we will describe the state of the art in the field of video games played "with the mind". In particular, we will consider the results of the OpenViBE2 project–one of the most important research projects in this area.

5.1. Introduction

Toward the end of the last decade, the availability of low-cost electrode headsets (electroencephalogram (EEG) based) paved the way for mass-market applications of BCIs. Although this equipment is less effective, more fragile and of lower quality than medical headsets, EEG headsets with up to 16 electrodes are now very easy to obtain for less than 300 euros, for example over the Internet. Consumer applications of BCIs in video games have therefore been a serious prospect for several years.

Video games as a sector are always open to the introduction of new interactive technologies. Consider for example the overnight success of the first game consoles based on player motion detection (Microsoft Kinect,

---

Chapter written by Anatole LÉCUYER.

♥

Nintendo Wii). Looking beyond "motion" control to "thought" control could therefore represent a promising avenue for the video games sector.

Since 2000, researchers and research labs have also been considering the scientific merit of combining BCI technology with virtual environments and video games. There are a number of recent articles on this topic, and interested readers can refer to [BOS 10, GUR 12, LEC 08, MAR 13, NIJ 09a, NIJ 09b].

Interacting with a video game through a BCI is a complex problem that remains largely open, even today [LEC 08]. There are numerous obstacles to be overcome in neuroscience, signal processing of electrical brain signals, the development of innovative interaction techniques and of course the design of more efficient and more suitable EEG video game headsets.

Several scientific challenges still remain to be addressed in different domains:

– *neuroscience*: many electrophysiological phenomena in the brain still need to be understood and modeled. New electrical markers for mental states relevant to video game applications still remain to be discovered and identified. In particular, we need markers that are more reliable, more robust, that can be more accurately classified, etc;

– *EEG signal processing*: players usually do not stand still. But muscle activity (blinking, tensing the jaw, moving the head, eyebrows, eyes, etc.) is a well-known source of noise and interference with in the electrical signals emitted by the brain, and can sometimes completely obstruct analysis. New signal-filtering techniques are therefore required to remove noise interference so that information can be reliably extracted to support video game applications of BCIs [FAT 07];

– *human–computer interaction*: the number of "mental commands" that can be successfully transmitted over a BCI is often limited (for example only one, two or three different commands based on motor imagery), and they are still fairly unreliable. Using the P300 paradigm allows the number of commands available to be increased, but does not necessarily increase the number of commands per unit of time (*bitrate*), and often requires visual attention to be focused on uncomfortable stimuli (flashing elements). We need interaction techniques that solve the problem of a low number of noisy commands, as well as other limitations currently associated with BCIs: latency, inaccurately classified commands, artifacts arising from muscle activity, learning difficulties, visual and/or cognitive fatigue, etc. (see Chapter 12 of Volume 1);

– *EEG equipment*: commercial EEG headsets are often still incompatible with the video games market. They are too expensive, slow and complex to set up, user-unfriendly (requiring gel) and additionally produce a very noisy signal (low-quality electrical signals). We need to design new sensors that are more effective, less expensive and easier to use, for example based on dry electrodes [GUG 12].

Given this context, the OpenViBE2 project (2009–2013) is unique. It is the first collaborative research project focusing specifically on the application and potential of BCIs in video games that has included industry players from this sector. The goal of the project was to study and demonstrate how players' mental states and brain responses can be used to adapt not just the way that players interact with the game but also the content of the game itself. The strength of the OpenViBE2 project lies in the cross-disciplinary character and complementary makeup of its panel of contributing experts. There are many different aspects to the target problem, which is complex and would represent an almost impossible challenge for any single partner working in a single area of specialization. In OpenViBE2, the full spectrum of necessary expertise was united in a single panel for the first time, collaborating in pursuit of a shared objective. For the first time, companies from the video game industry (UBISOFT, Kylotonn Games, Blacksheep Studio) entered into direct collaboration with academic research laboratories (Inria, INSERM, CEA-LIST, Gipsa-Lab, CHART/LUTIN) to study and develop video games based on brain activity. This singular arrangement helped to give focus to the scientific research over the course of the project, allowing the project to converge toward technological solutions that are better adapted to the constraints of the target field of application.

One recent and promising line of scientific research that was also explored in the OpenViBE2 project was the idea of considering BCIs not as a potentially inferior substitute for traditional player interfaces (joystick, mouse, gamepad), but rather as a new way of playing that can complement traditional techniques [NIJ 09b, GEO 10]. Thus, players can continue to use joysticks while simultaneously leveraging brain activity at certain key moments in the game. BCIs can also measure certain mental states (such as concentration, mental workload, or visual attention) for the purpose of adapting content or in-game interactions. For example, consider a tennis game in which the player must concentrate while serving (by standing still, so that muscle activity does not interfere with brain activity) to increase the chance of an ace. This shows that much still remains to be invented, and that new "gameplays" more suitable for BCIs will likely be suggested in future.

In the following section of this chapter, we will present a selection of prototypes developed during the OpenViBE2 project that are illustrative of the state of the art in this field and the use of BCIs in video games.

5.2. Video game prototypes controlled by BCI

A number of proofs of concept for video games "controlled by the brain" via BCI have been developed in academic laboratories in the past few years [BOS 10, NIJ 09a, NIJ 09b]. Below, we will present a few representative examples based on the main brain patterns that can be detected and exploited by BCIs: motor rhythms and the imagination of movements, the P300 and steady-state visually evoked potential (SSVEP), and control of levels of concentration/relaxation associated with alpha and beta rhythms.

5.2.1. *Video game based on the imagination of movement*

Our first example of a simple game takes place in the well-known universe of the *Star Wars* films, given the name of "Use-the-Force" [LOT 08]. The goal of the game is to lift up a spaceship using only brain activity, analogous to the notion of "force" and telekinesis in the films (see Figure 5.1 and Chapter 14). The game uses brain activity associated with imagining foot movement, which is measured by one or more electrodes placed at the top of the scalp. When players imagine moving their feet, the strength of the signal in the beta band measured by the electrodes slowly decreases. Shortly after ending the movement, there is a brief peak in beta activity. Most people are able to exploit this property of brain activity following a potentially lengthy learning process.

This video game was used to perform a study "out side the lab" with a relatively large group of subjects (21 participants). The goal was to evaluate how many people are able to learn to operate a game-based application of a BCI in more "difficult" and less controlled conditions than in a laboratory setting; in this case, the BCI was set up in a meeting room in the context of a conference [LOT 08].

Figure 5.1. *"Use-the-Force!": lift up a spaceship by imagining moving the feet (left = screenshot, right = participant in an experiment)*

In a second example, users instead had to imagine moving the hands (left hand vs. right hand). This is one of the few examples of a "multiplayer" game, each player equipped with an electrode headset and a BCI allowing them to play together using their brain activity within the same application (see Figure 5.2). This game, entitled "BrainArena" [BON 13], has two different modes for simultaneously analyzing the brain activity of both users: "collaborative" and "competitive". Two players can play together, either with a shared objective or against each other. The game is a simplified version of football in which the aim is to score goals at the right (or left) side of the screen by imagining a motion of the right (or left) hand.

This game was used to study the influence of the choice of collaborative or competitive mode on player performance and motivation [BON 13]. The study showed that some players find multiplayer more motivating than single player mode, allowing them to achieve better performance with the BCI.

5.2.2. *Video game based on P300 potential*

The "Brain Invaders" game [CON 11] was inspired by the Japanese video game "Space Invaders". The aim is to destroy enemy spaceships arranged in a grid formation on the screen (see Figure 5.3 and Chapter 14). Players must focus on the enemy ship that they wish to destroy. This game uses the evoked P300 potential that can be detected 300 ms after a rare, expected event (see Chapter 4 of Volume 1), such as the ship flashing. Each ship on the grid flashes randomly. When the ship on which the player is focusing flashes, a P300 signal should be observable in the electrical activity in the player's brain. The game can therefore identify the ships that the player wishes to destroy in the EEG signal by detecting the presence of P300 waves.

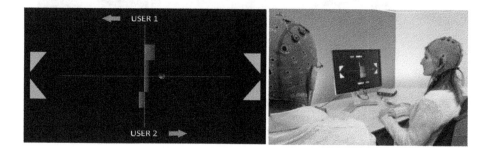

Figure 5.2. *"BrainArena": score goals on the right or left by imagining moving the right or left hand. Two players equipped with EEG headsets can play and score together, or play against each other*

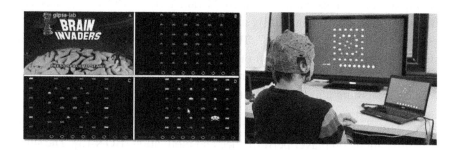

Figure 5.3. *"Brain Invaders": players can destroy enemy ships by concentrating directly on the target (randomly flashing spaceships)*

This game uses all of the most recent signal processing techniques developed by the OpenViBE2 project partners for eliminating muscle-related artifacts and more efficiently extracting P300 signals. This allows the ships to be destroyed more quickly, with virtually no learning required and minimal calibration [CON 11].

5.2.3. *Video game based on SSVEP potential*

In "MindShooter" [LEG 13], the user controls a spaceship at the bottom of the screen, and must destroy enemy ships at the top of the screen (Figure 5.4). There are three commands available: move right, move left and shoot. To activate these commands, the user must concentrate on the zone of the spaceship corresponding to the desired action: left wing, right wing or cannon. Each of these three zones flashes at a different frequency (e.g. 10, 12 and 15 Hz). The flashing frequency of the zone that the user is looking at can be detected directly in the activity in the visual regions of the subect's brain. This is an application of steady state visually-evoked potentials (SSVEPs, see Chapter 4 of Volume 1), which are associated with the user's attention: as the user concentrates on a certain region, the power of the frequency band corresponding to the flashing increases in the electrical activity emitted by the visual cortex. So, if for example the BCI detects an increase in the amplitude at the same frequency as the cannon in the visual cortex, the "shoot" command is triggered in-game.

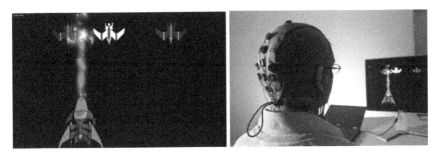

Figure 5.4. *"MindShooter": control a spaceship (move left/move right/shoot) by concentrating on different flashing areas of the ship (left wing/right wing/cannon) to destroy enemy ships*

5.2.4. *Video game based on concentration/relaxation tasks*

Mental concentration and relaxation tasks have also been used to design simple BCI games. Figure 5.5 illustrates this approach with the example of a game-based approach that is particularly impressive due to its highly immersive character and the use of cutting-edge virtual reality technologies. The application, named "Virtual Dagobah", was also inspired by the *Star Wars* movies and reproduces one of the movie sequences [LEC 13]: the training session of the hero Luke with his master, Yoda. The user, who plays Luke, must lift up a spaceship using only brain activity (analogously to the notion of "Force" in the movies). This application relies on brain activity associated with two different mental states: a state of heavy concentration and a state of relaxation. To lift the spaceship, the user must concentrate intensely. If he or she relaxes, the spaceship will sink. The EEG signal processing techniques used to identify these states require a preliminary training phase with player data saved in states of both "relaxation" and "concentration".

Figure 5.5. *Immersive game-based "Virtual Dagobah": application players can lift up a spaceship by concentrating intensively (or by relaxing). Here, the user is immersed in a highly realistic 3D scene because of virtual reality technology*

This application was implemented and tested in the Immersia virtual reality room at IRISA/Inria in Rennes. This is a 10 m × 3.5 m × 3.5 m virtual reality room with stereoscopic display and motion tracking. Thus, from users' perspective, they are standing in front of a full-scale virtual spaceship that is 6 m wide. Users experience a striking holographic effect because of the stereoscopic display, and their movements are tracked in real time. The application was tested with a low-cost wireless EEG headset.

5.3. Industrial prototypes: the potential for very different kinds of games

In the video games sector, there exist very unique genres of game with content and gameplay specially designed for specific target audiences. BCIs and EEG signals can be used in different ways, depending on the usage context and the type of game being considered. We will illustrate this principle in this section by describing a selection of different prototypes corresponding to games that are themselves very different, based on different BCIs. These are all industrial prototypes developed by experts in 3D and video games, showcasing the wide variety of possible applications: a classical game for entertainment directly developed from an existing game for the Nintendo Wii conole ("casual game" genre), a brain training-type game that uses EEG ("Brain Trainer" genre) and an applied game ("serious game" genre) for treating children with attention deficit disorders.

5.3.1. *Classical games for entertainment or "casual games"*

The game "Cocoto Brain" developed by Kylotonn Games is directly based on a successful game by Neko Entertainment for the Wii console by Nintendo (Figure 5.6). This is an example of a typical "defend-the-castle" game from the "casual" genre: the player must protect a princess by preventing enemies from getting too close. The game is based on SSVEP signals. The player must focus on targets shown above the heads of the enemies to neutralize them. These targets flash at different frequencies. An increase in the amplitude at the frequency of the flashing target on which the player is focusing can then be picked up directly from the brain activity (see section 2.3 and Chapter 4 of Volume 1). This enables players to destroy enemies directly by looking at them.

Cocoto Brain can be played on a PC with standard specifications. The game was developed and tested with an EPOC headset (Emotiv) that connects to the computer via bluetooth. The game may be started once an initial headset calibration phase is complete, which only takes 2 minutes. Note that in this game, the player can also continue to operate the mouse as usual to click and select options at the same time as issuing "mental commands".

Figure 5.6. *"Cocoto Brain" game: destroy the monsters to protect the princess in the center of the screen by concentrating on the flashing targets above their heads*

5.3.2. *Brain-training games or "Brain Trainers"*

An example of a "brain training" game that uses EEG was developed by Blacksheep Studio. In this genre of games, players perform different kinds of fun brain-training activities. Classical exercises are available such as visual searches and word searches. These in-game tasks are combined with real-time detection of the player's EEG brain activity (see Figure 5.7). One of the objectives of the game designers was to construct and integrate performance metrics and indicators that are directly associated with the player's EEG and brain activity. The developers also hope to modify the game so that it can adapt in real time to the mental state detected using EEG.

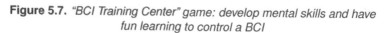

Figure 5.7. *"BCI Training Center" game: develop mental skills and have fun learning to control a BCI*

The game is called "BCI Training Center" and offers players the chance to directly practice certain BCI paradigms such as the P300. Here, the objective is to complete the game while improving personal performance for the detection of P300s. The game also allows players to visualize electrical activity in the brain in real time, color-coded and in the form of a topographic map. Users have the opportunity to see their brain work in real time, and can slowly learn to control it directly.

5.3.3. *"Serious games"*

An example of a "serious game" based on a BCI and designed for children with attention-deficit/hyperactivity disorders (ADHD) was developed by CLARTE. ADHD is one of the most common psychiatric disorders in children above the age of 5. Children with ADHD exhibit a combination of different symptoms, including attention deficits and high distractability (inability to concentrate on a single task for more than a few minutes), hyperactivity (uncontrolled and incessant motor agitation), and verbal and motor impulsiveness. This game was developed as a platform for treating ADHD using EEG. This platform, designed to be used in the context of therapy, uses neurofeedback techniques in combination with virtual reality equipment (Figure 5.8). Neurofeedback is a kind of biofeedback that relies on measurements of EEG activity to provide subjects with information about their brain activity (see Chapter 13 of Volume 1).

Figure 5.8. *A serious game for treating attention deficit disorders: children are immersed in a virtual classroom, and can complete exercises, some of which integrate EEG and neurofeedback, to improve their attention using their brain activity*

The application is organized into multiple neurofeedback scenarios that can be activated once the patient is immersed in the virtual environment and equipped with an EEG headset. These scenarios take the form of exercises, the success of which depends on the child's capacity to regain control over his or her brain activity in order to reach a certain mental state, validated by EEG. The virtual environment of this platform is a classroom with a set of interactive objects that can be used for neurofeedback scenarios. For example, in one of the scenarios, the child with ADHD is asked to watch a video on a screen in the classroom, the quality of which is directly linked to his or her EEG activity. To continue watching the video in good quality, the child must keep his or her brain activity in line with the conditions specified by the therapist. During the session, the therapist can test the stability of the patient's attention by triggering distractors such as a dog barking and a lorry driving past outside. There is also a method for measuring attention integrated into the platform, allowing the child's progress to be monitored. This platform for therapy can be used with various equipment setups, ranging from a PC with a 3D screen to a virtual reality room with multiple screens. The application of this approach and in particular of virtual reality in therapy must now be evaluated and validated clinically.

5.4. Discussion

We have presented a set of representative video game examples that use BCIs based on a variety of types of brain activity. Interested readers can complement this presentation by referring to recent review articles on this topic (see [BOS 10, GUR 12, LEC 08, NIJ 09a, NIJ 09b]). We have also described a selection of industrial prototypes developed in a collaborative project between academic laboratories and video games industry experts known as OpenViBE2. Throughout this project, games developers showed the most interest in types of brain activity that are easy to explain to the player and easy to learn, and relatively more robust (higher accuracy rates). One of the limitations of BCI applications in video games is the current low levels of reliability and robustness [LOT 11]. For example, SSVEP potentials were ultimately chosen over motor rhythms for the game Cocoto Brain. Industry experts were also greatly interested in the idea of using passive BCIs, detecting players' mental states not to explicitly control the video game but rather to adapt in-game content or interactions. One of the proofs of concept developed in the project was capable of adapting a virtual environment to the user's mental workload as directly measured by EEG in the context of haptic manipulation [LEC 13]. These applications considerably relax the constraints of real-time performance and BCI controllability and provide a foundation for designing original gameplay that can fully leverage the information provided by brain signals. This line of research is also very promising for the BCI community in a wider sense [GEO 10].

Video games controlled by a BCI are now a reality. Many games are indeed already available on the market. Today, it is possible to download BCI video games on the Internet from the websites and online stores of consumer EEG headset constructors, such as the company Emotiv. It is also possible to try out a number of simple games provided with the free software package OpenViBE (see Chapter 10).

There remain, however, a few obstacles that prevent mass scale diffusion of this technology. The most significant issue is probably still the extreme restrictiveness of electrode headsets. Despite efforts in this area by a few start-ups, the equipment available to consumers is often still incompatible with the requirements of the video games market. The ideal headset must be easy to set up, in a few seconds, for any type of user, must be quick to configure and must use dry electrodes. There is a number of other desirable properties: durable, easy to clean, wireless, compatible with audio headsets and of course tastefully stylized at an acceptable price. The introduction of such a headset could occur progressively; first as a secondary peripheral that complements classical controllers (mouse, keyboard, joystick), and later as an independent controller.

Large-scale trials conducted by the CHART/LUTIN laboratory at the Cité des Sciences et de l'Industrie in Paris with several hundred users showed that the general public has a real appetite for these new ways of interacting with video games. Players want new gaming sensations, and interacting with BCIs opens new avenues that must now be fully integrated, which will likely require new, more suitable types of gameplay to be devised. But at the same time, it seems that there are a number of factors that must be considered and that could yet be improved, such as system calibration, user learning curves and explanations about the way that BCIs work in order to avoid any apprehension or incorrect psychological interpretations of the nature of BCIs. Thus, there is still much research to be done into BCI usage to better understand the impact of this new technology and how it can be accepted by a potentially very diverse spectrum of players.

5.5. Conclusion

In this chapter, we described the state of the art in the field of video games controlled by a BCI. We discussed the results of the OpenViBE2 project, which showcased the wide variety of types of brain activity that can be used to develop these kinds of game, and the broad spectrum of applications and possible game types. Many prototypes have been developed, for example based on imagining a motion of the left and right hands to score goals, or in another example using the P300 potential to destroy spaceships in a remake of well-known Japanese game. Some online stores already allow users to download video games based on BCIs. But there are still a number of challenges that must be tackled before BCIs can qualify as a standard means of interaction with video games. In particular, the design and characteristics of consumer EEG headsets require improvement, and more research is necessary to examine this new area of BCI applications in more detail together with its constraints, advantages and unique qualities. Still, given what has already been achieved, and in light of the commercial success of innovative input devices such as those based on motion capture (Wii, Kinect), there is no question that the future of BCIs in video games will be bright.

5.6. Bibliography

[BON 13] BONNET L., LOTTE F., LÉCUYER A., "Two brains, one game: design and evaluation of a multi-user BCI video game based on motor imagery", *IEEE Transactions on Computational Intelligence and Artificial Intelligence in Games*, vol. 5. no. 2, pp. 185–198, 2013.

[BOS 10] BOS D.P.O., REUDERINK B., VAN DE LAAR B. *et al.*, "Brain-computer interfacing and games", *Brain-Computer Interfaces*, Springer, London, pp. 149–178, 2010.

[CON 11] CONGEDO M., GOYAT M., TARRIN N. *et al.*, "Brain Invaders: a prototype of an open-source P300-based video game working with the OpenViBE platform", *5th International Brain-Computer Interface Conference*, Graz, Austria, 2011.

[FAT 07] FATOURECHI M., BASHASHATI A., WARD R. *et al.*, "EMG and EOG artifacts in brain computer interface systems: a survey", *Clinical Neurophysiology*, vol. 118, pp. 480–494, 2007.

[GEO 10] GEORGE L., LÉCUYER A., "An overview of research on passive brain-computer interfaces for implicit human-computer interaction", *International Conference on Applied Bionics and Biomechanics – Workshop W1 Brain-Computer Interfacing and Virtual Reality*, Venice, Italy, 2010.

[GUG 12] GUGER C., KRAUSZ G., ALLISON B.Z. *et al.*, "Comparison of dry and gel based electrodes for P300 Brain–Computer interfaces", *Frontiers in Neuroscience*, vol. 6, 2012.

[GUR 12] GÜRKÖK H., NIJHOLT A., "Brain–computer interfaces for multimodal interaction: a survey and principles", *International Journal of Human-Computer Interaction,* vol. 28, no. 5, pp. 292–307, 2012.

[LEC 08] LÉCUYER A., LOTTE F., REILLY R. *et al.*, "Brain-Computer Interfaces, Virtual Reality, and Videogames", *IEEE Computer*, vol. 41, no. 10, pp. 66–72, 2008.

[LEC 13] LÉCUYER A., GEORGE L., MARCHAL M., "Toward adaptive VR simulators combining visual, haptic, and Brain-Computer interfaces", *IEEE Computer Graphics & Applications*, vol. 33, no. 5, pp. 18–23, 2013.

[LEG 13] LEGENY J., VICIANA-ABAD R., LÉCUYER A.,"Towards contextual SSVEP-based BCI controller: smart activation of stimuli and controls weighting", *IEEE Transactions on Computational Intelligence and Artificial Intelligence in Games*, 2013

[LOT 08] LOTTE F., RENARD Y., LÉCUYER A., "Self-paced Brain-Computer interaction with virtual worlds: a quantitative and qualitative study out of the lab", *4th International Brain-Computer Interface Workshop and Training Course*, pp. 373–378, 2008.

[LOT 11] LOTTE F., "Brain-computer interfaces for 3D games: hype or hope?", *6th International Conference on Foundations of Digital Games*, Graz Austria, pp. 325–327, 2011.

[MAR 13] MARSHALL D., COYLE D., WILSON S. *et al.*, "Games, gameplay, and BCI: The state of the art", *IEEE Transactions on Computational Intelligence and AI in Games*, vol. 5, no. 2, pp. 82–99, 2013.

[NIJ 09a] NIJHOLT A., "BCI for games: a state of the art survey", *Entertainment Computing-ICEC*, pp. 225–228, 2009.

[NIJ 09b] NIJHOLT A., BOS D.P.O., REUDERINK B., "Turning shortcomings into challenges: Brain–Computer interfaces for games", *Entertainment Computing*, vol. 1, no. 2, pp. 85–94, 2009.

PART 2

Practical Aspects of BCI Implementation

Analysis of Patient Need for Brain–Computer Interfaces

6.1. Introduction

The need of potential users of Brain–Computer Interfaces (BCI) is so great that it is no easy task to capture it. For a long time now, the technology has been maturing in the context of research laboratories, which despite being largely cross-disciplinary have all too often neglected to address purely clinical aspects. As a result, today, BCIs do not properly meet the needs of these patients. Fortunately, shared advances in fields closely related to BCIs (electronics, signal processing, artificial intelligence) are finally opening the hospital doors to this technology, finally allowing us to carefully examine the context in which these applications might unfold.

New technologies are becoming increasingly important in our daily lives; computer systems are the most obvious example. Having expanded past the simple status of ubiquitous work tools, computers are now penetrating ever further into our homes, to the point where almost two-thirds of adults possess a home computer, a statistic that increases each year. This trend is of course linked to the development of the Internet and the number of devices connected to it, each day opening new life-changing applications. This rapid

Chapter written by Louis MAYAUD, Salvador CABANILLES and Eric AZABOU.

transformation of our society is unfolding while one-tenth of the population suffers from motor deficiencies, a quarter of whom (2.5%) are affected by communication disorders [MCL 13]. Paradoxically, persons with disabilities (PWD) are often the first to use these new technologies as a method of compensating for their deficiencies and restoring social and family ties. Thus, information and communication technologies and their applications considerably improve the integration, independence and safety of PWD in numerous aspects of their daily life [BIG 07].

Naturally, in the specific sector of users with disabilities, many products are created by collaboration between the developers and future users. Unfortunately, groups of potential users are often small, and only rarely justify investment from industry, whose involvement is of course a key factor in any product's success. Often, the state intervenes in a providential capacity to make up for the lack of interest from private investors by providing grants for biomedical research. Such funding is ultimately awarded to research teams who are often unfamiliar with product development. Sometimes, researchers have never directly met with a patient and remain largely unaware of existing alternatives to the device they are developing. This is particularly true for BCI research.

This is the context in which we must analyze patient need for medical BCIs. We will begin by presenting the relevant groups of patients that will help us define this need, and we will briefly describe the tools that are currently available to these patients. Finally, we will see how the characterization of patient need can influence practical aspects of BCIs and in particular the method for recording electrical brain activity and the applications that have been developed for BCIs.

6.1.1. *Patient groups*

Occupational therapists, responsible for preparing patients for daily life, might tell you that there are as many types of disability as there are patients. Because of this, as much the result of variety in the underlying disorders as in the manifestations of these disorders, there are few assistive devices than can simply be given "as is" to patients. For example, wheelchairs must be adapted to the patient's weight, height, disability type and severity, so that each wheelchair requires numerous meticulous modifications before it can optimally serve the patient with the correct comfort. Anyone who has ever hiked in low-quality boots can understand how important these adjustments are, before even getting to the clinical needs of this fragile group of patients – which further counteract their desire for autonomy (risk of bedsores, fatigability). If BCIs are to be used as assistive devices, they must adapt to meet these delicate requirements. Before discussing the details of such clinical needs and constraints, we will first present the affected groups of patients and the tools available to them. The scientific community working on BCIs understandably first developed an interest in patients with locked-in syndrome (LIS) for whom the technology appeared to be the most useful. However, beyond this relatively small population, we will also look at a larger group of patients, namely those suffering from tetraplegia (paralysis in both the upper and lower limbs).

6.1.1.1. Tetraplegia originating from trauma

In the chronic posttraumatic phase, some patients experience near-total loss of all capacity for verbal and non-verbal communication. Not all of these patients are comatose; some patients retain non-negligible levels of awareness and attention (see Chapter 15). The residual functional capacities of this category of patients allows them to operate equipment via BCIs [LOO 11].

6.1.1.2. Amyotrophic lateral sclerosis

In patients suffering from amyotrophic lateral sclerosis (ALS), the progressive deterioration of motor neurons in the cerebral cortex and the anterior horn of the spinal cord causes the patient to slowly develop tetraplegia, in some cases with significant bulbar palsy, hindering phonation. These patients generally retain many high-level functions such as hearing, vision and language [KIE 11].

6.1.1.3. Multiple sclerosis

Some patients suffering from an advanced stage of multiple sclerosis (MS) find all forms of verbal and non-verbal communication very difficult [POL 11]. It has also been suggested that patients with loss of peripheral bladder nerve control could use this kind of interface to support the process of urinating [WOL 12].

6.1.1.4. *Guillain–Barré syndrome*

Guillain–Barré syndrome (GBS) is an inflammatory autoimmune disease of the peripheral nervous system. Once the disease spreads, some patients enter the plateau phase of the disease in critical neurological condition requiring mechanical ventilation with severe motor impairment in the form of tetraparesis or tetraplegia [YUK 12].

6.1.1.5. *Myopathies*

Myopathies correspond to deterioration of the muscle tissue. As myopathic conditions progress, patients in a severe functional condition can develop tetraplegia with respiratory and phonation difficulties rendering speech and movement impossible [DAL 11].

6.1.1.6. *Locked-in syndromes*

LIS is a neurological state in which the patient is awake and fully conscious, but is incapable of moving or speaking due to complete paralysis everywhere except the eyelids. Patients preserve full cognitive function. LIS can have a number of diverse etiologies: it can be the result of a stroke, or more rarely can occur following brainstem trauma or a neurodegenerative condition [CAR 13].

6.1.2. **Existing interfaces**

Researchers involved in the development of BCIs are often unaware that the need of their target population has always been fulfilled, at least partially, by other strategies, often low tech in nature. We believe that it is essential to briefly present these solutions to establish a context for BCIs: one assistive technology among many others, with which it competes directly. We will distinguish between universally available solutions (use of a visual keyboard on a screen for writing) and those designed specifically as an assistive device (either a pointing system or a scrolling system) thereby highlighting the specificity of each interface in relation to the physiological input signal it exploits (usually residual peripheral muscle activity).

To date, most accessibility interfaces are types of virtual keyboard, such as that illustrated in Figure 6.1. There are many types of keyboard, ranging from very simple to more complicated systems with a number of configurable settings and options [LAN 12].

Figure 6.1. *Example of a virtual keyboard (left) with rows that are illuminated sequentially at a predefined speed allowing the subject to make a selection by "clicking", for example with a button such as the one shown in yellow (right)*

Often, the user accesses the keys with a "pointing" system (mouse, trackball, headtracker) [SHI 09]. In these cases, the user's residual muscle activity is exploited, amplified and redirected to operate the interface. It is necessary to ensure that the patient can control the extent and the direction of the chosen movement in a reliable and continuous manner, no matter how weak this movement may be, e.g. movement of a finger, a hand or the head. It is important to note that the vast majority of patients are capable of operating this kind of interface.

When this is no longer possible, patients are often provided with a "scrolling" system, where the virtual keyboard scrolls automatically at a regular speed from row to row and then from letter to letter, until the user makes a selection by means of a button – a "clickable" interface whose function is to identify (to a certain degree of precision in time) a binary choice made by the subject [GHE 09]. The nature of the button is determined from assessment by an occupational therapist, depending on the subject's motor capacities. The goal is to find a movement that is reliable, reproducible and as little tiring as possible. There exist various types of buttons:

– mechanical (pressure buttons) can be placed in reach of the upper limbs or the head;

– breath switches, which use the act of voluntary exhalation that is generally present even in the most severe conditions;

– muscle switches, with a conductive pad 15 mm in diameter that can be placed on the skin (wrist, forehead, jaw, etc.) and a control panel with configurable sensitivity that reacts to muscle contractions performed at regular, configurable intervals.

Other technologies have been introduced more recently in the same vein as *Scatir*, which uses infrared technology [TAI 08]. It allows low-amplitude motion to be detected from a short distance away, without requiring physical contact with the sensor. These kinds of system involve a control panel connected to a sensor that is mounted on a flexible arm, which can, for instance, be installed on the frame of a pair of glasses to detect blinking with the eyelids.

In general, scrolling keyboards produce written messages relatively slowly, at a rate that is dependent on the scrolling speed. This type of accessibility system is offered to patients with significant motor impairments when pointing systems are no longer viable. To improve writing speeds, it is possible to complement the system with word-prediction software, which is automatically included with some types of keyboard. Paradoxically, the increase in cognitive load required by these solutions (the patient must think, identify and select the word) sometimes leads to a net decrease in the output rate (in letters per minute), which is exacerbated in patients with a limited capacity to concentrate and high fatigability.

6.2. Types of users

In order to be used with patients, medical equipment in general and assistive devices in particular must meet three sets of needs: that of the prescriber, that of the user and that of the beneficiary. In the case of assistive devices for communication, the beneficiaries are the patient and his/her relatives; the user is clearly the patient, but also to a certain extent the carer who must set up the system; finally, the prescriber is the person or body that decides to allocate financial resources to the acquisition and utilization of the assistance system. To illustrate this distinction, imagine a BCI communication system for patients that perfectly meets the patients' needs in terms of performance and comfort. If this system takes longer to set up than care staff can afford to give, it will not be used, as it does not fully meet the needs of the users. Similarly, if the system is too expensive, and its use requires the investment of significant human resources, it is highly likely that it will not suit the needs of the prescriber (the hospital), who is ultimately responsible for the decision as to whether to acquire the system. In practice, considering the needs of the beneficiaries, the users and the prescribers is an essential part of the process of defining an industrial solution that is likely to be adopted.

The goal of the prescriber is to find an advantageous balance between the cost and benefit of the purchase and subsequent usage of the system. How much is the investment, and what proportion would be covered by insurance? Similarly, in the context of clinical or hospital use, the prescriber must also consider the time investment and skillsets required to operate the system. Throughout the world, hospital human resources are under increasing pressure from financial optimization, ever since the introduction of service-based billing and the codification of services, meaning that a key factor in prescribing BCIs is the reduction of third-party involvement. As well as limiting the amount of time required by medical staff, the required qualifications must also be minimal. It is obviously impracticable to require the presence of an engineer to ensure that software solutions function properly. Similarly, the presence and attendance of a specialized EEG technician for setting up the system might not be realistic, such as in a typical critical care setup where BCIs could prove useful. We therefore cannot rely on users being capable of distinguishing noise from EEG signals. Consequently, it is the responsibility of the BCI designers to assist users as much as possible in the process of setting up the system, and in particular with electrode placement. This may require elaborate techniques to be implemented, either electronically (impedance measurements) or at the software level (signal quality indicators). These simple examples show how considering the prescribers' needs, which until now have largely been ignored, can deeply complicate the BCI design.

Clearly, it is necessary to place more focus on the study of the needs of users and beneficiaries according to the definitions given above. Below, we will present the results of a study performed with medical staff ($n = 34$) and patients ($n = 26$) in two centers in France that may be considered representative of care for patients with disabilities: the Raymond Poincaré hospital (52 participants, Paris hospital trust, Garches, Department 92) and the Saint-Roch hospital (eight participants, Nice) [MAY 13b]. In order to provide an international perspective, we will supplement this study with work performed with patients suffering from ALS [HUG 11, GRU 11], care providers [BLA 12], patients suffering from medullary trauma [COL 13] and surveys of PWD who have personal experience in operating BCIs [ZIC 10].

6.2.1. *Patient needs*

Although most existing BCIs were developed for purposes of communication, there is a rich body of literature showing that communication is not necessarily these patients' most immediate need. We showed earlier that patient needs understandably vary depending on the severity and the etiology of their condition. For patients with damage to the spinal cord, the primary need ranges from restoring control to the lower and upper limbs (legs and arms) to digestive function to sexual function, which has been shown by at least two independent studies of 500 patients with paraplegia and tetraplegia [AND 04, SNO 04, COL 13]. Equivalently, a study with no particular focus on BCIs showed that very low-tech assistance systems are by far the most commonly employed and the most appreciated by these patients: in particular, mechanical assistance systems such as supports and adjustable seats in bathrooms and anti-slip shoes for showering score highly both in terms of utility and user satisfaction [GRU 11].

There has been a non-negligible level of interest in general communication paradigms and systems for controlling the user environment, which achieved high levels of satisfaction despite low usage levels [GRU 11]. Inversely, computers are of course widely used with these patients to assist communication. Unfortunately, the level of satisfaction with these systems remains low. This suggests that the future prospects of BCIs are bright in the domain of communication while emphasizing the high levels of patient expectation.

It is interesting to note however that the analysis of patient needs reveals that almost half of them are currently unaware of the existence of BCIs [COL 13]; thus, when analyzing the wishes expressed by a large majority (80% of surveyed participants), we must be careful to account for the widespread misunderstanding and false expectations surrounding the technology. For example, in this study, 30% of participants requested that BCIs allow them to more easily operate their wheelchair "by thought". While such prototypes exist, none has ever reach the "beta" stage. This can be partially explained by the fact that satisfaction with wheelchair usage seems to be low, at least in patients with ALS [GRU 11]. However, given the relative autonomy of paraplegic patients, and the conspicuous absence of BCI-based solutions, we must conclude that this figure represents a positively biased perspective of the technology, which should be taken into consideration when analyzing the results. These needs naturally align with the capacity of BCIs to meet them: restoring communication naturally established itself as the principal application, not because it was the most frequently requested application by these patients, but because it remains the "simplest of the most frequently requested" applications.

In total, $n = 26$ PWD participated in the study, including 11 with LIS and eight patients at less advanced stages of ALS, two patients suffering from Duchenne muscular dystrophy, one patient with MS and four other miscellaneous conditions. Of these, only eight (13%) had full usage of their heads and only four (7.5%) had retained normal speech, meaning that despite being small the sample is representative of the potential BCI user base. All of these patients except one were equipped with assistive devices for communication, the most common of which were virtual keyboards (12/26), yes/no codes (3/26) and speech synthesis (3/26). The patients reported "average" to "good" levels of satisfaction with these systems (7/10 average for six participants). These applications were typically accessed by interfaces driven by scrolling systems controlled by a switch (6/26), pointing systems based on head movements (5/26) and pointing systems (mouse, trackball or joystick) operated by residual motion in the upper limbs (3/26). Users expressed high levels of satisfaction with these systems (9.3/10 average on an analogous visual scale).

This survey highlights first and foremost the importance that BSIs are easy to set up and configure (setup time less than 15 min in 82% of answers). At the same time, the estimated daily usage period was greater than 2 h. This particularly emphasizes the importance of mechanical comfort (identified as top priority by 72% of users) and the possibility of personalized configurations for the application (second priority for 79% of users and 62% of medical staff). For mechanical comfort, compatibility with the headrest was often quoted as a factor, while the most desired applications were in order of frequency: speech synthesis, web browsing, e-mails and home automation.

Within these groups of patients, it is important to contrast chronic and degenerative conditions (myopathies, MS, ALS) with disabilities that occur suddenly in an acute context (trauma, stroke, GBS). In the former case, the progression of the disease causes patients to slowly lose their capabilities before culminating in LIS. In the earlier stages, these patients will have the opportunity to perfectly master their assistance system of choice, which will progress along with them. In the latter case, an unexpected full loss of autonomy must be compensated from one day to the next.

In a certain sense, neurodegenerative patients have much higher expectations: they have already mastered one form of technical assistance that a hypothetical replacement BCI must outperform in terms of both comfort and performance (which non-invasive BCIs rarely achieve). Also, a number of strategies will have been formulated over time (non-verbal communication with carers) that additionally reduces dependence on the assistive device and consequently tolerance to potential defaults. By contrast, patients in an acute phase must compensate for a (often sudden and total) loss of control and communication, so they are generally less demanding. However, the acute context of these patients places other heavy restrictions on the usage of these systems: availability of a third party for installation, use of psychoactive drugs and sedatives, presence of mechanical noise (vibrating mattresses), other sounds (monitor beeps) and electromagnetic interference (electric bed, mattress, mechanical ventilation). These obvious factors might be less critical than they seem. Indeed, in a pilot study, a group of tetraplegic patients admitted to intensive care ($n = 15$) tested a BCI for communication without finding a statistically significant correlation between these factors and BCI performance [MAY 13b].

In addition to the obvious need for general improvements in BCI performance, it should be noted that BCI usage is sometimes associated with anxiety, which is characteristic of less adept patients. This phenomenon was identified very early on, even before much feedback was available from users who had used BCIs in real-life contexts. The source of this anxiety may be partly due to the technological complexity of the interface, the high cognitive burden required to operate it and a fear of failure that is exacerbated in these patients [BLA 12]. It is therefore necessary to be aware of this aspect of the patient experience and reduce as much as possible the anxiogenic character of the interface in terms of both its fatigability and, paradoxically, its high-tech appearance (electrophysiologic gel syringes, cables, LEDs, control panels). It is only by addressing *all* of the needs listed above that these systems can become successful, even despite the time and ingenuity that has been invested by a generation of researchers and engineers.

6.2.2. *Carers*

Although "functionality" is the main criterion for patient needs, care staff often care more about "ease of use", which is a striking example of the difference in perspective between these two groups [ZIC 10], highlighting the importance of properly investigating the needs of all parties. In view of this, $n = 34$ care staff agreed to answer our questions, of whom approximately half were occupational therapists (44%), and the rest of whom were physiotherapists, medical doctors, nurses and care assistants. Half of the participants were active in the area of re-education/rehabilitation, followed by, in descending order, intensive care units (13%) and home environments (8%).

The BCI applications preferred by care staff very strongly agreed with patient preferences, with a vast majority of answers ($> 90\%$) in favor of communication-related applications and in particular access to Internet-based technologies (browsing, e-mail, instant messaging). Unlike patients, who were relatively tolerant in terms of the time required to setup the system, these answers clearly reveal that any third-party involved needs to be strongly reduced (less than 30 min in 90% of answers), which agrees with existing data [ZIC 10]. Again, in this regard, the threshold at which BCIs cease to be viable is in the neighborhood of current levels of BCI performance, at least for communication-related applications. This shows that there does currently exist some demand for BCIs in communication, but that their usage remains limited even in the best of cases. Finally, the ideal expected performance for communication applications is of the order of five words per minute (over 90% of participants). This demonstrates the characteristic false expectations of the potential user base regarding BCIs, and emphasizes the misapprehension surrounding them that makes it particularly difficult to gather information related to user needs.

6.3. Interpretation of needs in BCI usage contexts

Gathering information about user needs is the necessary first step toward designing a successful interface. Translating these needs into technical specifications is however a non-trivial task, and requires some interpretation. The following section provides a few ideas for achieving this.

6.3.1. *Physical interfaces for reading brain activity*

The method of recording the brain activity interpreted by the BCI is central to the design, as it plays a role in determining setup time, cost, usage context, safety and system performance. Systems that are too expensive (magnetic resonance imaging and magnetoencephalography) or too invasive (deep electrodes, electrode microgrids implanted in the cortex) must be ruled out for now.

Overly expensive or overly cumbersome systems are not viable for obvious reasons, and overly invasive systems present a real risk to patient health when they are installed, and only have a limited lifetime. This is particularly true of intracortical electrode microgrids, which perform excellently, but which induce scarring after a few weeks, causing the signal quality to gradually drop and, with it, the interface performance. By contrast, systems that are based on electrocorticography (ECoG) are placed below the bone but outside of the brain (on the dura mater) are relatively safe to install and produce a good-quality signal with little deterioration over time. The system by far the most frequently used by computer research laboratories is the "electrocap" – a cap on which classical EEG electrodes have been placed in a predefined arrangement (the 10–20 international system). However, a recent study revealed that this method is unacceptable for more than one-fifth of patients [HUG 11] (in $n = 61$ ALS patients). The reason for this high rejection rate might be the poor esthetics of the cap, despite recent progress in this regard. Indeed, patients experience a degraded self-image, which is reinforced by the use of large and cumbersome equipment (such as electric wheelchairs). Adding cables creates a "Christmas tree" effect that patients naturally dislike. Finally, the "swimming cap" that is often used is a further deterrent to undecided patients. Although esthetics might appear insignificant given the necessity of communication, it is nonetheless a determining factor for potential BCI users and is partly responsible for the difficulty of including patients in clinical trials.

The importance of the choice of physical interface cannot be overstated in this chapter. Extended use of earphones that cover the ears, as some readers may have experienced themselves, leads to uncomfortable pain after a certain period (typically around 60 min). Similarly, for patients that intend to use a BCI for several hours, the slightest pressure on the scalp must be viewed as a potential source of pain.

This has in fact been observed in patients, with complaints ranging from overtight headsets that cause sweating to severe headaches [BLA 12]. New EEG-monitoring techniques have emerged to replace the existing cup-shaped sensors, but they are often complicated and lengthy to install. A number of ambitious promises have been made in connection with these techniques, sometimes culminating in unpleasant surprises. For example, the very widespread Epoc headset (Emotiv) engenders strong discomfort after 1 h of usage, mostly from the point at which pressure is applied to hold the headset in place [MAY 13a] (electrodes T6 and T7). It is clear that these kinds of design decisions are essential, and equipping LIS patients with this headset is out of the question, as the impact of this kind of discomfort on concentration could prevent them from informing the operator so that the session can be ended. We must additionally bear in mind that tetraplegic patients often experience oversensitivity on the scalp, which renders these considerations all the more critical. Although this particular shortcoming may not completely rule out the usage of this family of EEG headsets, it prompts us to proceed with the utmost caution, and reminds us that there is currently far too little feedback and precedence available from users who have operated these systems in real-life situations.

A survey of the 61 ALS patients mentioned earlier [HUG 11] also showed that more than two-thirds (71%) of the participants would be open to using an implant for recording electrical signals. This high proportion in favor of implants must not be allowed to go unnoticed, and becomes especially relevant in light of the above results. In particular, some invasive systems based on ECoG significantly improve system performance while reducing the time required for setup (once the initial surgery has been performed) and while addressing any esthetic concerns of end-users. We can hope that these techniques will be used more often once existing implants [MES 14] have been perfected and the risks associated with surgery have been balanced in favor of the benefit to users. The future of BCIs undoubtedly rests at least in part on this kind of physical interface.

6.3.2. *Analysis of brain activity*

The analysis of the needs of patients and their close friends and family shows that the expected level of minimum acceptable performance is in fact close to the actual performance levels of the BCI methods that are currently available for purposes of communication. The accuracy and the speed of the algorithms must therefore be improved. Fortunately, there is a consensus that patients are prepared to invest the necessary effort to feed algorithms with personalized data in order to reach satisfactory levels of performance [COL 13, MAY 13b]. The introduction of new mathematical representations of EEG signals together with the application of Riemannian geometry offers promising prospects both for the identification of noisy segments of the signal and for the identification of mental states or evoked potentials [BAR 13]. In order to meet the needs expressed by users, systems must improve to the point of requiring neither initial nor intermediary calibration, and must adapt their speed to the signal-to-noise ratio to produce commands with high and stable accuracy. Finally, as well as the obvious goal of improving system performance, it seems equally important to improve the user-friendliness and in particular user fatigue, which is one of the issues most commonly raised by patients [BLA 12].

Figure 6.2. *Three different usage cases for patients operating a BCI: (left) tracheotomized adult patient with Duchenne muscular dystrophy in intensive care unit; (center) tracheotomized patient with Guillain–Barré Syndrome in intensive care unit; (right) patient with amyotrophic lateral sclerosis (ALS) in her wheelchair. The first two patients are equipped with individually attached silver chloride (AgCl) electrodes, whereas the third patient (right) is equipped with a headset facilitating electrode placement*

6.3.3. *Applications and user interfaces*

Although there is a real interest in BCIs among patients and their carers [BLA 12, HUG 11, ZIC 10], it remains relatively clear that no application proposed so far can fully meet these users' needs [BLA 12]. A more pessimistic view of the analysis of patient needs might point out that the "real" performance of existing BCIs barely meets the needs of most patients; for example, communication interfaces – which are probably the most advanced application – possess maximum information transfer rates that are very close to the minimum rates described as acceptable by patients [HUG 11, MAY 13b]. However, in a context where individuals are defined by their personal information spheres, lack of access to new information technologies represents a "digital disability" on top of physical impairments, which undeniably increases the urgency of developing appropriate interfaces, some of which could be BCIs. More than ever, it is vital to construct dedicated applications for end-users that integrate real functionality. The applications suggested in the Tobi project[1] provide relevant examples that might serve to inspire the scientific community [LEE 13]. Despite this, it seems that these prototypes, which to the best of our knowledge are the most advanced of their kind, still only exist in a fenced-off research context. In general, these interfaces represent the deliverables of a project that is missing – in the best of cases – two of the critical steps of quality industrial development processes: unit testing and functional testing, and bug tracking for continuous software improvement. Often, the prespecifications phase is also neglected, despite being equally critical. This unquestionably dire state of affairs must of course be put into context with the maturity of the field, and we must recognize the quality work and effort that has been invested in these projects. The amount of funding currently in play (approximately 12 million euros for the Tobi project whose primary objective is "developing practical BCIs to improve the quality of life of disabled persons") gives an idea of the true difficulty of the endeavor.

6.4. Conclusions

In this chapter, we have seen that the potential BCI user base presents a number of different etiologies and a wide range of disabilities. In particular, we can distinguish between two groups of patients: chronic patients that are usually suffering from neurodegenerative diseases and patients hospitalized in an acute context with a different medical history, and relatively different limitations and needs.

The study of these groups of patients reveals widespread everyday usage of low-tech assistance systems with which patients are relatively satisfied. Although patients surveyed about BCIs specifically quote communication as

---

1 http://www.tobi-project.org/demos.

their primary objective, it is clear that they also have other more general expectations of assistance systems (mobility, upper limb control, digestive and sexual function). Furthermore, when attempting to identify patient needs in connection with this new technology, we have found it necessary to distinguish between the needs of patients and the needs of their prescribers. In order for a design to have a real chance at being widely adopted, it must meet all of these different types of need. This is probably part of the reason why BCIs have never quite managed to establish themselves as viable assistive devices (i.e. used outside of the context of biomedical research) yet. In particular, care staff are much stricter than patients regarding the presence and involvement of third parties to operate them. The importance of comfort has been raised (for non-invasive solutions) in connection with the method of recording electrical brain signals, and the future significance of ECoG has been emphasized for patients in chronic conditions. Finally, an unquestionable lack of industrial transfer of BCI-related research has been identified; the lack of interfaces designed with end-users in mind in particular stands in bitter contrast to the volume of scientific publications in this field.

The success of BCIs necessarily depends on properly meeting the needs listed in this chapter. There is a need for scientific development processes with the singular goal of making BCIs a clinically viable solution that can be used a manner that is both autonomous and fully integrated with the range of existing assistance systems [COL 13, PAT 08, GIL 11]. To achieve this, scientists and clinical interest groups need to unite to develop relevant and enduring solutions. This will probably also require the involvement of organizations and the search for funding specifically oriented toward engineering the transfer of this technology to the patient's bedside. Indeed, it is not an uncommon occurrence in the case of disability-related projects that the size of the target audience of the application is insufficient to justify industrial investment. In some cases, such as for the iBot project [HIL 04], remarkable technical achievements may still culminate in discontinuation during commercialization due to low sales figures. By contrast, there are many elegant examples of consumer applications arising from technologies developed for disabled audiences; the best-known example is the infrared remote control, which was originally conceived for a target audience with reduced mobility, developed by the engineer Adler, and finally brought onto the market by Zenith Electronics with the success that we are familiar with today. In the United States, this disconnect between the world of disabilities and the realities of the market gave rise to the concept of *Universal Design* [HIT 03], which describes the principle of considering the widest-possible spectrum of users when designing a product. The significant impairments characteristic of the disabled user base and the major restrictions imposed by their user environments guarantee a powerful *Universal Design* whose performance will gradually increase as the restrictions are lifted and the technology is migrated toward healthier users. For example, an industrial interest in the development of consumer wellness products based on neuromodulation (improving cognitive performances, relaxation) could serve as an industrial springboard for the proliferation of solutions that are viable for smaller patient groups.

6.5. Bibliography

[AND 04] ANDERSON K.D., "Targeting recovery: priorities of the spinal cord-injured population", *Journal of Neurotrauma*, vol. 21, no. 10, pp. 1371–1383, 2004.

[BAR 13] BARACHANT A., ANDREEV A., CONGEDO M. *et al.*, "The Riemannian potato: an automatic and adaptive artifact detection method for online experiments using Riemannian geometry", *Proceedings of TOBI Workshop IV*, pp. 19–20, 2013.

[BIG 07] BIGOT R., CROUTTE P., DAUDEY E., *La diffusion des technologies de l'information dans la société française*, Credoc, 2007.

[BLA 12] BLAIN-MORAES S., SCHAFF R., GRUIS K.L. *et al.*, "Barriers to and mediators of Brain–Computer interface user acceptance: focus group findings", *Ergonomics*, vol. 55, no. 5, pp. 516–525, 2012.

[CAR 13] CARDWELL M.S., "Locked-in syndrome", *Texas Medicine*, vol. 109, no. 2, 2013.

[COL 13] COLLINGER J.L., BONINGER M.L., BRUNS T.M. *et al.*, "Functional priorities, assistive technology, and Brain–Computer interfaces after spinal cord injury", *Journal of Rehabilitation Research and Development*, vol. 50, no. 2, 2013.

[DAL 11] DALAKAS M., "Review: an update on inflammatory and autoimmune myopathies", *Neuropathology and Applied Neurobiology*, vol. 37, no. 3, pp. 226–242, 2011.

[GHE 09] GHEDIRA S., PINO P., BOURHIS G., "Conception and experimentation of a communication device with adaptive scanning", *ACM Transactions on Accessible Computing (TACCESS)*, vol. 1, no. 3, p. 14, 2009.

[GIL 11] GILJA V., CHESTEK C.A., DIESTER I. *et al.*, "Challenges and opportunities for next-generation intracortically based neural prostheses", *IEEE Transactions on Biomedical Engineering*, vol. 58, no. 7, pp. 1891–1899, 2011.

[GRU 11] GRUIS K.L., WREN P.A., HUGGINS J.E., "Amyotrophic lateral sclerosis patients' self-reported satisfaction with assistive technology", *Muscle & Nerve*, vol. 43, no. 5, pp. 643–647, 2011.

[HIL 04] HILLMAN M., "2 Rehabilitation robotics from past to present – a historical perspective", *Advances in Rehabilitation Robotics*, pp. 25–44, 2004.

[HIT 03] HITCHCOCK C., STAHL S., "Assistive technology, universal design, universal design for learning: Improved learning opportunities", *Journal of Special Education Technology*, vol. 18, no. 4, 2003.

[HUG 11] HUGGINS J.E., WREN P.A., GRUIS K.L., "What would Brain–Computer interface users want? Opinions and priorities of potential users with amyotrophic lateral sclerosis", *Amyotrophic Lateral Sclerosis*, vol. 12, no. 5, pp. 318–324, 2011.

[KIE 11] KIERNAN M.C., VUCIC S., CHEAH B.C. *et al.*,, "Amyotrophic lateral sclerosis", *The Lancet*, vol. 377, no. 9769, pp. 942–955, 2011.

[LAN 12] LANCIONI G.E., SIGAFOOS J., O'REILLY M.F. *et al.*, *Assistive Technology: Interventions for Individuals with Severe/Profound and Multiple Disabilities*, Springer Science & Business Media, 2012.

[LEE 13] LEEB R., MILLÁN J.D.R., "Introduction to devices, applications and users: towards practical bcis based on shared control techniques", *Towards Practical Brain-Computer Interfaces*, pp. 107–129, Springer, 2013.

[LOO 11] LOOBY S., FLANDERS A., "Spine trauma", *Radiologic Clinics of North America*, vol. 49, no. 1, pp. 129–163, 2011.

[MAY 13a] MAYAUD L., CONGEDO M., VAN LAGHENHOVE A. *et al.*, "A comparison of recording modalities of P300 event-related potentials (ERP) for brain-computer interface (BCI) paradigm", *Neurophysiologie Clinique/Clinical Neurophysiology*, vol. 43, no. 4, pp. 217–227, 2013.

[MAY 13b] MAYAUD L., FILIPE S., PÉTÉGNIEF L. *et al.*, "Robust Brain-computer interface for virtual Keyboard (RoBIK): project results", *IRBM*, vol. 34, no. 2, pp. 131–138, 2013.

[MCL 13] MCLELLAN D., "Epidemiology of disability", *Principles and Practice of Restorative Neurology: Butterworths International Medical Reviews*, Butterworth-Heinemann, vol. 11, 2013.

[MES 14] MESTAIS C., CHARVET G., SAUTER-STARACE F. *et al.*, WIMAGINE®: Wireless 64-channel ECoG recording implant for long term clinical applications, 2014.

[PAT 08] PATIL P.G., TURNER D.A., "The development of brain-machine interface neuroprosthetic devices", *Neurotherapeutics*, vol. 5, no. 1, pp. 137–146, 2008.

[POL 11] POLMAN C.H., REINGOLD S.C., BANWELL B. *et al.*, "Diagnostic criteria for multiple sclerosis: 2010 revisions to the McDonald criteria", *Annals of Neurology*, vol. 69, no. 2, pp. 292–302, 2011.

[SHI 09] SHIH C.-H., HSU N.-Y., SHIH C.-T., "Assisting people with developmental disabilities to improve pointing efficiency with an Automatic Pointing Assistive Program", *Research in Developmental Disabilities*, vol. 30, no. 6, pp. 1212–1220, 2009.

[SNO 04] SNOEK G.J., IJZERMAN M.J., HERMENS H.J. *et al.*, "Survey of the needs of patients with spinal cord injury: impact and priority for improvement in hand function in tetraplegics", *Spinal Cord*, vol. 42, no. 9, pp. 526–532, 2004.

[TAI 08] TAI K., BLAIN S., CHAU T., "A review of emerging access technologies for individuals with severe motor impairments", *Assistive Technology*, vol. 20, no. 4, pp. 204–221, 2008.

[WOL 12] WOLPAW J., WOLPAW E.W., *Brain–Computer Interfaces: Principles and Practice*, Oxford University Press, 2012.

[YUK 12] YUKI N., HARTUNG H.-P., "Guillain–Barré syndrome", *New England Journal of Medicine*, vol. 366, no. 24, pp. 2294–2304, 2012.

[ZIC 10] ZICKLER C., KAISER V., AL-KHODAIRY A. *et al.*, "BCI-applications: requirements of disabled end-users and professional users", *TOBI Workshop*, p. 29, 2010.

Sensors: Theory and Innovation

To interface with the brain, we must first pick up its activity, or more specifically the electrophysiological activity by which it functions. Electrophysiological activity is the only kind of measurable activity to provide information with a temporal resolution of the order of milliseconds, corresponding to the time scale at which the brain functions. The level at which this activity is recorded can vary from the cells themselves to a very integrated view taken at the surface of the scalp. But at every level, sensors are responsible for providing the link between the tissue where this activity is measured and the systems responsible for amplifying, processing, visualizing and recording the data.

Electroencephalography (EEG) is a commonly used technique, measuring the potential at the surface of the scalp using metal electrodes (Figure 7.1(c)). These electrodes are usually connected to the skin via a conductive gel to ensure good contact. We will discuss the physical phenomena that occur at the interface between saline environments and the metal component of the electrode, the consequences of these phenomena, and how they may be characterized. If the precision of surface data is insufficient, it is possible in clinically justified situations to use invasive recording methods that are much more sensitive and that may be viable for certain BCI applications. All of these recording methods are subject to interference. More specifically in the case of EEG, we will see how using solid and/or active electrodes can

Chapter written by Jean-Michel BADIER, Thomas LONJARET and Pierre LELEUX.

improve some usage limitations, such as those associated with performance, comfort and stability, while simultaneously reducing the sensitivity to outside interference. We will also present recent research developments in the materials that are used for electrodes and skin interfaces.

Finally, we will discuss the recording technique of magnetoencephalography (MEG). Although this technique does not achieve the spatial resolution of invasive techniques, this method is not bound by some of the limitations associated with EEG. However, it is only viable for exploratory applications in connection with BCIs, for example precisely localizing target regions before inserting sensor implants, due to high requirements in terms of equipment.

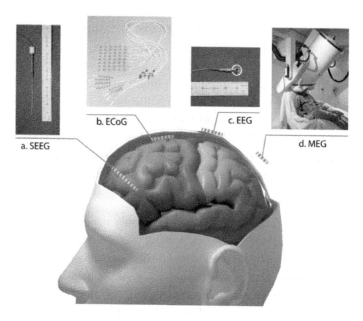

Figure 7.1. *Brain activity recording technologies: a) implant device composed of multiple electrodes used for stereoelectroencephalography (SEEG); b) electrode matrix Dixi medical for applications in electrocorticography (ECoG); c) cup-shaped electrode (Au) for use in electroencephalography (EEG); d) system for recording brain activity by magnetoencephalography (MEG)*

7.1. EEG electrodes

In the human body, ions are responsible for transporting charges released by the cellular potentials underlying electrophysiological phenomena. To measure this displacement of charge, we need a transducer, the electrode, to convert ionic current into electrical current that can be measured by our acquisition systems.

7.1.1. *Electrochemical model of the electrode*

Electrochemically, electrodes are electrical conductors placed in contact with a biological ionic aqueous solution (serum, mucous membrane, etc.) or synthetic solution called an electrolyte. At the electrode/solution interface, there is a redox reaction that creates a transfer of charge: the oxidized substance C_{Ox} transforms into the reduced substance C_{Red} by means of a transfer of n electrons:

$$C_{Ox} + n \cdot e^- \rightleftharpoons C_{Red}$$

The metal/electrolyte interaction creates a local change in the ion concentration in the region of the electrode. This results in a potential difference with the rest of the electrolyte, called the half-cell potential. This potential cannot be neglected, as it can influence low-frequency measurements by introducing a continuous component. Depending on the material used, the electrode may or may not be polarizable. If it is, changes in the ion concentration near the electrode induce a current in the electrode without any current strictly passing through the electrode/electrolyte interface. In this case, the electrode acts like a capacitor. In the context of biomedical measurements, if a polarizable electrode moves in the electrolyte, there is a change in the charge distribution in the region of the electrode and in its potential. This causes the measurement to experience a strong variation in the low-frequency potential, described as a motion artifact. For this reason, non-polarizable electrodes are preferred, for example made from silver/silver chloride (Ag/AgCl). In an ideal non-polarizable electrode, the current moves freely between the electrolyte and the metal, without inducing any change in the ion distribution around the electrode. In this case, the electrode acts as a resistor. In practice, non-polarizable electrodes are never perfect and have small capacitive effects [BUE 93, BRO 00].

7.1.2. *Electrodes in electrophysiology*

The above-mentioned model also applies in the case of invasive electrodes, i.e. electrodes implanted in the human body. Indeed, these electrodes are immersed in the physiological medium that surrounds each cell of the body. This medium is aqueous and strongly conductive, and thus acts as an electrolyte. Most of the electrodes currently used for electrophysiological applications in humans are however cutaneous, and use gel as the interface between metal and skin. This gel, which can be more or less liquid, is an ionic conductor (in extreme circumstances, a saline solution such as sweat would suffice). It must therefore remain stable for several hours (without evaporating over extended measurement periods) and can additionally have adhesive properties. Due to its liquid state, this gel creates a good contact with the skin and so can bypass thin layers of hair. Additionally, by humidifying the outer layer of the skin (*stratum corneum*), ordinarily an insulator, this layer becomes conductive, and so the gel greatly improves the contact impedance of the electrode.

In the case of electrophysiology, the working principle of a cutaneous electrode can be explained in terms of the phenomena that occur at both interfaces: electrode/contact gel and contact gel/skin. Figure 7.2 shows one possible model for the electrode/gel/skin system. The conductivity of the gel, the preparation of the skin, and the electrode performance are all parameters that affect the global impedance of the system and thus the quality of the recorded signal.

7.1.3. *Characterization of electrodes*

A simplified model of the electrode can be used for biopotential measurements (Figure 7.2). E_{hc} represents the half-cell potential, and the interface of the electrode is modeled as a resistor R_{int} and a capacitor C_{int} in parallel. The impedance can be calculated precisely in a laboratory setting (with a two or three-electrode system applying voltages at different frequencies) to investigate the inherent properties of the sensor. The geometry of the interface and the material composition of the sensor can then be adjusted to match the frequencies required for the measurement. For example, increasing the surface of the electrode interface reduces the impedance, whereas strong polarization increases the impedance at high frequencies. A simpler measurement of the impedance at a very low voltage applied between the electrode and another point of reference is taken when an EEG headset is put into place. This measurement verifies that the total impedance of the electrode/gel/skin system is low, meaning that the contact is good. Typically, the impedance values measured in these cases are around 5 and 10 kOhms at a frequency of 1 kHz.

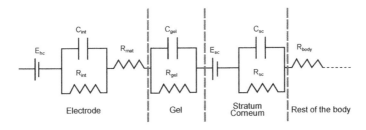

Figure 7.2. *Model of the electrode/gel/skin system. E_{hc} models the half-cell potential of the electrode and the components R_{int} and C_{int} represent the impedance associated with the electrolyte/metal interface. The contact gel and the stratum corneum are each represented by a capacitor and a resistor in parallel. The skin has the highest impedance in this circuit*

7.1.4. *EEG electrode matrices and headsets*

Even though some BCI applications can make do with a few electrodes, it is often desirable to cover the whole of the scalp. The standard clinical setup involves 21 electrodes in a standardized arrangement [LAS 59]. Electrode density can also be higher than this, reaching 128 or even 256 electrodes on the surface of the scalp. This can be useful for example when localizing the source of activity (see Chapter 2 of Volume 1, [CLE 16]). In this case, flexible headsets are used that allow electrodes to be rapidly placed (Figure 7.3). The challenge of ensuring good contact with the skin increases proportionally with the number of electrodes. Applying gel and achieving acceptable impedances for large numbers of electrodes greatly increases the time required for preparation. On the other hand, new solutions that integrate the electrolyte into the electrode [MOT 13], amplifiers that accept higher initial impedance values and electrodes with integrated electronic circuits (see section 7.3.4) can speed up the process. Finally, as the distance between electrodes decreases, there is an increased risk of conductive bridges forming between closely positioned electrodes due to excess electrolyte.

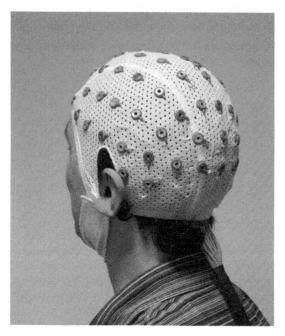

Figure 7.3. *Flexible EEG headset equipped with 64 electrodes. The headset holds the electrodes in place and ensures that they are quickly and homogeneously arranged. The electrodes have small holes through which gel is introduced using a truncated syringe*

7.2. Invasive recording

7.2.1. *The need for invasive recording techniques*

EEG records the potentials associated with extracellular currents generated by synaptic activity (see Chapter 3 of Volume 1, [CLE 16]). The distribution of these potentials is strongly affected by the skull, which has an estimated conductivity 20–80 times lower than the brain. This leads to an attenuation of the amplitude and a spatial blurring of the recorded signals. Similar to a translucent light filter, the skull acts as a low-pass spatial filter with a smoothing effect on the information picked up at the scalp [GEV 91]. This makes it more difficult to classify the various types of recorded activity according to their origin in the brain, and consequently more difficult to exploit in the context of BCIs. In clinical applications that require the highest standard of spatial resolution or reliable BCI solutions, it is necessary to record from inside the skull. The technique known as electrocorticography (ECoG, [CHA 13]) places the electrodes directly at the surface of the cortex. The technique of implanting the electrodes inside the brain is given the name of stereoelectroencephalography (SEEG, [LAC 07]).

7.2.2. *Electrocorticography*

Historically, this technique was developed by Wilder Penfield and Herbert Jasper in the 1940s for exploration with epileptic patients. Placing electrodes directly on the cortex through a hole in the skull was used among other methods to record atypical activity related to epilepsy and to identify regions for further surgery within the same session.

Today, electrodes are arranged in the form of a grid or strip with multiple contacts (Figure 7.1(b)). Recordings of the subject can be taken during surgery or afterward over the course of several days in an extended exploration process. Strips with a single row of recording contacts can be passed through an opening in the skull to reach regions that are not directly accessible. Still, ECoG recordings remain at the surface of the cortex, and do not easily provide access to deep brain structures.

In the context of BCIs, prostheses are implanted permanently. It can also be desirable to obtain signals in even smaller regions, for example the motor regions. In this case, even smaller electrode matrices are used, sensitive to more restricted neural populations and in sufficient number to maintain a sufficiently high sample rate [CHA 13]. Signals obtained by ECoG can be used to send commands to an effector, for example a robotic arm [HOC 12] or potentially even an exoskeleton [ELI 14]. One of the challenges is to position these electrodes on the correct regions of the brains during preparation of the implant. Magnetoencephalography (MEG, section 7.4) can be useful for this purpose.

7.2.3. *Stereoelectroencephalography*

This technique was developed by Jean Talairach and Jean Bancaud for presurgical exploration of epileptic patients [TAL 62]. SEEG, originally conducted during surgery for "acute" conditions, is now used for "chronic" conditions postsurgery, over several days. This allows the exploration phase, during which the brain region responsible for seizures is identified, to be distinguished from the remedial surgery phase. Each "electrode" is composed of a set of recording contacts. The number of contacts, typically between 5 and 15, depends on the length of the electrode, allowing different brain regions to be explored, from the most superficial regions to the deepest regions (Figure 7.1(a)). Before these electrodes are implanted, to avoid hemorrhage, the implant coordinates are precisely defined using stereotactic methods: a collection of measurements performed by several different imaging techniques (MRI, X-ray, etc.) to situate the skull within a fixed geometric reference system. The skull opening is restricted to the size of the screw that holds the electrode in place. This also helps to maintain a seal between the brain environment and the exterior.

From a technological perspective, the electrodes themselves are not particularly advanced. Each recording contacts consists of a hollow cylinder 2 mm in length and 0.8 mm in diameter (for electrodes commonly used in Europe). Each block is connected to the external circuit by an insulated conductor. Originally made from stainless steel, blocks are now available in platinum or alloys (platinum-iridium) compatible with MRI scans. Anatomical tests can therefore be performed once the SEEG electrodes are in place.

7.3. Latest generation sensors

7.3.1. Innovative substrate materials

Substrate materials, as we are referring to them here, constitute the inactive frame of the sensors, providing structure and support to the electrode. Depending on the application, these sections can take different appearances and have different compositions. Electrode implants (for SEEG) are usually rigid for better stability and are made of platinum-iridium to be more compatible with MRI and MEG. With these implants, there is a risk of damaging tissue during insertion, and in the long term there can be strong reactions from the biological tissue. In surface electrodes (for EEG or ECoG), the body of the sensor is plastic for flexibility, low production cost and favorable interactions with the skin.

Current research into a new generation of electrophysiological sensors has been focusing in particular on material *flexibility*. This allows the sensor to be more compatible with the three-dimensional (3D) structure of the skin and organs, providing better contact with active zones to reduce the contact impedance. Modern polymers are used to fulfill these requirements. Parylene, easily synthesizable, is now commonly used for sensor implants. Vapor delivered allows the formation of a substrate layer but also encapsulates and insulates the sensor. Combining excellent flexibility with a very thin cross-section (a few microns), it minimizes invasiveness [TAK 05, KHO 13]. Figure 7.4(a) shows an example of a parylene film supporting an electrode matrix in the context of ECoG and *in vitro* applications. Polyethylene terephthalate and polydimethylsiloxane are other examples of inert and flexible polymer films that are well known in connection with implants. Polyimides such as Kapton developed by the DuPont company, thicker and thus mechanically more resistant, are used for cutaneous electrodes such as those shown in Figure 7.4(b). To fully optimize sensor flexibility and minimize the immune response, research teams have suggested using a silk fiber-based substrate that is resorbed into the human body. Once dissolved, only the metal strips and insulators remain in contact with the biological medium [KIM 10].

a.   b.

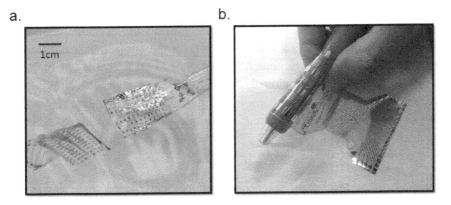

1cm

Figure 7.4. *Flexibility of organic substrates: a) matrix of organic active components built on a flexible substrate made up of parylene C (thickness 4 μm); b) matrix of electrodes for application in electromyography made of up Kapton polyimide with a thickness of 12.5 μm*

The other major axis of material improvement is *biocompatibility*. Currently, surface electrodes, and in particular their adhesive components, can sometimes lead to skin irritation, burns and other allergic reactions, especially over extended periods of contact. For invasive electrodes, the problem can be more critical, causing internal damage to tissue (for example fibrosis). Performing tests beforehand to evaluate the compatibility of the material with the cells is therefore crucial. Paralyene C, for example, interacts very well with tissues, and is the ideal candidate for long-term invasive sensors.

Another approach to surface sensor design is to integrate sensors into textile components. Combining good flexibility, mechanical resistance and healthy skin contact, clothes can be used to support sensors. These might be classical electrodes woven into the textile fibers, or can be the fibers themselves, endowed with conductive properties by the addition of polymer inks [ZEN 14, TSU 11]. This model of electrode enclosed in simple clothing has seen a number of developments in medical, wellness and sport applications, and could be used in the next generation of EEG headsets.

7.3.2. *Interface materials*

7.3.2.1. *Conductive polymers*

Conductive polymers belong to the family of organic materials. Discovered in the 1970s, they have since been the subject of a number of research studies. Used as luminophore materials in OLEDs, they also play a fundamental role in developing thin-film transistors and photovoltaic cells. The use of conductive polymers for the interface with biological tissue is a new field of research in organic electronics with extremely promising prospects. In this field, known as organic bioelectronics, conductive polymers are used to improve the biotic/abiotic interface.

Let us list a few of the advantages of these materials: they are easily biocompatible and can be easily integrated onto flexible substrates. They allow mixed conduction, both ionic and electronic, which is essential for biological systems whose activity depends on ionic flow. Finally, a non-negligible benefit of these materials is their excellent impedance when in contact with biological tissue. The combination of high electrical conductivity and high ionic permeability creates a significant reduction in the electrode/tissue impedance. Consider the simple example of poly(3,4-ethylenedioxythiophene). The conjugated structure of this polymer when used in combination with the right stimulants (such as polystyrene sulfonate) allows conductivity of the order of 1,500 S/cm to be achieved, which is equivalent to that of conventional semiconductors. The use of this material was validated for recording physiological signals in higher quality than conventional materials [LEL 13].

7.3.2.2. Contact gels

Much effort has been invested into developing electrodes that do not require liquid electrolytes. The gel that is commonly used dries out after a few hours, at which point the impedance between the electrode and the skin significantly increases, resulting in a deterioration of the signal quality. Additionally, in cases with high electrode density (which might foreseeably be the case in certain BCI applications), conductive bridges (short-circuits) between adjacent electrodes arise more frequently. Finally, the time required to set up a multielectrode system is significantly higher, jeopardizing the comfort of the patient or subject (applying the gel can take over half an hour). But removing the electrolyte increases sensitivity to motion artifacts during recording. Some solutions suggest applying only a tiny quantity of gel by pressure on the electrode [MOT 13]. This system, although innovative, is very complex to implement. Another solution is to use ionic gels [LEL 14, ISI 15]. These gels are salt compounds that take a semiliquid state at room temperature. Their excellent ionic conductivity and thermal and chemical stability provide long-term stability to physiological recordings. The organic nature of these gels means that their formulation is very open, allowing the integration of other compounds (adhesives, enzymes, proteins) to adapt to the usage context. These ionic gels are not water compounds, so they do not evaporate. Thus, they provide stability in the electrode/skin impedance over extended recording periods (see Figure 7.5). This new type of interface material will allow longer applications, which is good news for BCIs.

7.3.3. Interface topography

Standard Ag/AgCl electrodes suffer from several drawbacks, notably the necessity to prepare the skin and apply a conductive gel, which can lead to damage or discomfort. One laboratory-developed solution that may be particularly viable for long-term recordings involves dry electrodes with a non-flat contact structure. This 3D structure can be defined at the macro-, micro- or nanoscales. The outermost layer of skin, composed of dead cells, is called the *stratum corneum*, and has high resistance to the EEG electrical field. This layer of skin is removed by abrasion before conventional electrodes are placed. A micrometric 3D structure allows this layer of skin to be penetrated (without pain for the subject), which reduces the contact impedance. Additionally, the active surface of the electrode is increased without changing the overall size of the electrode, which improves the signal quality. These kinds of electrode are now simple to produce using 3D printing [SAL 12]. Nanoscale pins, such as carbon nanotubes, can be added to the surface of a dry electrode to improve comfort while preserving good signal quality [LOP 14]. Macropins have also been suggested to bypass the hair barrier, providing excellent impedance values. This allows EEG signals to be recorded at a level of quality comparable to standard electrodes, without requiring gel and removing the obstacle of hair [FIE 13]. These new electrodes simplify the preparation phase but are highly sensitive to motion and sometimes lack mechanical grip.

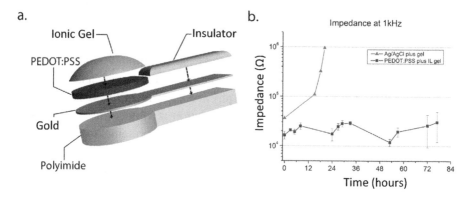

Figure 7.5. *Organic interface materials: a) breakdown of the materials in an organic electrode. The flexible polyimide substrate is covered by a layer of conductive metal such as gold. Next, interface materials such as poly(3,4-ethylenedioxythiophene):polystyrene sulfonate (PEDOT:PSS) followed by ionic gel are used to improve the quality of the signal and the stability of the recording over time; b) evolution of the impedance between the electrode and the skin in the case of a conventional Ag/AgCl electrode and an electrode of the type shown in (a) with an ionic gel component*

7.3.4. *Active sensors*

7.3.4.1. *Electrodes with integrated amplifiers*

For most EEG recordings, the so-called passive electrodes are preferred. These electrodes are inexpensive, easy to manufacture and sometimes disposable. Passive electrodes simply record the potential and relay it to the acquisition system. "Active" electrodes on the other hand are in fact a system composed of a passive electrode and electronic circuits integrated into the same device. This integrated circuitry often contains filters and amplifiers that improve the signal quality as close as possible to the source. Research into active electrodes began at the end of the 1960s, but they were exclusively used for ECG, where the amplitude of the measured signals is rarely less than 100 μV [RIC 67, RIC 68a, RIC 68b, POR 74, KO 74]. Active electrodes were first validated for EEG applications in the early 1990s by Babak Taheri, a researcher at the University of California. In 1994, he designed the first multitrack system of dry active electrodes. It was shown that the performance of these electrodes equaled that of more conventional Ag/AgCl electrodes. Today, active electrode systems are available commercially from companies such as BioSemi (Amsterdam, The Netherlands) and BrainProducts (Gilching, Germany, Acticap series).

The major advantage of active electrodes is an improved signal-to-noise ratio in recordings by better adapting the impedance to the skin. Advances in microelectronics have allowed increasingly advanced generations of sensors to be developed. In the 1970s, for example, a simple MOS operational amplifier was developed, confirming the potential value of this new type of electrode. Over the following years, progress in micromanufacturing technology and integrated circuitry made it possible to integrate miniaturized bipolar transistors and onboard power sources. The latest generation of active electrodes are less sensitive to electromagnetic interference and are compatible with standard acquisition systems.

One example of an active electrode that is suitable for BCIs is the g.SAHARA model (Cortech Solutions), able to record cognitive P300 waves as well as auditory and visual evoked potentials. In both BCI applications and classical EEG, active electrodes have a number of desirable properties (resistance to external interference, *in-situ* amplification, etc.) but have not yet been widely adopted.

7.3.4.2. *Transistors, another path for active electrodes*

We described the advantages of using organic materials for substrates and interfaces above. It is also possible to use these materials in the active components of transistors.

Transistors are semiconductive active components with three terminals: the drain, the source and the gate. They can be used as switches, amplifiers or even biosensors. Here, we will discuss their potential in the context of BCIs. Organic thin-film transistors can be divided into two categories. The first is the category of organic field effect transistors: in this case, the channel made from semiconductive organic material is insulated from the measurement environment, and the recorded modulations of the current in the channel are induced by modifying the interface capacitance. The other category is that of electrochemical transistors (Figure 7.6). This time, the channel is directly in contact with the electrolyte and is permeable to the ions in the surrounding medium. The modulations of the current in the channel correspond to oxidation or reduction reactions in the conductive polymer that modify its resistance.

Organic transistors provide the solution to a number of design and manufacturing constraints: these materials are easy to modify structurally, given that the field of organic chemistry is well understood. They can also be used in methods of direct pattern transfer such as material jet printing. Finally, their crystalline structure supports both ionic and electronic conduction, which as noted above is ideal for interfacing with biological tissues due to the ionic nature of most of the activity that we wish to measure.

The performance of organic transistors was validated for recording neurological activity in the context of electrocorticography by Khodagholy *et al.* [KHO 13], the preferred technique for invasive BCIs. Achieving a gain of almost 30 dB in the signal-to-noise ratio compared to an electrode of similar size located near the transistor, the latter was even capable of recording deep activity that was invisible to surface ECoG.

These new devices seem promising for BCI applications. Organic materials used as flexible substrates conform perfectly to the biological tissue being measured. As for organic interface materials, they provide high-quality recordings that can last for longer periods suitable for certain planned BCI applications, such as communication and control of the user environment.

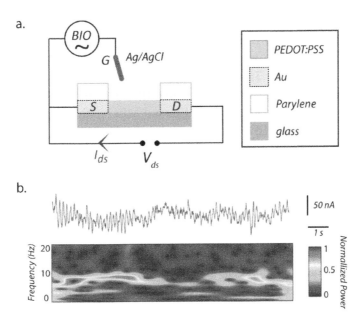

Figure 7.6. *An organic electrochemical transistor (OECT): a) schematic diagram of an OECT. The biological signal measured at the gate (G) will modulate the current in the channel (source-drain); b) application of OECT in EEG. Detection of the alpha rhythm, confirmed by time-frequency analysis, validates this innovative and miniaturized technology (the device is $100 \times 100 \, \mu m^2$). For a color version of this figure, see www.iste.co.uk/clerc/interfaces2.zip*

7.4. Magnetoencephalography

7.4.1. *The source of the signal*

MEG is the magnetic counterpart to EEG. *A priori* MEG is not an ideal recording method for BCIs as it is not portable, and requires the subject to remain immobile inside a fixed machine. However, MEG possesses a certain number of properties that EEG does not, which makes it useful for developing and prototyping BCI scenarios.

Similarly to EEG, synaptic activity is the origin of the ionic currents that create the signals picked up at the surface of the scalp. Synaptic activity takes the form of a (primary) intracellular current that equalizes ionic concentrations in the cell membrane. This current locally modifies the distribution of charge and induces a secondary current that equalizes electric charge. This secondary current, which travels through various different tissues in the head, is the source for EEG. Every electric current also generates an associated magnetic field. This is particularly true for the intracellular current, which is stronger than the extracellular current, but which is not accessible by EEG. The major difference between EEG and MEG is that the extracellular currents picked up by EEG are affected by differences in conductivity between the different environments in the head.

The magnetic fields generated by the intracellular currents, representing the principal component of the MEG signal, are not affected by these environments. MEG does not have the smoothing problem associated with EEG mentioned above (see section 7.1.2). Therefore, sources are easier to identify and to localize with MEG (Figure 7.7) than with EEG. It is also possible to perform simultaneous EEG and MEG recordings, assuming that the electrodes are made from compatible materials. Finally, MEG has practical advantages such as faster placement of a greater number of sensors and better spatial coverage. Its primary drawback other than cost is the requirement that the subject must remain immobile during the recording.

7.4.2. Equipment

Recordings are performed in a chamber that strongly attenuates any exterior magnetic fields. Current MEG systems are based on the use of a Superconducting QUantum Interference Device (SQUID). They are highly sensitive (at femto-Tesla scales, 10^{-15} T) and only operate in superconductive conditions. This requires the system core to be cooled with liquid helium, which has a boiling temperature (4 K or -269C) close to absolute zero [PER 07].

To measure the magnetic field, each SQUID is coupled to a "coupling" coil. Variation in the magnetic field passing through the coil induces an electric current that is detected by the SQUID (Figure 7.8). Unlike EEG, MEG systems do not strictly require a reference (EEG measures a potential difference between two electrodes, see Chapter 8). However, some MEG systems (CTF, 4D neuroimaging) use additional sensors located away from the head to measure residual magnetic activity in the isolation chamber so as to eliminate any external contribution. Elektra systems use other techniques (signal space separation, [TAU 04]) that only require the information recorded by the sensors located around the head.

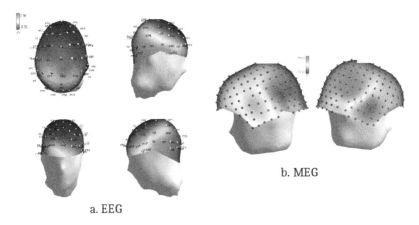

b. MEG

a. EEG

Figure 7.7. *Maps of the potential a) and the field b) recorded after the same auditory stimulus 100 ms after emission of sound. The stimulus is a pure note at a frequency of 500 Hz. The data represent averages (evoked activity). Note the diffuse topography at the surface of the scalp in EEG that decomposes into a couple with one positive pole and one negative pole in MEG. Each of these dipolar topographic patterns can be attributed to a source in each hemisphere. For a color version of this figure, see www.iste.co.uk/clerc/interfaces2.zip*

7.5. Conclusions

Sensors in general, and in particular electrodes, are the first segment of the acquisition and processing chain. They determine the quality of the acquisition, and therefore condition the exploitation of the acquired signal. We have seen there are difficulties in connection with the biological/electronic interface, and that many issues are far from being resolved. Achieving tolerance to motion and electromagnetic interference and in particular stability over time is the major challenge presented by BCIs. Although EEG electrodes have changed little since EEG was first introduced, recent technological progress, new materials and new equipment suggest that major advances may be on the horizon.

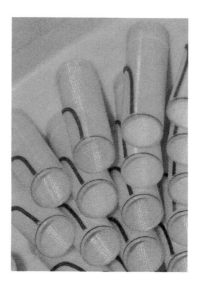

Figure 7.8. *Coupling coil of a magnetometer. Partial view of the sensor after removing the external envelope. Each coil, at the top of the cylinder, is kept at a temperature close to absolute zero in this space. The coils detect variations in the local field transmitted to the SQUID by the induced current. A second coil mounted at the base of the opposite cylinder allows the system to act as a gradiometer. The cylinder is 5 cm long, and the coil is 1.8 cm in diameter*

Invasive recordings are used for experimental work in animals or in specific clinical conditions in humans. The sensitivity and specificity of cortical recordings allows the detection of critical and adapted information for BCIs, and elevates this recording technique to a preferential status for the most ambitious clinical applications on condition that the correct cortical regions are identified for recording. MEG, in addition to providing a signal that is richer than EEG and its potential as a high-performing tool for developing algorithms, can help to identify candidate regions for cortical electrode implants.

7.6. Bibliography

[BRO 00] BRONZINO J.D., *The Biomedical Engineering Handbook* , 2nd ed., vol. I, CRC Press, 2000.

[BUE 93] BUERK D.G., *Biosensors: Theory and Applications*, CRC Press, 1993.

[CHA 13] CHARVET G., SAUTER-STARACE F., FOERSTER M. *et al.*, "WIMAGINE: 64-channel ECoG recording implant for human applications", *IEEE Engineering in Medicine and Biology Society*, 2013.

[CLE 16] CLERC M., BOUGRAIN L., LOTTE F., (eds), *Brain–Computer Interfaces 1*, ISTE, London and John Wiley & Sons, New York, 2016.

[ELI 14] ELISEYEV A., MESTAIS C., CHARVET G. *et al.*, "CLINATEC(®) BCI platform based on the ECoG-recording implant WIMAGINE(®) and the innovative signal-processing: preclinical results", *IEEE Engineering in Medicine and Biology Society*, pp. 1222–1225, 2014.

[FIE 13] FIEDLER P., FONSECA C., PEDROSA P. *et al*,. "Novel flexible dry multipin electrodes for EEG: signal quality and interfacial impedance of Ti and TiN coatings", *35th Annual International Conference of the IEEE*, EMBS, 2013.

[GEV 91] GEVINS A., LE J., BRICKETT P. *et al.*, "Seeing through the skull: advanced EEGs use MRIs to accurately measure cortical activity form the scalp", *Brain Topography*, vol. 4, no. 2, 1991.

[HOC 12] HOCHBERG L.R., BACHER D., JAROSIEWICZ B. *et al.*, "Reach and grasp by people with tetraplegia using a neurally controlled robotic arm", *Nature*, vol. 485, no. 7398, pp. 372–375, 2012.

[ISI 15] ISIK M., LONJARET T., SARDON H. *et al.*, "Cholinium-based ion gels as solid electrolytes for long-term cutaneous electrophysiology", *Journal of Materials Chemistry C*, pp. 8942–8948, 2015.

[JAS 58] JASPER H., "Report of the committee on methods of clinical examination in electroencephalography: 1957", *Electroencephalography and Clinical Neurophysiology*, vol. 10, no. 2, pp. 370–375, 1958.

[KHO 14] KHODAGHOLY D., DOUBLET T., QUILICHINI P. *et al.*, "In vivo recordings of brain activity using organic transistors", *Nature Communications*, vol. 4, p. 2133, 2014.

[KIM 10] KIM D-H., VIVENTI J. *et al.*, "Dissolvable films of silk fibroin for ultrathin conformal bio-integrated electronics", *Nature Materials*, vol. 9, pp. 511–517, 2010.

[KO 74] KO W.H., HYNECEK J., "Dry electrodes and electrode amplifiers", in MILLER H.A., HARRISON D.C. (eds), *Biomedical Electrode Technology*, Academic Press, New York, pp. 160–181, 1974.

[LAC 07] LACHAUX J.P., JERBI K., BERTRAND O. *et al*,. "BrainTV: a novel approach for online mapping of human brain functions", *Biological Research*, vol. 40, no. 4, pp. 401–413, 2007.

[LOP 13] LOPEZ-GORDO M.A., SANCHEZ-MORILLO D., PELAYO VALLE F., "Dry EEG electrodes", *Sensors*, vol. 14, pp. 12847–12870, 2014.

[LEL 13] LELEUX P., BADIER J.M., RIVNAY J. *et al.*, "Conducting polymer electrodes for electroencephalography", *Advanced Healthcare Materials*, vol. 3, pp. 490–493, 2013.

[LEL 14] LELEUX P., JOHNSON C., STRAKOSAS X. *et al.*, "Ionic liquid gel-assisted electrodes for long-term cutaneous recordings", *Advanced Healthcare Materials*, vol. 3, pp. 1377, 2014.

[MOT 13] MOTA A.R., DUARTE L., RODRIGUES D. *et al.*, "Development of a quasi-dryelectrode for EEG recording", *Sensors and Actuators A*, vol. 199, pp. 310–317, 2013.

[PER 07] PERNIER J., *Electro et magnétoencéphalographie, Biophysique, techniques et méthodes*, Hermes-Lavoisier, 2007.

[POR 74] PORTNOY W., DAVID R.M., AKERS L.A., "Insulated ECG electrodes", in: MILLER H.A., HARRISON D.C., (eds), *Biomedical Electrode Technology*, Academic Press, New York, p. 41, 1974.

[RIC 67] RICHARDSON P.C., "The insulated electrode: a pasteless ECG technique", *Proceedings of 20th ACEMB*, vol. 9, p. 15.7, 1967.

[RIC 66a] RICHARDSON P.C., "New construction techniques for insulated electrocardiographic electrodes", *Proceedings of 21st ACEMB*, vol. 10, pp. 13A1, 1968.

[RIC 68b] RICHARDSON P.C., "Some new electrode techniques for long-term physiological monitoring", *Aerospace Med.*, vol. 39, pp. 745–750, 1968.

[SAL 12] SALVO P., RAEDT R., CARRETTE E. *et al.*, "A 3D printed dry electrode for ECG/EEG recording", *Sensors and Actuators A*, vol. 174, pp. 96–102, 2012.

[TAK 05] TAKEUCHI S., ZIEGLER D., YOSHIDA Y. *et al.*, "Parylene flexible neural probes integrated with microfluidic channels", *Lab Chip*, vol. 5, pp. 519–523, 2005.

[TAL 62] TALAIRACH J., BANCAUD J., BONIS A. *et al.*, "Functional stereotaxic exploration of epilepsy", *Confinia Neurologica*, vol. 22, pp. 328–331, 1962.

[TSU 12] TSUKADA S., NAKASHIMA H., TORIMITSU K., "Conductive polymer combined silk fiber bundle for bioelectrical signal recording", *PLoS ONE*, vol. 7, no. 4, 2012.

[TUA 04] TUALU S., KAJOLA M., SIMOLA., "Suppression of interference and artifacts by the signal space separation method", *Brain Topography*, vol. 16, no. 4, pp. 269–275, 2004.

[ZEN 14] ZENG W., SHU L., LI Q. *et al.*, "Fiber-based wearable electronics: a review of materials, fabrication, devices, and applications", *Adv. Mater.*, vol. 26, pp. 5310–5336, 2014.

8

Technical Requirements for High-quality EEG Acquisition

This chapter emphasizes the fundamental principles of instrumentation and the technology and the practice for which standards must be adopted in order to ensure the recording of high-quality digital signals, within the context of electroencephalography (EEG).

Surface EEG is a method for cerebral exploration that measures the electrical activity of the brain by means of electrodes placed on the scalp. The electrical signal at the basis of EEG is the resultant of the summation of synchronous postsynaptic potentials originating from a large number of neurons. This electrical signal has a low amplitude (25V) because the recording electrodes are separated from the cortical surface by the scalp, the skull, a layer of cerebrospinal fluid and the meninges. In order to be accurately analyzed, these signals are considerably amplified by an acquisition system that consists of several elements (Figure 8.1):

– the totality of the electrodes placed on the scalp;

– the amplifiers of the electrical signals;

– the frequency filters;

– the analog-to-digital converters.

Chapter written by Emmanuel MABY.

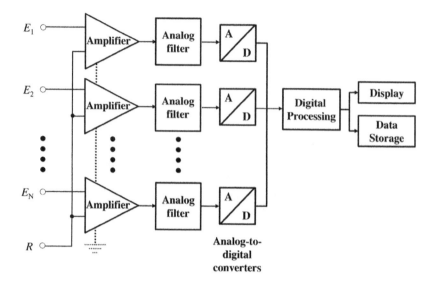

Figure 8.1. *Acquisition chain of EEG signals*

8.1. Electrodes

The electrodes used in scalp EEG are sensors measuring an electrical voltage on the surface of the skull. The quality of the electrode-skin contact is measured by an impedance expressed in ohm (Ω) whose value is lowest when the conductivity is high.

8.1.1. *Passive electrodes*

The term of passive electrode implies that the electrode functions as a simple metal sensor that establishes an electrochemical contact with the epidermis by means of a salt electrolyte. The measurement of the electrical effects related to brain activity is therefore effected through a conversion of the variations in charged ionic concentrations at the level of the scalp into an electric current in the metal part of the electrode. The most commonly utilized electrodes are silver and silver chloride electrodes (Ag/AgCl) whose conductive contact with the epidermis is facilitated through a conductive paste containing chloride of sodium[1].

---

1 See Chapter 7 on sensors for more details.

8.1.2. *Active electrodes*

Active electrodes contain an electronic circuit that processes the electric signal to correct:

– the problems related to a wide impedance range of the electrode;

– the capacitive coupling between the cable and sources of interference;

– movement artifacts of cables and connectors.

This improvement is achieved by a buffer circuit that allows the impedance conversion. The buffer itself consists of an operational amplifier so as to amplify the immunity to electrical noise of the cables.

8.2. Montages

8.2.1. *Monopolar montage*

8.2.1.1. *Common reference electrode*

In a referential montage, each scalp electrode (known as "measurement" electrode) is evaluated against a "reference" electrode (for example placed on the nose, Figure 8.2(a)). In theory, the voltage (v) measured on each pair corresponds to the signal collected under the single measurement electrode (this is then referred to as monopolar montage). However, since it can never be ultimately neutral, the reference electrode has a real impact on the measurement of v obtained with the measurement electrode. It is therefore important to choose the most neutral reference electrode possible in the defined study context. The examples of placement chosen for the reference electrode in the literature are the ears lobes, the skin on the mastoiditis (behind the ears), the nose, the chin, some cephalic electrodes (Cz, FPz) and the base of the neck.

Nevertheless, the reference to the linked ears sometimes used in EEG studies is not advisable. As a matter of fact, it sets both hemispheres to the same potential which affects the distribution of intracranial currents originating EEG voltages.

8.2.1.2. *Average reference*

A number of acquisition systems, such as the ANT Neurosystem, use an average reference, known as Wilson's reference [WIL 34], corresponding to a virtual average reference voltage defined by the average of the potentials of all the electrodes. The calculation of the average reference is based on the assumption that, when sources are dipolar, the sum of the voltages of a closed surface is equal to zero [BER 85]. However, this assumption is nonetheless valid with a very large number of electrodes only (high-density EEG using more than 128 electrodes). Otherwise, the average reference can sometimes favor the activity of a predominant sensor capturing a large amplitude signal.

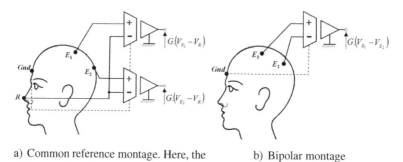

a) Common reference montage. Here, the reference electrode is placed on the nose

b) Bipolar montage

Figure 8.2. *Amplifiers montage. The floating ground of the amplifiers is here connected to a Gnd electrode placed on the subject's forehead*

8.2.2. *Bipolar montage*

In a bipolar montage, the pair of electrodes includes two electrodes known as "measurement" electrodes placed on the scalp. The potential difference measured in each pair corresponds to the algebraic difference of the signals registered at each "measurement" electrode (Figure 8.2(b)).

8.2.3. *Ground electrode*

The ground electrode, usually placed on the forehead, is used during the recording of EEG data to function as a common reference point for the electronics for all the voltages in the system. Reducing the impedance of the ground electrode will at the same time make it possible to considerably reduce the electrical noise.

8.3. Amplifiers

In practice, a single electrode does not allow for cortical bioelectrical activity be measured on the surface of the scalp. The electroencephalographic signal corresponds to the difference in electrical potential recorded between two electrodes using common ground differential amplifiers. Depending on the EEG acquisition systems, different combinations of electrodes or EEG montages can be considered.

8.3.1. *Gain*

The measurement of the voltage between a pair of electrodes is carried out by means of a differential amplifier. It achieves the subtraction of the measured potentials and amplifies this differential signal by a factor called the amplification chain gain. Furthermore, bioelectric signals produced by the brain being of the order of a few microvolts or tens of microvolts, the amplifier has an adjustable gain to enable on output, signals of a few volts in order to make use all the dynamics range of the analog-to-digital converters.

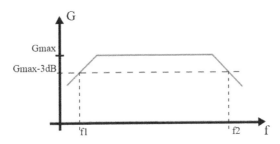

Figure 8.3. *Frequency response of the amplification chain gain*

In addition, the gain of the amplification chain depends on the frequency of the incident signal. There is a range of frequencies (referred to as bandwidth of the amplification channel) for which the amplifier works at constant gain (Figure 8.3). A quality amplifier presents a broad bandwidth, which means that it is potentially capable of amplifying signals in a reliable manner whose frequency content reliably is broad.

Moreover, the efficiency of the amplification also depends on the quality of the voltage on input at the amplifier, itself depending of the impedances of the electrodes and of the input impedance of the amplifier. Considering the potential difference V_E measured between the two electrodes E_1 and E_2, Z_1 and Z_2 the impedances of the two electrodes and Z_{in} the input impedance of the amplifier, then according to Osselton [OSS 65] the amplitude of the signal applied to the differential inputs is approximate to:

$$V_i = V_E \cdot \frac{Z_{in}}{Z_1 + Z_2 + Z_{in}}$$

Thus, to get the smallest loss of the EEG signal, it is necessary that $\frac{Z_{in}}{Z_1 + Z_2 + Z_{in}} \approx 1$, which means that $Z_{in} \gg Z_1 + Z_2$ and therefore that the amplifiers have an input impedance much higher than the impedances of the electrode.

8.3.2. Differential amplifier

Ideally, an EEG channel amplifies and records the voltage measured between two electrodes placed on the scalp. In practice, these electrodes capture two kinds of signals:

– the physiological signals of cerebral origin that is looked for to be recorded;

– the interfering signals that can be physiological as the electrocardiogram and/or generated by the electrostatic activity of the environment inside which the subject is placed, such as the 50/60 Hz sector.

The purpose of the differential amplifier is to amplify the useful signals and to reduce interference signals that are superimposed to the useful signal during transmission in a common manner on both transmission wires (Figure 8.4).

This amplifier is characterized by the common-mode rejection ratio (CMRR), which expresses the capability of a differential amplifier to reject the common voltage of its two inputs (common mode). It is considered that an amplifier is perfect when its input impedance and the CMRR are of infinite value.

Figure 8.5 shows the equivalent circuit diagram of an amplifier connected to the electrodes. If $V_E = V_{E_1} - V_{E_2}$ is the potential difference applied in differential mode between the "+" and "−" inputs, and if the gain amplifier G is perfect, then the output voltage verifies: $V_{\mathrm{s}} = G \cdot V_{\mathrm{E}}$.

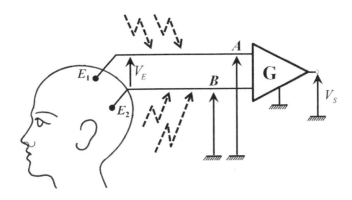

Figure 8.4. *Amplification of useful signals in the presence of interference signals*

Unfortunately, the amplifier is not perfect and three interfering components (V_{CI_i}) overlap with the amplified signal, such that:

$$V_{\mathrm{s}} = G \cdot V_{\mathrm{E}} + V_{\mathrm{CI}_1} + V_{\mathrm{CI}_2} + V_{\mathrm{CI}_3}$$

If a signal V_{mc} is applied in common mode (Figure 8.5), that is to say on both the "+" and "−" inputs with regard to the ground, ignoring the influence of the sources impedances, the residual parasitic voltage is defined by:

$$V_{\mathrm{CI}_1} = G . \frac{V_{\mathrm{mc}}}{TRMC}$$

It is therefore necessary that the CMRR be very large to cancel out the ratio $\frac{V_{\mathrm{mc}}}{TRMC}$ and therefore to remove the interfering component V_{CI_1}.

8.3.2.1. *Influence of the input impedances of the useful signal*

The effect of this rejection ratio can be mitigated by a difference between the impedance values of the sources ($Z_1 \neq Z_2$). As illustrated in Figure 8.5, if a common-mode voltage appears between the ground electrode and the electrodes (E_1 and E_2), then this difference ($Z_1 \neq Z_2$) causes a differential mode voltage to occur that will be amplified by the gain G. Applying Ohm's law and the conservation of current [FER 01], not taking the impedances of the electrodes with respect to the input impedance of the amplifier into account, a parasitic component will be obtained:

$$V_{Cl_2} = G.V_{mc}.\frac{Z_2 - Z_1}{Z_{in}}$$

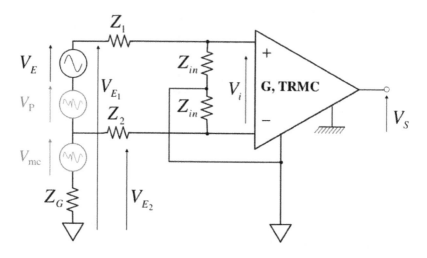

Figure 8.5. *Equivalent electrical diagram of the amplification of useful signals in the presence of interfering signals V_{mc} and V_P*

To reduce this component proportional to the difference of impedance of the sources, it is therefore paramount that the electrodes impedance be low and that the input impedance of the amplifier be great. This process called "potential divider effect" [HUH 73] shows the importance of the reduction of common-mode voltages where possible.

In addition, the variations in electrical potential between the surface of the skin and deeper layers result in a parasitic potential difference V_P between the electrodes E_1 and E_2. On output, a third interference component is induced:

$$V_{Cl_3} = G.V_P$$

For this type of interference, the use of an amplifier with a TRMC greater than 100 dB and high input impedance does not guarantee that good quality EEG signals be obtained. Thus, only a reduction of the impedance of the skin [PIC 72] allows the elimination of this interference component V_{CI_3}.

8.3.2.2. *Driven-right-leg circuit*

If the difference of impedance in the electrodes is not low enough and the input impedance of the amplifier not large enough, then the "voltage divider effect" will be significant. To reduce this common-mode noise, Winter and Webster [WIN 83] proposed a configuration named "driven-right-leg" (DRL). Thus, some amplification systems, for example Biosemi, feature this DRL circuit that retrieves the common-mode signal throughout all electrodes and then amplifies it with a negative factor. This signal is then injected back into the body of the subject using an electrode in order to reduce common-mode noise (Figure 8.6).

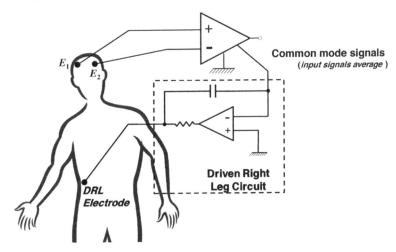

Figure 8.6. *"Driven-right-leg" circuit reducing the interferences of the common mode*

The name, DRL, has been preserved since its first use in the field of electrocardiography, although the electrode used in the case of EEG recording is not necessarily placed on the right leg of the subject. It may be located on the lower right portion of the abdomen, which is away from sources of bioelectrical signal such as the ECG. With the DRL circuit, the suppression of common-mode noise will be largest when the frequency of the captured signals is low. This device compensates for the decrease in the CMRR of the amplifiers applied to low-frequency signals. In practice, the DRL circuit enables an increase in the CMRR up to 50 dB at 50 Hz and thus a near suppression of electrostatic interferences from the mains supply.

8.4. Analog filters

The use of a quality amplifier that has the widest bandwidth possible does not imply that it be desirable to analyze all the frequencies comprised in the signal.

Naturally, the signal picked up by electrodes consists not only of useful activities, those that one aims to study, but also of other parasitic activities. Thus, to avoid the saturation of the amplitudes created by a very slow drift of the potential due to the movements of the electrodes or to sweating [PIC 72], it is necessary to apply a high-pass analog filter. The function of the latter is to reduce the gain of amplification for frequencies below a given frequency called cutoff frequency.

On the other hand, the finality of the low-pass filter is to eliminate high-frequency electrical phenomena related to muscle artifacts and to the background noise of the amplifiers. It is also essential in the stage preceding the conversion of analog signals to digital values (see Figure 8.5).

For frequencies higher or lower than the cutoff frequency, the variations in the gain depending on the frequency are not occurring in an "all or nothing" fashion but according to an exponential law. The slope characterizing this law is the slope of the attenuation that is expressed in dB/octave or dB/decade: the larger the attenuation slope, the more selective the filter.

8.5. Analog-to-digital conversion

After being amplified, the analog signal that constitutes the voltage describing the electrical activity of the brain is then converted into a discrete curve consisting of a sequence of regularly sampled numerical point values.

At each tic of the internal clock of the acquisition computer, the amplitude of the analog signal injected into the converter is measured and stored in memory. In this way, the computer has a sequence of amplitude values available describing the original curve: the analog signal has become a digital signal. The quality of the digital analog conversion depends on two characteristics of the converter.

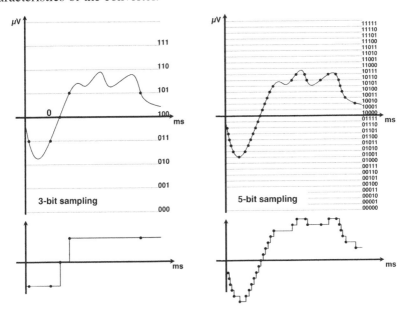

Figure 8.7. *Conversion of the analog signal into a digital signal. With a resolution of 3 bits (eight levels of amplitudes), the digitization of the analog signal does not allow the fine estimation of the analog signal*

Its *resolution* is measured in bits. The number of resolution bits represents the maximum number of digits that the computer is capable of processing at each sampling to represent the amplitude of the signal. A converter whose resolution is of N bits can address 2^N different amplitudes: the more significant the resolution of the converter is, the more accurate the amplitude measurements will be (Figure 8.7). However, an increase in resolution translates into an increase in the cost of data storage. Most systems have a minimum resolution of 12 bits that amounts to 4,096 different values of EEG potential.

The second characteristic that influences the quality of the conversion is its sampling frequency F_e, expressed in hertz. The higher it is, the closer the digital signal gets to the original signal. Therefore, it has to be correctly chosen. With too high values, the volume of the numeric values will be unnecessarily large. When it is too low, variations in the signal between two measurements will be lost.

The choice of the right sampling frequency is the result of a compromise; it should ideally correspond to a frequency twice higher than the maximal frequency of the signal under study (Nyquist–Shannon theorem). When this theorem is not respected, low parasitic and non-existing frequencies appear instead of the high frequencies initially present in the analog signal.

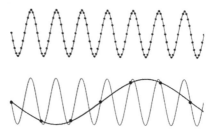

Figure 8.8. *Analog signal sampling. On the top, properly sampled signal. On the bottom, aliasing due to subsampling*

In Figure 8.8, the signal subsampled shows a lower frequency than the analog signal – one cycle compared to eight cycles for the analog signal. This phenomenon is known as aliasing.

Thus, analog signals with frequency components above $F_e/2$ cause parasitic frequencies lower than $F_e/2$ to appear after sampling. For example, a frequency component $F_e/2 < f_0 < F_e$ produces a frequency at $F_e - f_0$. Figure 8.9 represents the spectrum of a signal consisting of two frequencies $F1$ and $F2$. After digitization, the frequency $F1$ lower than $F_e/2$ did not generate any interference, whereas the frequency $F2$ (70 Hz) larger than $F_e/2$ (50 Hz) causes an aliasing component to appear at 30 Hz ($F_e - F2$).

To avoid this phenomenon, all spectral components whose frequency is higher than $F_e/2$ should be suppressed prior to sampling by applying by convention a low-pass filter (see Figure 8.4) with a cutoff frequency at least lower than $F_e/3$.

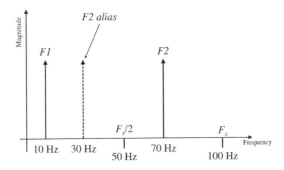

Figure 8.9. *Spectrum of the continuous signal and the sampled signal (dotted)*

8.6. Event synchronization with the EEG

Among the different brain activity analysis protocols, a large number of studies are based on evoked potentials (EP) by stimulation (*event-related potential*).

This type of protocol allows cognitive and sensory processes to be explored by means of numerous responses evoked by stimulation and require a very accurate synchronization of the stimuli presented with the EEG signals to avoid the following problems:

– *Delay*: the moment of presentation of the stimulus is marked with a constant delay of a few milliseconds and the evoked responses are then shifted in time. This delay should then be taken into account to estimate the latencies of the components of the EP (Figure 8.10(b));

– *Jitter*: the delay between the presentation of the stimulation and its time marking is unstable. This generates variable shifts of the evoked responses and therefore a significant attenuation of the average evoked responses (Figure 8.10(c)).

According to the EEG acquisition systems, there are two solutions: hardware marking or software marking.

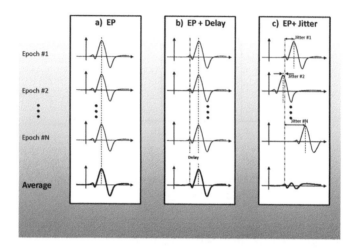

Figure 8.10. *Evoked responses and averaging: influence of temporal accuracy of the marking of the presentation of stimuli a) No time, b) constant delay and c) variable delay (jitter)*

8.6.1. *Hardware marking of events*

In the context of studies of EP or of synchronous brain–computer interfaces (BCI), it is essential to anticipate the feeding of marker (trigger) to indicate all types of events, such as the presentation of a stimulus or the start of a session. For some systems, such as the Brainampsystem (BrainProducts), this marker is treated by an external "trigger" input whose signal is sampled at the same frequency as the EEG signals. This trigger is a signal sent through the parallel port (coded in 8 bits) of the stimulation computer. This transistor–transistor logic (TTL) signal makes it possible to indicate the presentation moment of a stimulus, but also its code to identify it from among the other types of stimulations.

In Figure 8.11(a), when a stimulation (visual in this case) is presented, an event is simultaneously sent through the parallel port. A TTL signal is sent through the 8 D0–D7 channels indicating the moment of the presentation of stimulus and the value of the code. In Figure 8.11(b), it can be observed that an event has been sent at instant 4.45 s and with a code equal to 7. This marking being achieved via a TTL analog signal, the transmission of this code is almost immediate. Thus, temporal accuracy depends on the software used for the presentation of stimuli and on the process to send the trigger (software process performing the transmission on the parallel port).

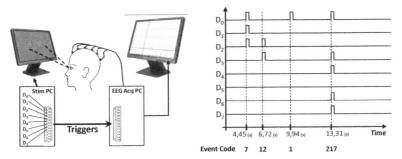

a) Event marking by parallel port trigger transmission

b) Transmission of 8-bit word by parallel port

Figure 8.11. *Material marking of events*

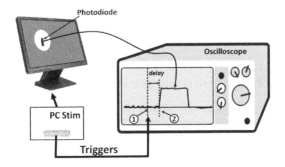

Figure 8.12. *Device allowing for the characterization of the delay between the transmission of the trigger and the presentation of visual stimulation*

To evaluate this accuracy, an experimental device shown in Figure 8.12 can be implemented. In the case of a presentation of visual stimulation (in this case a white disc), a photodiode is placed to measure the difference in luminance at the place of appearance of the stimulus. The signal of this photodiode is then analyzed by an oscilloscope whose measurement is initiated by the trigger sent through the parallel port. The delay between the transmission of the trigger (①) and the presentation of the stimulation (②) can therefore be characterized.

8.6.2. *Software marking of events*

For some wireless EEG systems (whose data are transmitted via Bluetooth), such as the Emotivsystem, it is impossible to address the triggers by an external path. Therefore, the solution that allows the marking of temporal events and their synchronization with the EEG signal is a software solution to be developed and adapted to the protocol.

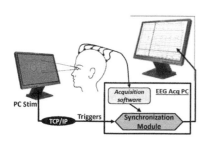 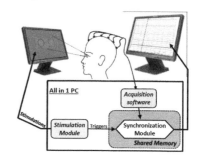

a) Events marking by sending triggers via a TCP/IP protocol

b) Events marking by trigger transmission via shared memory

Figure 8.13. *Software marking of events*

Two avenues of development can be considered:

– stimuli are presented to the subject by an external program that sends the triggers via a TCP/IP protocol to a fusion and synchronization software module (Figure 8.13(a)). This module is designed to synchronize the EEG data stream with the triggers;

– the stimulation system and the acquisition of EEG data are carried out by the same computer. The stimuli are presented to the subject by a program that sends the triggers to a fusion and synchronization software module by means of shared memory (Figure 8.13(b)). This module is designed to synchronize the EEG data stream with the triggers.

In both cases, it is essential to be able to characterize the temporal accuracy of this software marking because delays or jitters may appear if the software synchronization is not perfect. To carry out this measurement, a device inspired by Badcock *et al.* [BAD 13] can be implemented. In this case, as shown in Figure 8.14, the stimulation computer presents the visual stimulus to the subject and sends a trigger using a TCP/IP protocol to the synchronization software module with the EEG data stream. A photodiode is placed on the screen and its signal is attenuated in amplitude by a transmission module (to have an amplitude comparable to the EEG signals) and injected into one of the electrodes of the helmet (Emotivin the illustration).

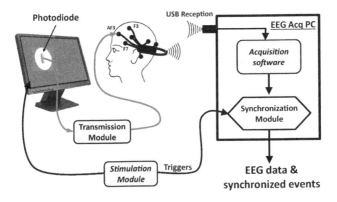

Figure 8.14. *Device for measuring the temporal accuracy of the events software marking*

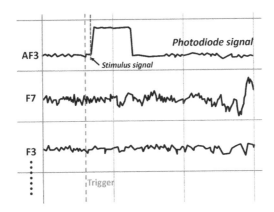

Figure 8.15. *EEG signals recorded after software trigger and EEG data synchronization. The dotted line shows the moment of occurrence of the trigger resynchronized with respect to the EEG signals*

In Figure 8.15 we can observe from the EEG tracings after synchronization, the instant of the presentation of the visual stimulus initiated by the transmission of the trigger and the signal of the photodiode on one of the EEG sensors. The delay between the software processing of the trigger and the presentation of the stimulus can then be measured.

8.7. Conclusions

Concerning the acquisition of quality surface EEG signals, it is paramount to use a system composed of elements whose characteristics must be optimally defined. Thus, it is preferable to have the following minimal configuration:

– the input impedance of the amplifier must be greater than 100 MΩ;

– the CMRR must be greater than 110 dB;

– the sampling frequency must be greater than 200 Hz but must be chosen according to the electrophysiological components under study (minimal frequency of 1,000 Hz for EPs with average and delayed latencies or 3,000 Hz for the EPs of the brainstem);

– the resolution of the analog-to-digital conversion must be greater than 16 bits and the EEG must be described with a minimal resolution of 0.5 $\hat{A}\mu V$;

– the minimal number of sensors is less critical because it depends on the experimental protocol. A conventional study of EPs, for example including a topographic representation, requires the use of 32 electrodes. On the other hand, some protocols such that of Kaiser *et al.* [KAI 11] based on motor mental imaging make use of only three electrodes (C3, Cz, C4).

In the field of BCIs, several types of EEG acquisition arise according to the context of its use. In the laboratory, EEG acquisition systems are often those used in conventional electrophysiology protocols. These systems are very efficient but seldom ergonomic and very expensive. In BCI applications outside laboratories, it is important to use cheap and portable systems. In conclusion, the choice of an EEG acquisition system is a compromise between its accessibility (ergonomics and price) and the quality of the captured signals that impact the performance of BCIs.

8.8. Bibliography

[BAD 13] BADCOCK N., MOUSIKOU P., MAHAJAN Y. *et al.*, "Validation of the Emotiv EPOC® EEG gaming system for measuring research quality auditory ERPs", *PeerJ*, vol. 1, p. e38, 2013.

[BER 85] BERTRAND O., PERRIN F., PERNIER J., "A theoretical justification of the average reference in topographic evoked potential studies", *Electroencephalography and Clinical Neurophysiology/Evoked Potentials Section*, vol. 62, no. 6, pp. 462–464, 1985.

[FER 01] FERREE T., LUU P., RUSSELL G. *et al.*, "Scalp electrode impedance, infection risk, and EEG data quality", *Clinical Neurophysiology*, vol. 112, no. 3, pp. 536–544, 2001.

[HUH 73] HUHTA J. C., WEBSTER J. G., "60-Hz interference in electrocardiography", *IEEE Transactions on Biomedical Engineering*, vol. 20, no. 2, pp. 91–101, 1973.

[KAI 11] KAISER V., KREILINGER A., MÜLLER-PUTZ G.R. *et al.*, "First steps toward a motor imagery based stroke BCI: new strategy to set up a classifier", *Frontiers in Neuroscience*, vol. 5, 2011.

[OSS 65] OSSELTON J., "Acquisition of EEG data by bipolar, unipolar and average reference methods: a theoretical comparison", *Electroencephalography and Clinical Neurophysiology*, vol. 19, no. 5, pp. 527-528, 1965.

[PIC 72] PICTON T., HILLYARD S., "Cephalic skin potentials in electroencephalography", *Electroencephalography and Clinical Neurophysiology*, vol. 33, no. 4, pp. 419-424, 1972.

[WIL 34] WILSON F.N., JOHNSTON F.D., MACLEOD A. *et al.*, "Electrocardiograms that represent the potential variations of a single electrode", *American Heart Journal*, vol. 9, no. 4, pp. 447–458, 1934.

[WIN 83] WINTER B., WEBSTER J., "Driven-right-leg circuit design", *IEEE Transactions on Biomedical Engineering*, vol. 30, no. 1, pp. 62–66, 1983.

9

Practical Guide to Performing an EEG Experiment

This chapter describes the main steps to successfully perform an electroencephalography experiment on humans. It details all aspects of the planning of the study, the implementation of experimental equipment and describes the different stages of experimentation. All these concepts are the result of experience acquired during numerous experiments in classical electrophysiology performed in the laboratory. As a result, some steps are to be adapted according to the applications of the BCI.

9.1. Study planning

9.1.1. *Legislation and ethics*

Any experimentation in electroencephalography is carried out within a legal administrative framework that ensures the safety of participants. The experimental protocol must therefore be inserted inside a rigorous framework in order to perform all the necessary administrative procedures upstream.

Within this framework, it is necessary that the premises of the experimentation be approved by the agency[1] in charge of verifying if the facilities are suitable for research and compatible with the safety of persons.

Chapter written by Emmanuel MABY.
1 In France, this approval is issued by the Agence Régionale de Santé (ARS).

There are numerous conditions that must be checked: the building must adhere to the standards in force, first-aid devices must be present inside the premises and a well-defined emergency procedure must be established. Finally, a specific request must be carried out if the experiments are to be conducted with a pathological subject or a child.

An authorization from the agency[2] that evaluates the safety and the quality of the materials used during the research is also required. The objective is to ensure that the safety of individuals participating in biomedical research under the conditions established by the experimental protocol is guaranteed.

Similarly, an approval from the ethics committee[3] in charge of the protection of persons is mandatory. Its mission is to provide an opinion ranging from administrative procedures (information notice, informed consent, possible compensations being due) to experimental conditions (collection and use of data). Finally, personal data collection and processing (ID number, name, address, telephone number, etc.) are subject to a legislative framework aiming to protect the privacy of filed subjects and individual freedoms. It will thus be mandatory to apply for an authorization to the authorities[4] in charge of ensuring the protection of personal data in digital format.

9.1.2. *Subject selection criteria*

In the context of the experimental protocol, the experimenter must specify the criteria of selection of the subjects to be involved in the study. Among the criteria, some are related to the suitability of the person to carry out an experiment in electroencephalography. Exclusion factors include pregnancy, claustrophobia, drug addiction or neurological diseases. On the other hand, the inclusion criteria related to the study are: age, sex, academic level, visual acuity, hearing acuity, IQ, etc. They are precisely defined to constitute a representative group of populations in order to respond to the questions posed

---

2 In France, this authorization is issued by the *Agence Nationale de Sécurité du Médicament et des Produits de Santé* (ANSM).

3 In France this committee is called the *Comité de Protection des Personnes* (CPP).

4 In France, this authorization is issued by the *Commission Nationale de l'Informatique et des Libertés* (CNIL).

in the protocol. Similarly, the number of participants in the experiment must be sufficient to demonstrate the significance of the experimental results and to support the generalization of these results.

9.1.3. *Experiment organization*

The organization of the experiment must be optimized to meet the efficiency and reproducibility requirements of the study but also the comfort and the well-being of the subject. Thus, the protocol can be established by separating the experimental conditions into blocks (inspired from "block design" protocols [ADD 69]), or it can take into account the variability of measures and the fatigue of the subject by randomly distributing the conditions throughout the experiment ("mixed design" [KRA 00]). Regardless of the "design" being used, the experience is divided into blocks of trials. The duration of each block and the sequence of the different blocks must be defined such that the variability of the electrophysiological measurements over time have the least possible impact. Short breaks are enforced between blocks of consecutive tests, which help the subject to stay focused but also to prevent possible muscle artifacts by allowing the subject to relax and reposition herself/himself so that she/he regains a comfortable position between the blocks.

Among the parameters of the experimental protocol, the most difficult to control are the strategies implemented by the subjects to complete the tasks that are required. It is therefore essential to describe in detail how the subjects will be informed of the experimental situation and about the task that has to be performed. For example, in situations where patients have to actively respond to stimuli, instructions must clarify the subjects if they ought to pay particular attention to the speed or to the accuracy of the answer. These instructions are provided in writing to the subject and are intended to ensure the replicability of the recording conditions. They also must reassure the subjects so that they be in the best possible state of mind, as well as motivated. At the end of the experiment, the subject participating in the study fills in a questionnaire to confirm that he/she has understood the task, to know the strategies that he/she has developed and to his/her opinion of the experiment.

Before initiating the measurement campaign with volunteers, it is recommended that the researcher attempt the experiment to evaluate the feasibility of the task and the associated mental load. Finally, it is mandatory to at least carry out a pilot experiment that allows for the verification of all the technical aspects, the clarity of the instructions, the course of the experience as well as its duration.

9.2. Equipment

9.2.1. *Recording site*

The laboratory where the recording of the electroencephalogram (EEG) signals takes place may be organized as described in Figure 9.1.

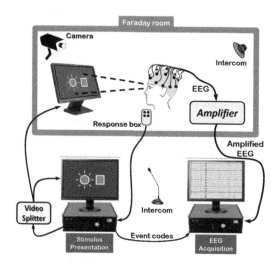

Figure 9.1. *Main elements of an EEG recording laboratory*

In conventional electrophysiology, the ideal condition would be that the experiment take place in an electrophysiology Faraday room to decrease the influence of artifacts due to the mains supply and sufficiently far removed from electrostatic and/or electromagnetic sources such as an magnetic resonance imaging or a surgical suite. It is also advisable to install the highest number of electrical appliances outside this recording room.

However for some BCI applications, electroencephalography experiments cannot be carried out in the laboratory. Thus, to protect themselves from electrical interference, it is paramount to employ completely galvanically decoupled EEG systems (wireless or fiber optic devices), battery-powered and preferably making use of active electrodes.

Regardless of the room (Faraday or not), it is preferable to perform the recordings at room temperature not exceeding 20°C to prevent any sweating of the subject. As a point of fact, sodium chloride and lactic acid in sweat interact with the metal of the electrode and combine with the change in potential of the skin and sweat glands [SAU 79]. Therefore, an artifact can appear in the form of a very slow component (0.1–0.5 Hz) (Figure 9.2), which can nonetheless be reduced by applying a high-pass filter, except in the study case of a slow component such as thecontingent negativity variation [WAL 64].

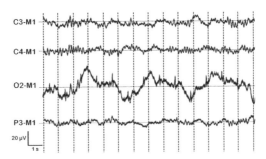

Figure 9.2. *Sweat artifact present in the O2-M1 derivation (tracings over 14 s)*

In experiments using visual stimuli, the subject must be placed at a minimal distance of 50–70 cm from the screen in order to optimize the visual field. It is very important that the subject be sitting in an adjustable, stable seat, very comfortable and with the correct support. In an uncomfortable position, the subject will tend to move a lot and therefore create artifacts of movement from the electrodes (Figure 9.3).

In addition, muscle tension at the level of the neck will increase with the duration of the experimentation and generate a muscle artifact (Figure 9.4). Apart from the generated artifacts, an uncomfortable position will also tend to distract the subject, resulting in an alteration of the involvement of the subject to perform the intended task.

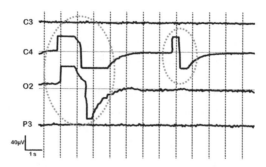

Figure 9.3. *Artifact due to electrode movement (tracings over 12 s)*

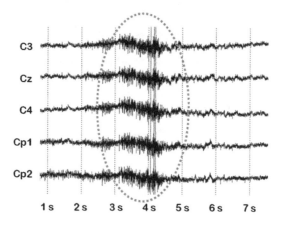

Figure 9.4. *Muscle artifact*

For the purpose of performing the acquisitions in the best conditions, the subject is placed in an acoustically isolated recording room. To comply with the optimal safety rules, the room is equipped with a camera to observe the subject without disturbing him/her and an intercom to communicate with him/her (Figure 9.1). During experiments using sound stimuli, noise disturbances external to the recording room must be the most attenuated possible so as to not disturb the stimulation. By being isolated, the subject is less distracted by the work of the researcher and thus can concentrate totally on the task at hand. Finally, all precautions to make the recording site as welcoming as possible will be beneficial to ensure that patients are comfortable in a vacuum.

9.2.2. *Stimulation system*

The stimulation system must fulfill three objectives:

– send sound, visual or tactile stimuli via the available equipment (screen, headphones, etc.);

– record the behavioral responses of the subject via the available hardware (response button, keyboard, etc.);

– synchronize the different elements being used (stimuli and/or answers) with the EEG recording.

There are several commercial software to control the stimulation system (Presentation, E-Prime, PsyScope, PsycoPy®, etc.). In the context of the study of the responses evoked by stimulation, the management of the time to transmit stimulations and the marking of the EEG by these events is crucial (see Figure 8.6). Thus, the choice of parameters such as the model of the sound card or the presentation mode has an incidence on the temporal accuracy of stimuli. Similarly, an acquisition with EEG systems that feature an external trigger channel implies that the stimulation computer include a parallel port.

The choice of the type of stimulation is an element to be taken into account. Traditionally, cathode ray tube (CRT)-type screens were used in research. They have a very short luminance transition time and do not induce any latency between the transmission of the stimulation and its presentation on the screen. However, they are no longer commercialized and are replaced by liquid crystal display (LCD)-type of screens that have, for their part, a much bigger transition time. The voltages in response to stimuli presented by these screens are thus of lower quality. In order to overcome this problem, a possible solution is the use of active-matrix organic light-emitting diode (AMOLED)-type screens that would show the same qualities and the same temporal accuracy than CRT screens.

Finally, regardless of the type of stimulation, it is mandatory to measure the temporal management of the presentation of stimuli to evaluate possible latencies or jitters (see Figure 8.6).

9.2.3. *Acquisition system*

Concerning the acquisition system of surface EEG signals, the elements of the experimental protocol lead to the implementation of particular technical means, for example:

– the study of voltages of the brain stem (including the analysis of components of early latencies smaller than 10 ms [BOS 84]) forced the experimenters to use acquisition systems having a minimum sampling frequency of 3 kHz to achieve good quality measurements;

– the reconstruction of intracranial sources activated from the EEG surface recordings [BAB 05] implies that the measurements be achieved with an high-density EEG system, that is with a minimum number of 96 sensors.

Therefore, in the majority of research works in electrophysiology, the EEG acquisition systems are composed of:

– 32–96 electrodes (passive or active);

– different-sized electrode caps (head circumference: 54–60 cm);

– software and/or hardware that allows the measurement of impedances;

– 32–96 channels compatible amplifiers;

– batteries in order to power amplifiers;

– EEG data fusion module and trigger (via parallel port);

– acquisition software enabling the recording of EEG signals: recording in an open and documented format, possibility of establishing a workspace gathering all acquisition parameters.

9.3. Experiment procedure

The early stages of the experimentation correspond to all the work carried out upstream: study planning, administrative permissions, instructions drafting, development of the experiment and trials with pilot subjects. Once these steps are performed, the EEG experiment itself involves the following procedure.

9.3.1. *Recruiting of subjects*

The steps are as follows:

– advertise a call for the participation of volunteers by means of all types of communication, whether they be written messages (brochure, letter, poster, etc.), e-mail messages (posting on a website, in a forum, etc.) or radio or broadcast messages. During this call, the context of the study, the duration of the study, the name of the laboratory, the address of the experiment site, the experimental period and inclusion criteria are clearly indicated;

– agree with the participant about the appointment by specifying the date, the place and the time of the experiment. Any confusion has an impact on the organization of the experimenter;

– instruct the subject that his/her hair must be clean and free of hairspray, oil, cream, lotion or any other product. His/her hair should be washed and rinsed with clear water the night before the examination or the morning itself (no conditioner or oil after shampooing). Also properly indicate that he/she should not be under the influence of drugs and that he/she must be in the best mental and physical conditions during the experiment.

9.3.2. *The day before the experiment*

Since the experiment is being planned as part of a well-defined schedule, it is essential to prepare it as much as possible in advance to avoid any waste of time:

– print the information notices, the instructions and the consent form;

– power up the stimulation computer and open the planned stimulation guidelines;

– power up the acquisition computer and verify or configure the workspace (for example the destination of the files of the recorded data);

– check all connections (amplifiers, batteries, acquisition computer);

– power the amplifiers;

– visualize the signal to verify the proper connection of amplifiers;

– prepare the syringes by filling them with conductive gel.

9.3.3. *The day of the experiment*

The steps are as follows:

– welcome the subject by presenting oneself (name, function, involvement in the study) and by conducting a tour of the site. Be courteous so that the subject feels as confident as possible;

– give information notices to the subject and explain the experiment as precisely as possible by providing him/her written instructions;

– ensure that he/she signs the informed consent form. This signature indicates that the subject is aware of the procedure and purpose of the experiment and agrees to participate thereto;

– install the subject by asking him/her to make all the necessary adjustments for his/her comfort when seating;

– if the experience is based on auditory stimuli, perform a hearing threshold to adjust the amplitude of sounds;

– if the experience is based on visual stimulation, ask the subject to make use of his/her means of visual correction and adjust the distance of the subject relatively to the screen. Based on the experimental paradigm, it is also necessary to perform a visual calibration (contrast, balance and color saturation, brightness);

– locate the positions of the ground (on the forehead or on the shoulder) and of the reference electrodes (on the nose for instance, see section 8.2.1.1);

– using abrasive cream (e.g. Nuprep) and a cotton swab, rub the skin at the location of the reference and ground electrodes. This allows the elimination of dead cells, impurities and the excess of sebum to improve conductivity;

– degrease the forehead as well as the scalp with a compress soaked with 70°C alcohol;

– select the right cap size. Measure the head circumference (hat size) at the level of the middle of the forehead and the rear of the skull (inion) using a measuring tape. In adults, the size of the caps varies generally from 54 to 60 cm in 2 cm increments. If the measurement falls between two sizes, choose the larger. The electrodes are distributed on this cap in a standard fashion based on the International System [JAS 58] adapted to the number of electrodes (Figure 9.5);

– place the cap on the head of the subject securing it either using a chin strap or a chest belt. Adapt the position of the cap such that the Cz electrode be placed on the vertex, that is halfway between the nasion and the inion (Figure 9.5);

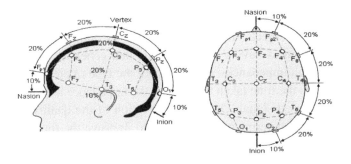

Figure 9.5. *10-20 International System*

– connect the electrodes to the acquisition computer and start the software for the impedance measurement;

– place the ground and the reference electrodes (except the average reference EEG systems that do not feature a reference electrode) and add the conductive gel with the prefilled syringe to improve contact and consequently the impedance;

– ensure that the impedances of the reference and ground electrode are smaller than 5 kΩ. Effectively, the impedances of the measurement electrodes depend on the impedances of the reference and ground electrodes. Therefore, if one of these two electrodes presents a bad impedance, then the impedances of the measurements electrodes will be impacted. As a result, the reference and ground electrodes must be prepared and verified first, before addressing the other electrodes;

– address the electrodes placed on the cap according to the implementation schema (for example start with the electrode Fp1);

– use the syringe in order to release the hair situated under the electrode to gain access to the scalp and apply the conductive gel. There should be enough gel to ensure contact while avoiding creating a conductive bridge between two electrodes;

– renew for all electrodes;

– record the impedance values of each electrode from the measurement software. The goal is to obtain impedances below 5 kΩ. If this is not the case, some gel must be added and/or rub the scalp with the tip of the needle (painless for the subject). For active electrodes that operate at higher impedance, the quality of the signal will not be deteriorated for impedances neighboring 15 kΩ. In some subjects, it is more difficult to obtain good impedances; subjects with baldness having a thicker scalp that generates low conductivity and therefore high impedances. Regardless of the type of electrodes, there is a tradeoff between the time taken to improve the impedance and the real quality gain of the recorded signal. Only an observation of the quality of the signal can indicate if the experimenter should try to improve the impedances of the electrodes;

– stop the impedance measurement software;

– where required, connect the electrodes to the amplifiers;

– start the EEG data acquisition software;

– verify the quality of the signal by estimating the amount of artifact of the mains supply (Figure 9.6);

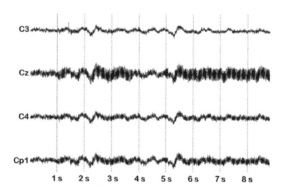

Figure 9.6. *Interferences originating from the mains. Artifact on the electrode Cz*

– improve the impedance of the electrodes that exhibit this type of artifact by adding conduction gel or by rubbing the scalp with the tip of the needle;

– verify that the obtained signal is properly electrophysiological. To this end, ask the subject to achieve tasks that generate visually detectable artifacts such as:

- blinking and performing saccades (lateral eye movements without moving the head) to observe the ocular artifacts (Figure 9.7);

- clenching the jaw to observe the muscles artifact (Figure 9.4);

- shutting the eyes to observe the alpha rhythm (Figure 9.8).

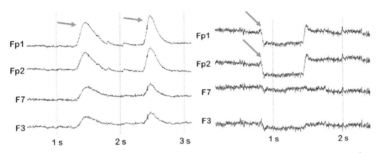

a) Artefact generated by the blinking of the eyes

b) Artefact generated by ocular saccades

Figure 9.7. *Ocular artifacts*

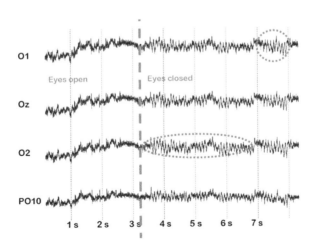

Figure 9.8. *Alpha rhythm present during a period with eyes closed*

– also use this verification to show these artifacts to the subject who will then be able to understand the significance of her behavior during the experiment and the impact it may have on the recorded EEG signals;

– recall any instructions to motivate, but also reassure, the subject. Always use the same instructions so that all subjects undergo the same conditions when performing the tasks. Clear and precise, these instructions guarantee the optimal performance of the subject;

– initiate the acquisition of EEG signals;

– initiate the stimulation presentation script;

– visualize the signals during the experiment to ensure their quality;

– verify the behavioral outcomes during the experiment to control the involvement of the subject to perform the task;

– allow the subject to have several breaks. Take the opportunity to eventually remotivate the subject in the case of a tedious experiment.

9.3.4. *After the experiment*

The steps are as follows:

– once the experiment is complete, remove the cap and the electrodes;

– conduct a debriefing with the subject to acknowledge if he/she had correctly understood the task and to know what strategies he/she has used and his/her overall impression on the experiment. This debriefing can also include a questionnaire to obtain a more objective answer from the subject;

– allow the subject to wash his/her hair, providing shampoo, a towel and a hairdryer;

– dispose of single-use equipment in the garbage;

– wash the cap with soapy water, rinse it and immerse it in a disinfectant solution for 15 min. Rinse and dry on a suitable support;

– gently clean the electrodes with a soft-bristle toothbrush and soap. Rinse and immerse them in a disinfectant solution for 1 min. Let them dry on a towel placed on flat surface;

– recharge all batteries;

– store the data acquired on a storage space.

9.4. Bibliography

[ADD 69] ADDELMAN S., "The generalized randomized block design", *The American Statistician*, vol. 23, no. 4, pp. 35–36, 1969.

[BAB 05] BABILONI F., CINCOTTI F., BABILONI C. *et al.*, "Estimation of the cortical functional connectivity with the multimodal integration of high-resolution EEG and fMRI data by directed transfer function", *Neuroimage*, vol. 24, no. 1, pp. 118–131, 2005.

[BOS 84] BOSTON J., MØLLER A., "Brainstem auditory-evoked potentials", *Critical Reviews in Biomedical Engineering*, vol. 13, no. 2, pp. 97–123, 1984.

[JAS 58] JASPER H., "The ten twenty electrode system of the international federation", *Electroencephalography and Clinical Neurophysiology*, vol. 10, pp. 371–375, 1958.

[KRA 00] KRAUTH J., *Experimental Design: A Handbook and Dictionary for Medical and Behavioral Research*, Elsevier, New York, vol. 14, 2000.

[SAU 79] SAUNDERS M., "Artifacts: activity of noncerebral origin in the EEG", in *Current Practice of Clinical Electroencephalography*, Raven Press, New York, 1979.

[WAL 64] WALTER W., COOPER R., ALDRIDGE V. *et al.*, "Contingent negative variation: an electric sign of sensori-motor association and expectancy in the human brain", *Nature*, vol. 203, pp. 380–384, 1964.

PART 3

Step by Step Guide to BCI Design with OpenViBE

10

OpenViBE and Other BCI Software Platforms

Modern Brain–Computer Interface (BCI) designs are often principally implemented on the software level. We begin this part of the book by describing BCI software systems. These BCI platforms are collections of open source software tools that assist in implementing, exploring and using BCI. In particular, the platforms provide off-the-shelf versions of the common BCI paradigms and components. These can then be applied or adapted as needed.

In this chapter we give a high-level introductory overview of such platforms. Our presentation is centered on the OpenViBE platform. We also contrast it to other well-known BCI platforms.

10.1. Introduction

A functional implementation of a BCI consists of signal acquisition hardware and signal processing software, the latter running on a normal computer. The main challenge of the software is to transform the sampled measurements from the acquisition hardware into discrete commands. To achieve this, the software typically performs standardization, processing and classification of the signal segments, and finally shows the results to the user

---

Chapter written by Jussi LINDGREN and Anatole LECUYER.

as feedback (see [WOL 02, GRA 10]). These steps are illustrated in Figure 10.1.

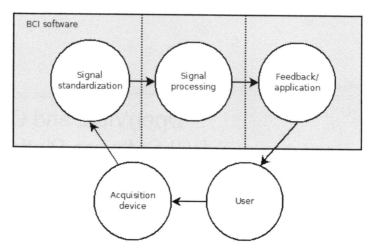

Figure 10.1. *Current BCI systems have several software modules (in gray). With the user and the acquisition device included, the BCI system forms a feedback loop. The software stages are separated by dotted lines emphasizing that these modules can be separate applications*

The scope of BCI software systems (platforms) ranges from the low-level signal processing to high-level example applications. The systems may expose different levels of detail to different kinds of users. For example, a researcher may be interested in technical details, whereas an end-user may just want to control some BCI-driven application as simply as possible. However, at the time of writing, BCI is challenging to deploy as easily as a mouse or a keyboard: the known approaches are often not reliable enough and may require a setup stage. For this reason, in this chapter we mostly consider the BCI platforms as development and experimentation toolkits for researchers, clinicians and enthusiasts who are interested in tinkering with BCI and its components.

While doing research and exploration, the benefits of using open source components in BCI are well known [MEL 07, VID 11]. If common components of BCI software systems are available and can be freely reused, the work can be focused on exploring new directions instead of having to re-develop the basic components. In addition, if components from established software platforms are used, the BCI investigator can be more confident of their quality as they have been field tested by a larger audience. Finally, basing BCI research on published systems allows external parties to more easily understand and reproduce the experiments – a major point of importance in research.

In the following sections we will give a high level outlook on what the BCI platforms offer to those working on BCI. We recall the basic BCI workflows and conceptual components, while illustrating how these are implemented by the existing software systems. We especially focus on the OpenViBE software, and discuss how some other platforms contrast with it. Due to the specific features of each platform changing over time, we do not attempt to present detailed feature lists here (for a more feature-oriented review, see [BRU 13]). The web pages of the individual platforms are the most up-to-date sources for feature-related information.

10.2. Using BCI for control

It is customary to imagine several different use-cases and corresponding roles in BCI. These are the author, the operator, and the user. Those in different roles are interested in different aspects of the system. An *author* is the designer who builds the BCI system from hardware and software components. After the author has assembled the system, it can be used for application control or experimentation. Unlike established control devices such as a mouse or a keyboard, a BCI solution is not currently a plug-and-play approach. Instead, using BCI may require an *operator*, an assistant who sets up and monitors the BCI system to ensure that it keeps working appropriately. In some situations, the *user* who interacts with the BCI-controlled application may be unable to handle these setup tasks himself. Ideally, the BCI software should make the role of the operator as small as possible.

For ease of exposition, we start from a situation where a typical BCI system architecture has already been designed and implemented. Before BCI can be used for some practical purpose, the operator may have to perform the following steps:

– *Setup*: the first step is to setup the hardware and perform the software installation. After this, the operator may need to start an acquisition application manually (as in OpenViBE, see Figure 10.4). This application is typically provided by the software platform. Next, the operator connects the signal acquisition sensors to the user while monitoring that the signal quality is appropriate. The software used may assist in this by providing tools for visualizing the signal (Chapter 8, section 10.4). The software may also be able to show signal quality statistics from the acquisition hardware, for example impedance measurements in EEG (see Chapter 8).

– *Training*: generally the user needs to be instructed about the system. The user needs to know what is expected of him, either mentally or otherwise. Additionally, the software system itself may need to be trained (calibrated). Due to the differences between individuals, the accuracy of the BCI may be improved by optimizing the signal processing to the particular user and setting. For this calibration, the measurements relayed by the acquisition hardware are recorded by the software, usually in interaction with the user via a specific interaction paradigm (see Chapter 4 of Volume 1, [CLE 16]). For example, in the SSVEP paradigm, the user has to focus on flickering objects. After the data has been recorded, the recordings are analyzed by the software using statistical, automated methods to learn how to discriminate between the flicker conditions from the measured cortical activity. Figure 10.2 (left) illustrates a training display (sometimes called a *stimulator*) that helps to collect data for the calibration of SSVEP pattern detection. After enough data has been collected and the statistical analysis is complete, the system can be switched into an application control mode.

– *Controlling an application*: after the previous stages, the user can finally start to interact with a BCI application. This application may be bundled with the BCI platform, or be a custom application made for some specific purpose. The BCI software packages commonly provide ready-to-use demo applications. For example, OpenViBE provides P300 spellers (Chapter 13) and an SSVEP based game (see Chapters 3, 5 and 14). We show the SSVEP game [LEG 13] in Figure 10.2 (right).

10.3. BCI processing stages

While the user interacts with a BCI application, the BCI software processes the signal in real time and attempts to translate it into commands. We now turn to take a look at these processing stages. They are of interest to the author who works on building BCI systems and improving them. The author's concern are the underlying technical aspects related to designing, parameterizing, testing and debugging the BCI systems.

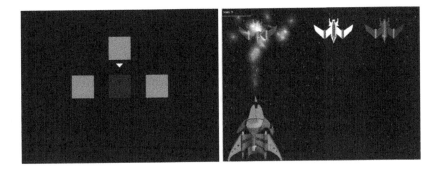

Figure 10.2. *Example of BCI calibration and BCI use with the SSVEP paradigm. Left, SSVEP training stimulator. The squares are flickering with different frequencies while the user is attending to them in turns. At the same time, EEG measurement data is recorded to train a three-class classifier. Right, a shooting game [LEG 13] controlled by focusing on the three different parts of the ship. The parts flicker with the same frequencies that were used in the training, and the predictions from the trained classifier are used as control commands to the game*

First, we consider the signal processing the software performs during BCI. This typically consists of several repeated stages ([WOL 02], see Chapter 12 of Volume 1, [CLE 16]), recalled here for completeness: signal acquisition (standardization), signal processing and classification, and finally feedback. The stages are shown in Figure 10.1 and they are iterated until the BCI-based control is terminated. Of these stages, the acquisition and processing stages are also performed during the system training stage we discussed in the previous section:

1) *Signal acquisition*: when BCI is used as a source of commands for an application, the first stage is to acquire data reflecting brain activity. Regardless of the signal source (for example EEG electrodes, fNIRS or ECOG, see Chapters 7, Chapters 3 and 2 of Volume 1, [CLE 16]), the signal is transferred from the sensors to a computer where the actual signal processing is performed algorithmically. At the time of writing, there are no established standards for the signal format or for controlling the acquisition device. Instead, every manufacturer has its own proprietary, specific interfaces. For the development of BCI-based applications this can be inconvenient, if compatibility with each acquisition device has to be separately programmed. To address this situation, the BCI platforms often provide signal acquisition components that standardize from different hardware devices to the signal format of the platform. This converted data can then be processed independently of the

manufacturer specific conventions. Different platforms provide the acquisition component for different sets of acquisition devices[1].

2) *Signal processing*: the BCI systems have tools to perform different kinds of transformations on the acquired signal, including different kinds of filtering. The purpose of these transformations is either to highlight important aspects of the data, or to clean the signal from noise and other artifacts that may contaminate the signal (such as the country specific electrical artifact of around 50/60hz in EEG, related to the power supply). After this clean-up, the software may allow the signal to be subjected to further feature extraction transformations intended to alleviate finally translating parts of the signal into commands [WOL 02]. All the BCI platforms described in this article provide a multitude of signal processing filters for cleaning and altering the data. These tools include for example temporal and spatial filters (see Chapter 6 of Volume 1, [CLE 16]), signal arithmetic, and feature extraction techniques such as Common Spatial Patterns and Fourier band power features (see Chapter 7 of Volume 1, [CLE 16]).

3) *Classification*: the classification stage translates a segment of the processed signal into a discrete prediction of the user state. This prediction is equivalent to a command such as a key press. Often the used classifier is estimated during a separate training stage using a statistical machine learning algorithm. The algorithm optimizes the classifier to the properties of the data, attempting to find a classifier configuration that predicts well similar future data. The BCI platforms provide established algorithms for training classifiers, including Linear Discriminant Analysis and Support Vector Machines (Chapter 9 of Volume 1, [CLE 16]).

4) *Feedback*: in the last stage the predictions from the classifier are used to control some application such as a speller or a game. For historical reasons, this stage is often called a feedback stage, as it may be the only medium that concretely demonstrates the effect of the brain activity to the user. The author has several choices here: whether to use some application provided by the software platform, to modify it, or if an entirely new application is needed. As the applications are typically external programs with a limited purpose, changes may require programming[2].

---

1 Please consult each platform's online documentation about the current device support.

2 It is possible that tools such as Unity – http://www.unity3d.com/ – can be used to create applications with less programming.

10.4. Exploring BCI

When an author tries to improve BCI, he can focus on any of the components of Figure 10.1. The most important choice after the selection of acquisition hardware is perhaps the selection of the BCI interaction paradigm (SSVEP, P300, motor imagery, ...). This selection not only dictates how the user will interact with the application, but also what kind of signal processing, training protocols, and user applications are suitable. Sometimes the platforms offer pre-made, fully working examples of common paradigms. One starting point for further exploration then is to take an existing example and modify it.

For example, if the goal is to improve accuracy of the BCI, the author may change various components: the acquisition hardware, the parameters of the current setting, the signal processing, or perhaps the classifier learning algorithm. How this is done depends largely on the BCI platform. Some platforms might present the signal processing chains in a scripting language like Matlab (BCILab, FieldTrip, BioSig). Others might offer a graphical user interface that allows to change the parameters of the BCI paradigm in question (BCI2000, BCILab). The third alternative is to offer a graphical framework for editing signal processing chains in general (OpenViBE, Figure 10.5).

The platform also affects how new signal processing blocks are most easily implemented. In Matlab-based platforms, new techniques are most naturally Matlab scripts. With these platforms it is also possible to implement parts in C++. This can be useful for optimizing algorithms with loops, recursion or branching, as these may be inefficient on an interpreted script language such as Matlab. On the other hand, in C++ based platforms such as OpenViBE and BCI2000, algorithms are typically implemented in C++. These platforms still allow implementing processing blocks using Matlab or Python, an approach that may be especially convenient for rapid prototyping.

If the author wants to use signal processing optimized to a particular user, this can be done using machine learning techniques (see Chapter 9 of Volume 1, [CLE 16]). Aside from the challenges related to machine learning in general (for example model selection and overfitting), an additional encumbrance in this approach is that the training data needs to be gathered individually from each user, possibly before each use. This requires a paradigm-specific stimulator to guide the user to the right kind of brain activity until enough data has been collected (for example see Figure 10.2 (left)). BCI platforms can aid in the data collection stage by providing example scripts and stimulators. While these are running, the platform records the processed data and the expected states of the user based on the training protocol.

However, there is no strict need for the stimulator to be a part of the platform. For training classifiers and feature extraction techniques, it is sufficient that the stimulator provides information of the user state to the platform, which then attaches these as event markers to the signal data. How the event markers can be sent to the platform is platform specific, and approaches such as TCP/IP may be available. Markers may also be accepted by the acquisition hardware. One possibility is to send markers to the acquisition device via a serial port in the computer running the stimulator.

Like the stimulator for data collection, the application controlled by BCI can also be independent from the platform (as in the game show in Figure 10.2 (right)). In this case the events flow from the BCI platform to the application, consisting of discrete commands obtained from the classifier. These commands can be transmitted to the controlled application in various ways. Possibly the most established way is the TCP/IP connection (for example OpenViBE and BCI2000). OpenViBE also supports the VRPN protocol especially made to control virtual reality environments [TAY 01]. Currently there is no established standard to encode or transmit commands or data from BCI, so each platform may have different conventions.

Finally, a recurring task in developing BCI is debug and analysis. It is common in designing and operating BCI to look at the data to discover potential problems. Problems such as badly connected electrodes in EEG may be revealed by an impedance check provided by the hardware, whereas other problems, such as interfering noise, may only be clear in some appropriate visualization. Another reason to visualize data is to gain insight into improving the signal processing. It can be illustrative to look at the data after different kinds of transformations to see if the signal has changed as expected and if the encountered issues have been mitigated. For these reasons, the platforms offer visualization tools. Figure 10.3 shows some of the common types of visualizations in EEG-based BCI: signal data, band power histogram, and a spectrogram (see Chapter 13 of Volume 1, [CLE 16]). In addition to allowing debugging BCI, visualizations can be useful on their own, for example in training the user to control his brain activity in the neurofeedback paradigm (see Chapter 13 of Volume 1, [CLE 16]). Some platforms, such as OpenViBE, provide their own custom visualization tools which can be applied at different points of the processing chain. With platforms based on Matlab, it is also possible to apply Matlab's generic plotting tools.

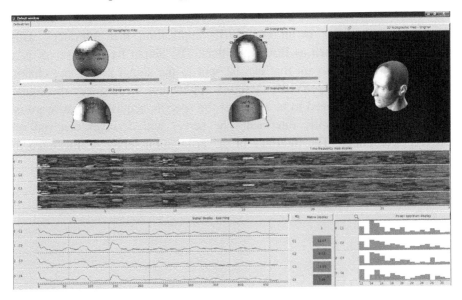

Figure 10.3. *Some visualizations of EEG data from OpenViBE. Top left, 2D topographic map. Top right, 3D topographic map. Center, 2D Power Spectrum over time. Bottom left, plot of signal over time. Bottom right, the Fourier Power Spectrum of the last data chunk. Anomalies such as noise or artifacts can sometimes be easy to spot in such displays. For a color version of this figure, see www.iste.co.uk/clerc/interfaces2.zip*

10.5. Comparison of platforms

We now turn to take a look at the platforms and their main properties. The currently established BCI platforms appear to be OpenViBE, BCI2000, BCILAB, Biosig and Fieldtrip. We first describe OpenViBE and then discuss the other systems. The reader may also be interested in other published platforms and proposals, for example BCI++, xBCI, TOBI, and BF++ [BRU 13].

10.5.1. *OpenViBE*

OpenViBE[3] is a C++ -based software platform designed for real-time processing of biosignal data [REN 10]. One of its most distinguishing features is its graphical language for designing signal processing chains. Understanding the central tools and concepts of the software is sufficient to start exploring BCI with it.

Acquisition Server is an OpenViBE application that interfaces with acquisition devices such as EEG amplifiers. The output from the server is a standardized signal stream that can be sent to the signal processing chains assembled with the OpenViBE Designer application. In this way the signal processing does not need to be aware of the specific acquisition hardware or its manufacturer specific interface. The server and designer can run on different computers. The interface of the acquisition server is illustrated in Figure 10.4.

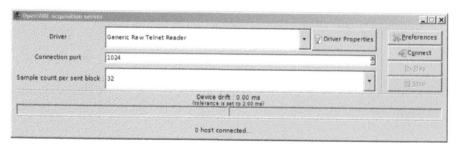

Figure 10.4. *OpenViBE Acquisition Server application. The used hardware device can be selected from a drop-down menu and its properties can be configured. Upon pressing Play, the Acquisition Server starts to send measurement data to client applications such as Designer*

Designer is the main application in OpenViBE that BCI authors and operators work with. The application is illustrated in Figure 10.5. Designer is used both to construct and to execute signal processing chains. Due to the graphical design language provided, new experiments and signal processing chains can be constructed without programming, if the author is familiar with basic signal processing components. However, not every imaginable

---

3 http://openvibe.inria.fr/.

component is provided with OpenViBE, and in such cases some programming may be needed.

In Designer, a *box* denotes almost any component that is meaningful to place somewhere in a signal processing chain. In OpenViBE, components such as filters, displays, classifiers, file readers and writers, etc. are all implemented as boxes. In Designer, the author is able to access all the boxes from a tree view, as seen on the right in Figure 10.5.

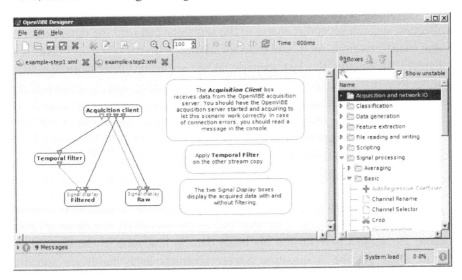

Figure 10.5. *OpenViBE Designer is a design and playback application for signal processing chains and BCI experiments. Processing chains are made by connecting series of modules (boxes) in one or more directed acyclic graphs. Different scenarios appear as tabs in Designer, and may be used to represent different stages of the experiment (for example data recording, training, and control)*

Scenario is a collection of one or more signal processing chains. When designing a scenario using Designer, the author simply drags and drops the required boxes onto a workspace, sets their parameters, and connects them in an appropriate manner. An example scenario can be seen in Figure 10.5. In the figure, the chain reads data from the acquisition server, creates a filtered version of it, and finally displays both the filtered and the original (raw) signal.

Experiment Workflow denotes the steps that must be taken in order to ultimately run the BCI control loop (Figure 10.1). In a typical OpenViBE workflow, the author designs a few different scenarios that implement the training and the use stages of BCI. These scenarios are run manually in a sequence by the operator. Often the first scenario is designed to collect the training data while instructions are provided to the subject, with the subject presumably behaving accordingly. For example, the scenario might prompt the user to imagine left- or right-hand movements in turns in the motor imagery paradigm. Meanwhile, a box in the scenario writes the recorded data to the disk along with the related event markers describing the state that the user is supposed to be in according to the instructions. After the data collection stage, a second scenario in the sequence can read the data, perform some transformations on it, and train a classifier with the processed data (see Chapter 12). Finally, the last scenario in the sequence implements the BCI online loop by constantly repeating the signal processing, evaluating the trained classifier and finally sending the results to some application as commands. Usually this application runs outside OpenViBE and the commands are provided to it over VRPN [TAY 01] or TCP/IP. In this way any application or environment that can accept commands over such channels can in principle be controlled by BCI.

OpenViBE is bundled with several examples of BCI paradigms: motor imagery, P300 and SSVEP. In addition, some scenarios are included that enable the subject to visualize his brain data in real time in the manner of Figure 10.3. As the Acquisition Server abstracts away hardware specific details, these same BCI scenarios can be used with different data sources. In practice, small changes in the scenario may be in order, for example to accommodate for the different number of electrodes in the EEG headset used.

At the time of writing, OpenViBE is supported by Inria (French Institute for Research in Computer Science and Automation). In addition there is a startup company named Mensia Technologies that can provide OpenViBE support for commercial users.

10.5.2. *BCI2000*

BCI2000 [MEL 07] is another C++ -based BCI platform[4]. An impressive amount of different kinds of BCI experiments have been carried out using

---

4 http://www.bci2000.org/

BCI2000 over the years [BRU 13]. BCI2000 provides external applications with runtime access to the internal parameters of the system, allowing the software to be controlled by scripting and external convenience interfaces.

Conceptually, BCI2000 has four different modules: source (data acquisition and storage), signal processing, user application, and operator interface. The source module corresponds to OpenViBE's Acquisition Server, and the signal processing module reflects a signal processing scenario in OpenViBE. In both platforms, user applications and stimulators should be external (i.e. to run as independent processes, possibly on different computers). The last module, operator interface, ties the other modules together and allows changing the parameters of the BCI setting and to run it. In OpenViBE, Designer is used for this purpose. The main difference is that the BCI2000's operator interface is not intended as a signal processing design tool as well.

The modularization of the two platforms is achieved in a different manner. In OpenViBE, a single Acquisition Server supports many different amplifiers. Signal processing chains of different types are all assembled graphically in the same Designer application. In BCI2000, different amplifiers and different signal processing chains have their separate executables as compiled instances of the source and signal processing concepts, respectively. At startup, the specific instances of the four modules are launched, and then controlled by the operator interface.

BCI2000 provides support for signal acquisition from various sources, has a wide palette of signal processing tools, classifiers, and visualizations and pre-designed BCI paradigms. One very useful feature of BCI2000 are its modules for offline analysis of the signal, for example r^2 plots for specific signal periods, topographic displays and so on [MEL 07]. The reader is advised to look for the most recent feature list from the web page of the project.

10.5.3. *Matlab-based platforms*

OpenViBE and BCI2000 are collections of C++ programs and have to be recompiled if low-level modifications are needed. Matlab[5]-based platforms,

---

5 http://www.mathworks.com/

on the other hand, appear as collections of Matlab scripts which can be modified while Matlab is running, making restarting an experiment or analysis relatively quick after any changes. Another benefit is that Matlab is an established framework for data analysis, and the BCI data can be handled just as any matrix data in Matlab. Also, plotting tools, filters and other data handling functions provided by Matlab and its toolboxes can be used. This setting makes offline analysis and prototyping convenient using large, prerecorded datasets. On the other hand, the Matlab-based platforms may assume that the author is essentially able to program in Matlab.

BCIlab[6] is a Matlab-based platform for BCI that aims to provide the latest technical advances of the field [KOT 13]. BCIlab has a graphical user interface where the operator/author can select and modify a reference paradigm (here denoting the whole BCI setting and its parts). BCILab features some interesting technical choices. One is that the signal processing components are evaluated in a lazy fashion: they are only executed if there is another component demanding the output they produce. In OpenViBE, signal processing is performed when there is data to process, regardless of whether there is anything needing the output. Another novelty in BCIlab is that it can try to propose meaningful orders for signal processing plugins. In OpenViBE, the scenario author has to manually order the components.

Fieldtrip[7] is another Matlab-based platform [OOS 11]. Fieldtrip was originally designed for offline EEG data analysis, with support added for BCI later in the form of the Fieldtrip buffer. Fieldtrip is intended for an advanced audience and does not provide a graphical user interface. Instead, the experiment control is done with scripts. The release cycle of Fieldtrip has also been very rapid, one release per day. The other platforms featured in this chapter are more traditional, with fewer releases per year – although the users may be able to get development versions from the code repositories of the platforms.

Biosig[8] is a platform that does not attempt to provide complete, pre-made BCI paradigms or real time signal acquisition [VID 11]. Instead, Biosig appears as a signal processing toolbox, with large set of functionality for

---

6 http://sccn.ucsd.edu/wiki/bcilab/
7 http://www.fieldtriptoolbox.org/
8 http://biosig.sourceforge.net/

artifact removal, filtering, feature extraction, classifiers and prediction quality statistics. Like Fieldtrip, Biosig is intended for advanced users who are experienced in the field and comfortable with scientific programming.

10.6. Choosing a platform

All BCI platforms discussed in this chapter have established themselves in different communities where they have been used in research, clinical trials, and countless publications [BRU 13]. A newcomer to the field may be convinced that the platforms provide many useful features, but be perplexed about choosing a platform. A straightforward way would be to look at the features offered by each software, and see if they match the needs. Table 10.1 shows the central properties of the discussed platforms. As can be seen, on this level there are clear similarities. On the level of the actual signal processing components provided, the platforms have larger differences which can be studied on their corresponding web pages (not shown). What is more difficult to estimate is the amount of development work required when the platform does not provide some necessary feature. The only way to find out may be to attempt the implementation.

In practice the selection of the platform may not only depend on the features or the ease of use, but may be dictated by the environment: working in a lab, it is natural to select the platform that the lab already uses, and benefit from the expertise and the custom tools of the colleagues. Another approach is to use different platforms and their components for different purposes. For example, in some situations OpenViBE could be used for real-time processing or signal acquisition, and a Matlab-based solution for offline or statistical analysis of the obtained data. As the software systems themselves are free (except for the possible Matlab dependency), the main cost paid for the mix-and-match approach comes from the time investment required to learn how to work with each platform. Given their similarities, mixing platforms may very well be feasible today, and eventually tools may emerge that allow interchanging components and makeing communication between systems easier, such as TOBI[9] and LabStreamingLayer[10].

---

9 http://www.tobi-project.org/
10 https://github.com/sccn/labstreaminglayer/

System	Platforms	License	Language	Interfaces	Around since
OpenViBE	Windows, Linux	AGPL3	C++	Python, Matlab	2009
BCI2000	Windows, Linux, OS X	GPL	C++	Python, Matlab	2001
BCIlab	Windows, Linux, OS X	GPL	Matlab	Matlab	2010
Fieldtrip	Windows, Linux, OS X	GPL	Matlab	Matlab	2003
Biosig	Windows, Linux, OS X	GPL	Matlab/C++	Matlab/C++	<2003

System	Dependencies	GUI	Scriptable	Origin
OpenViBE	Open source	Yes	Graphically	Inria (France)
BCI2000	Open source / None	Yes	Yes	Wadsworth Center (USA)
BCIlab	Matlab	Yes	Yes	Swartz Center (USA)
Fieldtrip	Matlab	No	Yes	Donders Institute (Netherlands)
Biosig	Matlab / Octave	Yes	Yes	TU Graz (Austria)

Table 10.1. *Some properties of the BCI platforms. On this level, they appear similar. In practice, the workflows, details and available plugins vary significantly. In the table, the 'dependencies' column may be of specific interest. This indicates the other software required by the platform. Typically open source dependencies are available free of charge*

Platforms may also have their downsides, especially if commercialization of the result is intended. In this case, a BCI platform may have its biggest role in the rapid prototyping and exploration phase but not be a part of the eventual product. This is because the platform and its potential dependencies introduce storage requirements, and the presence of the platform may be difficult to hide from the user experience. Also, the restrictive open source licenses may not be compatible with commercialization efforts. The eventual full application may be better implemented without the platform (similar ideas have been presented before, for example [KOT 13]).

10.7. Conclusion

Exploration of BCI can be carried out by using open source software systems. These platforms provide a multitude of free tools to experiment with the current BCI interaction paradigms. Several possibilities for customizing the offered baseline solutions are possible, ranging from simple parameter tuning to constructing entirely new approaches to BCI. On each platform, signal processing chains and experiment flows provided can be fully modified in platform-specific ways, such as by a graphical editor, using a scripting language, or by C++ programming. The publicly available source code makes it possible to attempt any improvement imaginable. The only limits are posed by the technical skill of the author.

For software platforms themselves, some future challenges remain. For example, the current platforms may be complicated to use for non-expert audiences. Using different parts from different platforms together may require a significant amount of work due to different interfaces, formats and conventions used by each. The platforms may be large in size and depend on other complex software, making it difficult to utilize them in resource-constrained situations such as on tablets, or embedded in games. Open source licensing may also make it difficult to base commercial work on the platforms. Another obstacle can arise from the lack of hardware drivers for different operating systems. Some manufacturers only provide Windows specific drivers to their acquisition devices, effectively making it impossible to develop the corresponding acquisition stage on systems such as Linux or OS X. However, all these software limitations can be solved by engineering and do not require scientific breakthroughs. In this sense, addressing these challenges appears to be only a matter of time.

10.8. Bibliography

[BRU 13] BRUNNER C., ANDREONI G., BIANCHI L. *et al.*, "BCI software platforms", *Towards Practical Brain-Computer Interfaces*, Springer Berlin Heidelberg, pp. 303–331, 2013.

[CLE 16] CLERC M., BOUGRAIN L., LOTTE F. (eds), *Brain–Computers Interfaces 1*, ISTE, London and John Wiley & Sons, New York, 2016.

[GRA 10] GRAIMANN B., ALLISON B., PFURTSCHELLER G., "Brain-Computer Interfaces: A gentle introduction", in *Brain-Computer Interfaces*, pp. 1–27, Springer, 2010.

[KOT 13] KOTHE C.A., MAKEIG S., "BCILAB: A platform for Brain–Computer interface development", *Journal of Neural Engineering*, vol. 10, no. 5, 2013.

[LEG 13] LEGÉNY J., VICIANA ABAD R., LÉCUYER A., "Towards contextual SSVEP-based BCI controller: smart activation of stimuli and controls weighting", *IEEE Transactions on Computational Intelligence and AI in games*, IEEE Computational Intelligence Society, vol. 5, no. 2, pp. 111–116, 2013.

[MEL 07] MELLINGER J., SCHALK G., "BCI2000: a general-purpose software platform for BCI research", in *Brain-Computer Interfaces*, MIT Press, 2007.

[OOS 11] OOSTENVELD R., FRIES P., MARIS E. *et al.*, "Field trip: open source software for advanced analysis of MEG, EEG, and invasive electrophysiological data", *Computational Intelligence and Neuroscience*, vol. 2011, 2011.

[REN 10] RENARD Y., LOTTE F., GIBERT G. *et al.*, "OpenViBE: an open-source software platform to design, test and use Brain-Computer interfaces in real and virtual environments", *Presence: Teleoperators and Virtual Environments*, vol. 19, no. 1, 2010.

[TAY 01] TAYLOR II R.M., HUDSON T.C., SEEGER A. *et al.*, "VRPN: a device-independent, network-transparent VR peripheral system", *Proceedings of the ACM Symposium on Virtual Reality Software and Technology*, 2001.

[VID 11] VIDAURRE C., SANDER T.H., SCHLGL A., "BioSig: the free and open source software library for biomedical signal processing", *Computational Intelligence and Neuroscience*, vol. 2011, 2011.

[WOL 02] WOLPAW J., BIRBAUMER N., MCFARLAND D. *et al.*, "Brain–Computer interfaces for communication and control", *Clinical Neurophysiology*, vol. 113, no. 6, 2002.

11

Illustration of Electrophysiological Phenomena with OpenViBE

As we have seen in previous chapters, numerous neurophysiological markers are used for brain–computer interfaces (BCIs), such as motor imagery, P300, the steady-state visual evoked potentials (SSVEP) or mental workload. Each of these markers correspond to particular electrophysiological phenomena, notably event-related synchronizations/desynchronizations or evoked potentials. The objective of this practical implementation chapter is to present how to use OpenViBE software to visualize these different phenomena. First, we will see how to implement an OpenViBE scenario to visualize electroencephalographic (EEG) signals in real time in order to, for example, verify the quality of the signals and to visualize artifacts such as electrooculograms (EOG) or electromyograms (EMG). Then, we will see how to visualize alpha oscillations and then other phenomena such as beta rebound following the movement of the feet or SSVEPs. Before going into detail, the interested reader can learn more on the main[1] concepts of the use of OpenViBE with introductory videos available on the OpenViBE software website. EEG data examples and OpenViBE scenarios mentioned in this chapter can be downloaded for free on the following web page: http://openvibe.inria.fr/brain-computer-interface-book/.

Chapter written by Fabien LOTTE and Alison CELLARD.
1 http://openvibe.inria.fr/openvibe-video-tutorial-english/.

11.1. Visualization of raw EEG signals and artifacts

11.1.1. *Visualization of raw EEG signals*

One of the most simple and basic operations that can be achieved with OpenViBE, and yet that is almost indispensable, consists of visualizing raw EEG signals that are being measured. As a point of fact, this operation is necessary to ensure that the signals measured by each sensor are of good quality and not abnormally noisy (electrical noise, insufficient or missing gel, faulty electrode, etc.). The visualizing of raw EEG signals is simply done by connecting two boxes only inside OpenViBE (see Figure 11.1). The first box, *acquisition client*, will recover the signals measured in real time by the acquisition server (see Chapter 10), at the address specified in the parameter *acquisition server hostname* of the box (double click on the box to access its settings). The second box is *signal display*, a box that simply displays the signals and stimuli (OpenViBE events) that it receives on the input. Thus by connecting the output *signal* of the *acquisition client* box to the input *signal* of the *signal display* box, then by launching this scenario, it is possible to visualize in real time the raw EEG signals being continuously measured.

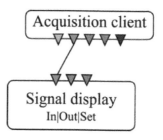

Figure 11.1. *A very simple OpenViBE scenario to visualize the recorded EEG signals in real time*

Since the EEG signals are raw, it is very difficult to perceive the electrophysiological phenomena of cerebral origin therein. As we will mention in the following sections, it is necessary to preprocess these signals in order to correctly visualize these phenomena therein. On the other hand, artifacts can already be observed in the raw signals, notably electrophysiological signals of non-cerebral origin such as EOGs or EMGs.

11.1.2. *Visualization of EOG and EMG artifacts*

If your subject is still "connected" to the EEG measurement device, ask him/her to blink several times repeatedly. You will then see perturbations of the EEG signals, in the form of small "peaks", particularly for the electrodes the closest to the eyes (for example Fp1 or Fp2), as is the case in Figure 11.2(a). These are EOG artifacts due to the movements of the eyes and are not of cerebral origin.

Now ask your subject to clench their jaw several times. You will see another type of perturbation of the EEG signal, with the appearance of high-frequency large amplitude signals, mainly on the peripheral electrodes (frontal electrodes F, Fp or temporal TP) as shown in Figure 11.2(b). These are EMG artifacts, that is to say electrical signals of muscular origin. As mentioned in the previous chapter, both the EOGs and the EMGs are artifacts polluting the EEG signal and that may interfere with the functioning of a BCI.

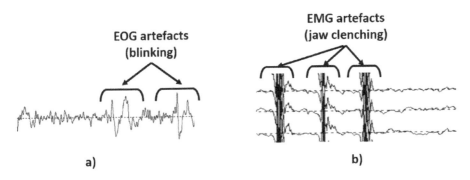

Figure 11.2. *(a) Examples of EOG artifacts measured by the EEG sensors. (b) Examples of EMG artifacts*

11.2. Visualization of alpha oscillations

If EMG or EOG artifacts can be seen in the EEG signals when the subject clenches the jaw or blinks, this means that something is being correctly measured with the sensors. On the other hand, the EOG and EMG signals have much higher amplitudes than the EEG signals. Therefore, if something is measured it does not mean that the signal being measured is of sufficient quality to measure the EEG. A common test that is performed to verify that the EEG is also being measured is the "alpha rhythm test". The alpha rhythm is very prominent and visible in the EEG. In particular, when the subject closes his eyes, an alpha "burst" must be observed (that is an increase in the amplitude of alpha oscillations) in the occipital electrodes, that is to say in the electrodes located above the visual cortex. The visualization of this occipital alpha rhythm can be fairly simply achieved with OpenViBE. Compared with the previous scenario visualizing the raw signals (see Figure 11.1), it suffices to add only two boxes. The first box, the *channel selector*, will select the electrodes of interest, in our case the occipital electrodes, such as O1, Oz or O2. The second box, the *temporal filter*, will filter the signal in the alpha band, for example between 8 and 12 Hz. It is possible to specify the parameters of the filter by double clicking on the box, and by selecting notably different values for both parameters *low/high cut frequency (Hz)*. The signals can then be visualized as previously. The resulting scenario is visible in Figure 11.3.

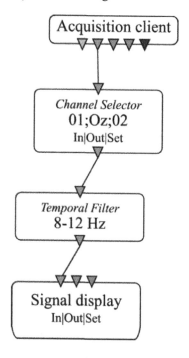

Figure 11.3. *An OpenViBE scenario to visualize the occipital alpha rhythm*

Normally, if you ask the subject to close his eyes, we must see an increase – usually pronounced – in the amplitude of the EEG signals (which are filtered in 8–12 Hz and therefore represent the alpha rhythm). This increase should continue as long as the subject keeps their eyes closed, and the amplitude of the EEG signals in the alpha band should return to its original level when the subject reopens the eyes. This phenomenon can be seen in Figure 11.4.

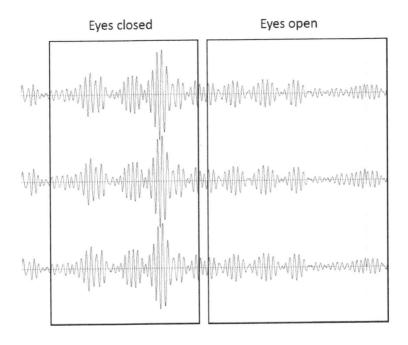

Figure 11.4. *The occipital alpha signals, here visualized with OpenViBE, and whose amplitude increases when the subject closes his/her eyes. The signal represented here is the EEG signal filtered in 8–12 Hz, for electrodes PO7, Oz and PO8*

11.3. Visualization of the beta rebound

Now we focus on the visualization of another signal, the "beta rebound". The "beta rebound" is an increase in the amplitude (that is an event-related synchronization) of the beta rhythm (around 20 Hz), which occurs particularly in motor areas when the subject stops performing a real or an imagined movement. For example, when a subject performs a movement of the feet and then stops, the power of the beta rhythm around the Cz electrode (situated above the areas of the motor cortex of the feet) will increase sharply, and then return to its basic level. This is thus, just as the "alpha rhythm test" mentioned previously, an increase in the amplitude of a rhythm. This beta rebound, however, is not as salient as the alpha rhythm. Therefore, we need further signal processing. In particular, we will use a Laplacian spatial filtering (see Chapter 6 from Volume 1, [CLE 16]) around Cz to amplify the signal coming from this part of the cortex, as well as to calculate the band power of the signal, so as to better visualize the rebound. These operations are performed by the OpenViBE scenario shown in Figure 11.5. This scenario achieves the following operations:

1) the EEG signals are first filtered in the beta band (here, between 16 and 24 Hz), using the *temporal filter* box, as previously;

2) the five electrodes necessary for the Laplacian filtering around Cz, namely FCz, C1, Cz, C2, and CPz, are selected with the *Channel Selector* box;

3) a *Spatial Filter* box is used to apply a Laplacian spatial filter. This box multiplies the input signals by spatial filters represented by a matrix (parameter *spatial filter coefficient* of the box), this matrix representing the weights to be given to each input sensor. Here, the weights -1 are applied to FCz, C1, C2 and CPz and 4 to Cz to perform a Laplacian filter;

4) the power of the signal is then calculated over a sliding window of a second. To this end, we:

a) decompose the input in windows of 1 s long, with (for example) 100 ms of overlap between two consecutive windows. This is carried out by the *time-based epoching* box that makes it possible to break down the signal into windows of a given size (parameter *epoch duration* of the box), with a given interval (parameter *epoch interval*) between two consecutive windows,

b) computes the square of the signal with the *Simple DSP* box. This box enables any simple mathematical operation to be applied to the signal, here the square ($x \times x$ where x is the input signal),

c) computes the average of the resulting signal (that is the square of the beta oscillation) over the input window (here a window of a second) with the box *signal average* that just calculates the average of the signal over the window it receives,

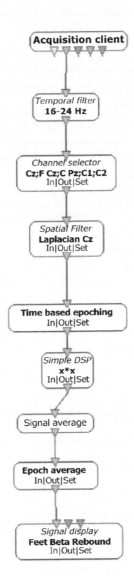

Figure 11.5. *An OpenViBE scenario to visualize the beta rebound in Cz, occurring after the subject have finished performing a (real or imagined) movement of the feet*

d) slightly smoothes the resulting signal by averaging the four latest measurements with the *epoch average* box.

The result is a continuous measurement of the power of the beta rhythm in a Laplacian montage around Cz. It can be visualized with the *signal display* box as previously. If the subject is asked to stamp their feet, it should be seen that this measure gently and slightly decreases (this decrease is not always easily visible) as long as the subject stamps their feet. When we ask him/her to suddenly stop, we should see a sharp increase in this measure of the beta band power, as is the case in Figure 11.6: this is the beta rebound.

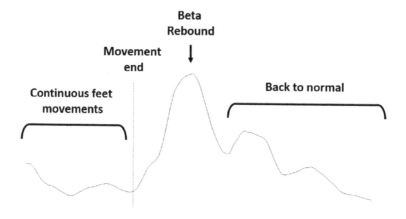

Figure 11.6. *The beta rebound (ERS) occurring after a motion of the feet, visualized here by displaying the band power within 16–24 Hz with OpenViBE, around the Cz electrode, in a Laplacian montage*

This measure can be used to create a BCI detecting imagined movements of the feet, as is the case in the application "use-the-force" described in Chapters 5 and 14.

11.4. Visualization of the SSVEP

Another signal that can be visualized is the SSVEP, that is an increase in the amplitude of occipital EEG signals for the oscillations at the frequency of a flashing visual stimulus to which the user directs his/her attention (see Chapter 4 of Volume 1, [CLE 16]). In other words, if the user directs his/her attention to a visual object flashing at 15 Hz, the amplitude of his/her occipital EEG signals (for example for the electrode Oz) will increase at the frequency of 15 Hz. To see this phenomenon, we will analyze a file of EEG signals captured during a SSVEP experiment called the "SSVEP shooter", which is provided with OpenViBE. The analyzed EEG signals are also provided with OpenViBE. In this application, the user is required to watch a red square flashing with two others, these three squares flashing at 12, 15, and 20 Hz. The OpenViBE scenario of this application sends a different stimulation (an OpenViBE event) for each instruction, that is for each square that the user has to watch. To observe the SSVEP, the spectrum of the occipital EEG signals will thus be calculated (here for the electrodes O1, Oz and O2, that will be averaged together), separately averaged for several trials of each stimulation. In other words, we will average separately the spectra that are obtained when the user stares at the square flashing at 12 Hz, that flashing at 15 Hz and the one flashing at 20 Hz. To this end, we can use the scenario shown in Figure 11.7.

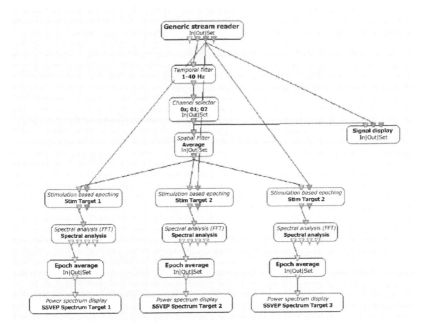

Figure 11.7. *An OpenViBE scenario to visualize the steady-state visual evoked potentials (SSVEP) in the occipital electrodes (O1, Oz, O2) for stimulations at 12, 15 and 20 Hz*

In this scenario, we first read the file of the EEG signals recorded during an SSVEP experiment by means of the *generic stream reader* box. Next, the signals are filtered in the 1–40 Hz band with a *temporal filter* to remove the low frequencies. As a matter of fact, since the EEG signal has a $1/f$ spectrum, the very low frequencies have a much higher amplitude than the others, and would thus hide them during their visualization. Because there is interest in the occipital electrodes, the electrodes O1, O2 and Oz are then selected with the *channel selector* box, then the signals from these three sensors are averaged using the *spatial filter* box, which here assigns a weight of 1/3 to each of the three electrodes. We will then look at the spectrum of the resulting signal for each visual stimulation, that is to say when the subject must look at each of the three squares. To do this, the *stimulation-based epoching* box is used that will slice a window of the EEG signal following the reception of a stimulation. Here, each of the three stimulations corresponding to each square is being used, each in a different box. A 4-s window is chosen (in the parameters of the box). The spectrum of the resulting signal is then calculated with the *spectral analysis* box, several spectra thus obtained are then averaged with the *epoch average* box (here, the last five spectra obtained for each stimulation are averaged), and the result all together is visualized with the *power spectrum display* box. After the scenario has been run long enough to have gathered at least five spectra of 4 s for each stimulation, the spectra represented in Figure 11.8 can be seen.

In this figure, amplitude peaks can be clearly observed for frequencies 20, 15 and 12 Hz for the EEG signals captured when the user was looking at the square flashing at 20, 15 and 12 Hz, respectively. These are the SSVEP.

11.5. Conclusions

By using OpenViBE, it is relatively easy to visualize in real time, or to replay and to visualize afterward (off-line), EEG signals to picture therein different electrophysiological phenomena. To this end, the procedure consists of temporally and spatially filtering the signals, eventually averaging them, then visualizing them or visualizing their spectra. These different tools can be used to visualize phenomena other than those illustrated here, for instance evoked potentials such as the P300, which will be discussed in Chapter 13 notably.

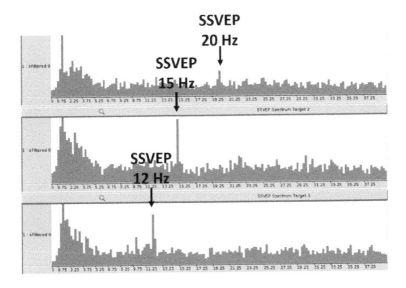

Figure 11.8. *The average spectra of the EEG signals in O1, Oz and O2 for stimulations at 20 (on top), 15 (in the middle) and 12 Hz (at the bottom). A peak amplitude can be clearly seen therein for the stimulation frequencies, that is at 20, 15 and 12 Hz*

11.6. Bibliography

[CLE 16] CLERC M., BOUGRAIN L., LOTTE F. (eds), *Brain–Computer Interfaces 1*, ISTE, London and John Wiley & Sons, New York, 2016.

12

Classification of Brain Signals with OpenViBE

12.1. Introduction

The objective of this chapter is to illustrate, with the software OpenViBE, the classification phase in the processing chain of a BCI, that is how to recognize the brain activity of the subject, source of information and commands within brain–computer interfaces. This phase follows the phases of data acquisition, preprocessing and feature extraction. It is followed by the translation into commands of the mental state recognized by the system.

The following sections therefore present how to train the parameters of a classifier from learning examples, how to evaluate the performances of the resulting classifier and how to use it to automatically classify new signals.

OpenViBE's scenarios and electro encephalographic data sets to reproduce the treatments presented in this chapter are available on the website of OpenViBE: http://openvibe.inria.fr/ brain-computer-interface-book/.

OpenViBE is a software suite consisting of processing modules called boxes. All processing boxes related with this chapter are available in the *classification* category. They are accessible via the boxes tree located on the right-hand side of the OpenViBE Designer interface (see Figure 12.1). The

Chapter written by Laurent BOUGRAIN and Guillaume SERRIÈRE.

boxes can also be easily found by using the search feature situated above the boxes tree. The main boxes to use for training are: for classification, *classifier trainer* and *classifier processor*, and for evaluation, *accuracy*, *confusion matrix*, *ROC curve* and *kappa factor*.

12.2. Classification

Discrimination, commonly referred to as classification, consists of assigning an element in a class from a set of predefined classes (see Chapter 9 of Volume 1, [CLE 16]). Machine learning methods allow this function to be trained from examples.

12.2.1. *Classification algorithms*

OpenViBE basically offers a set of well-known methods for performing automatic classifications. Among the available methods, we have linear methods such as linear discriminant analysis and nonlinear methods such as vector support machines (or SVM) and artificial neural networks, i.e. multilayer perceptron (MLP). The list of classification methods available can be accessed on the OpenViBE website in the documentation of the *classifier trainer* box. This box allows the selection of the classification method to be used (*Algorithm to use* field, see Figure 12.1).

12.2.1.1. *The classifier trainer box*

The *classifier trainer* box, enabling the definition of the type of learning, is available in the *classification* category (see Figure 12.1).

This box has by default three inputs. The first input receives a trigger stream. Only the selected stimulation triggers the learning process. When this stimulation is received, all the feature vectors are labeled and sent to the classification algorithm, and the training is launched. Then, a configuration file containing the parameters of the classifier is stored. It will be used online by the *classifier processor* box. It is possible to add other inputs if there are more than two classes to discriminate. The stimulation *OVTK_StimulationId_TrainCompleted* is sent through the single output of the box when the training of the classifier is complete. The parameters of the box are the following:

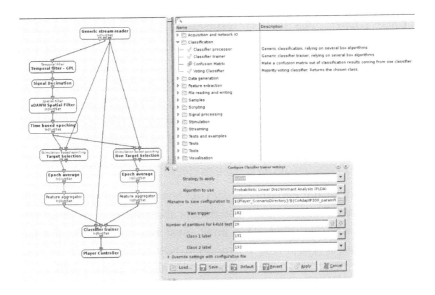

Figure 12.1. *The classifier trainer box (in yellow) required here to learn the parameters of the classifier input examples belonging to two classes. This box is available in the classification category of the boxes tree located on the right side of the Designer. The setup parameters, accessible through double clicking on the box, are visible in the window at the bottom right*

– *Strategy to apply*: the selection of "OneVsAll" or "OneVsOne" (described in sections 12.2.2.1 and 12.2.2.2 respectively) will start the training and the combination of a set of binary classifiers, that is to say that discriminate two classes, to obtain a discrimination of a greater number of classes. The selection of "native" will indicate that a single classifier will be used;

– *Algorithm to use*: this field corresponds to the type of classifier to use. The list available will depend on the strategy selected in the field *strategy to apply*;

– *Filename to save configuration file*: this field corresponds to the file in which the parameters of the classifier will be saved after training;

– *Train trigger*: this field corresponds to the stimulation received at the input that will trigger the training process;

– *Number of partitions for k-fold test*: this field corresponds to the number of partitions that will be used in the context of cross-validation (see section 12.3.2.2);

– *Class i label*: this field corresponds to the stimulation that will be associated with each class.

Depending on the strategy or on the classification algorithm being used, some parameters can be added or removed from the list. The parameters added will be passed to the algorithm during its initialization. The parameters added during the selection of the strategy to apply will be described later.

12.2.1.2. *The classifier processor box*

The objective of the *classifier processor* box is to provide for each input that it receives the predicted class and details about the reasons of this result. This box has only one input. This input must be connected to the feature vector stream to be classified. Whenever a new feature vector arrives, the classification process is triggered and a stimulation corresponding to the predicted class is transmitted through the first output. The second output contains one or more distances with a separator hyperplane if the classifier being used provides them. Otherwise, the matrix will be of dimension 0. The format of this output directly depends on the classification algorithm and on the strategy used by the *classifier processor* box. The third output contains one or more probabilities if the classifier provides them. Otherwise, the matrix will be of dimension 0. The format of this output directly depends on the classification algorithm and on the strategy used by the *classifier processor* box.

12.2.2. *Classification strategies*

A large number of problems amount to having to distinguish between the elements of two classes, for example when it is necessary to detect if an evoked potential is present or not in the signal after the presentation of a stimulus (see Chapter 4 of Volume 1, [CLE 16]). More generally, the elements that have to be recognized belong to more than two classes. This is the case, for example, when it is necessary to detect several mental tasks (calculating, motor imaginary, object visualization, etc.). In this case, there are different strategies available because some classification algorithms allow for discriminating two classes only or yield better results by combining several binary classifiers.

12.2.2.1. *1-vs-all*

This method decomposes a multiclass classification into a set of binary classifications whose combination makes it possible to determine the class. In the context of the one-versus-all coupling strategy, each classifier will be trained to discriminate a particular class from the others. Then, using a confidence indicator provided by the classifiers, the most probable class is determined. This strategy does not take additional parameters.

12.2.2.2. *1-vs-1*

This method breaks down a multiclass classification into a set of binary classifications such as the 1-vs-all strategy. However, here, each classifier discriminates two particular classes. The results of each classifier are grouped together to predict the final class. In OpenViBE, three different syntheses are available: the vote, a method developed by Hastie and Tibshinari [HAS 97] (referenced as HT in the software) and a method developed by Price *et al.* [PRI 94] (referenced as PKPD). This classification strategy thus introduces an additional parameter, namely *pairwise decision strategy*, which makes it possible to select the method that will be used to determine the class from the results of each binary classifier.

12.2.2.3. *Native*

Some algorithms are intrinsically capable of performing non-binary classifications. They thus inherently allow that a multiclass classification be intrinsically obtained without undergoing a binary classification decomposition. In OpenViBE, only the MLP and linear discriminant analysis are capable of natively accepting more than two classes. This is not the case for Support Vector Machines since the libSVM library used by the software performs a 1-vs-1-type of coupling to obtain a classification in more than two classes.

12.2.3. *Illustration of motor imagery recognition*

The files containing recorded signals as well as the scenarios used in this section are available on the OpenViBE website at http://openvibe.inria.fr/brain-computer-interface-book/.

Suppose that we aim to recognize if a user performs a motor imagery of his/her right hand or a motor imagery of his/her left hand (see Chapter 4 of

Volume 1 [CLE 16]). As a first step, a set of trials is recorded for which the subject performs imageries of each hand according to the indications given on the screen. This record contains a series of signals corresponding to the imagery of the right hand and to the imagery of the left hand in a random order as well as a series of labels designating their respective class. Second, this recording is reread. The features associated with each trial are calculated and provided as input to the *classifier trainer* box (Figure 12.2). The *classifier trainer* box stores the parameters of the learned classifier in a file. A similar chain to that constituted for learning is applied to a new series of trials originating from the electroencephalographic system or for the purposes of this illustration a file containing other recorded signals. The *classifier processor* box rereads the classifier parameters and provides for each trial a class and eventually details on the reasons for this classification (Figure 12.3).

12.3. Evaluation

Once the learning is carried out, it is important to validate the processing chain and the classification system. Notably, the classifier will have to be evaluated. OpenViBE provides several useful tools in order to extract performance measures. These metrics must be obtained from data that were not used to parameterize the classification model in order to estimate the performances that the classifier will obtain from new cases.

12.3.1. *Measures*

The reader can refer to Chapter 9 of Volume 1 [CLE 16] for details on the performance metrics presented in this section.

12.3.1.1. *Accuracy*

The accuracy or correct classification rate corresponds to the percentage of cases correctly classified from the total number of cases. The *classifier accuracy measure* box provides a means to obtain this metric.

12.3.1.2. *Confusion matrix*

The confusion matrix is achieved by the *confusion matrix* box present in the *classification* category. This box has two inputs: the actual and the predicted classes (Figure 12.4). The confusion matrix is generated by comparing the elements in a pairwise fashion. The parameters of the box are the following:

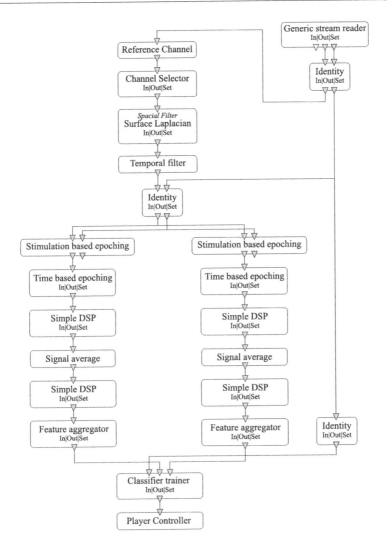

Figure 12.2. *Illustration of the usage of the classifier trainer box in a processing chain for the discrimination of two motor imageries. A file containing the recordings is replayed through the generic stream reader box. The recorded channels are named, selected, combined and filtered, respectively, using the reference channel, channel selector, surface Laplacian and temporal filter boxes. The data are then transmitted to two channels for the extraction of features that select the trials corresponding to a particular class, extract a time window during which the motor imagery has taken place and calculate a power index, respectively, using the stimulation-based epoching, time-based epoching, simple DSP and signal average boxes. All of these features are organized into a matrix that is provided as input to the classifier trainer box. The player controller box is here waiting for a stimulation corresponding to the end of the experiment to terminate the scenario*

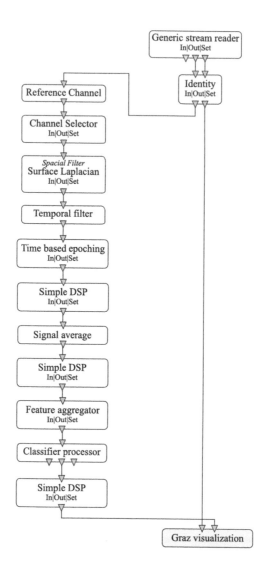

Figure 12.3. *Illustration of the usage of the classifier processor box in the processing chain for the detection of motor imageries. A similar chain to that constituted for learning is applied to a new series of trials originating from the electroencephalographic system or for the purposes of this illustration of another data file. The classifier processor box rereads the parameters of the classifier and provides a class for each trial*

– *Percentage*: this field corresponds to the formatting of the data in the matrix. If the value is true, the box will then provide percentages, otherwise occurrences;

– *Sums*: this field corresponds to the addition or not of a column and a row containing the sum of each row/column. This option is useful when percentage is set to false;

– *Class i*: this field corresponds to the stimulation identifying class i.

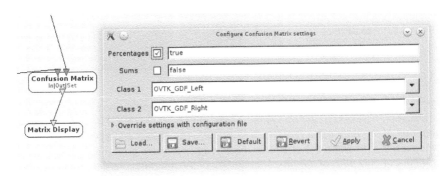

Figure 12.4. *The confusion matrix box accepts as parameters stimulations such as labels of classes (here, OVTK_GDF_Left and OVTK_GDF_Right for motor imageries of the left hand and the right hand) that it associates to form the confusion matrix, which is then transmitted on output. The right-hand side of the screenshot shows the configuration window of the box*

It is possible to add classes to the confusion matrix. To this end, a parameter should be added to the box by means of the graphical interface. It will then suffice to fill in its value in the same manner as for the two inputs by default.

The output of the box is of the matrix type. In order to display it and analyze the results that it contains, the *matrix display* box has to be used. This box is available in the *visualization/basic* category. A visual such as that shown in Figure 12.5 is then obtained.

12.3.1.3. *ROC curve*

The receiver operating characteristic (ROC) curve is a means to visualize a subset of the types of errors proposed by the confusion matrix and to determine the decision threshold that has to be used to find a good compromise between the number of false positives and that of true positives (Figures 12.6 and 12.7).

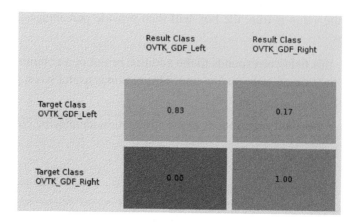

Figure 12.5. *Confusion matrix displayed by the display matrix box in the case of a classification between motor imageries of the left hand (OVTK_GDF_Left) and motor imageries of the right hand (OVTK_GDF_Right). The displayed values correspond to percentages. Therefore, the imageries of the right hand are properly classified by the classifier but only 83% of the motor imageries of the left hand. Target class and result class, respectively, correspond to the actual class and the predicted class*

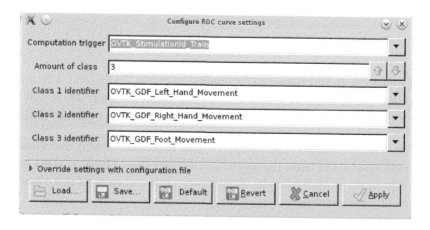

Figure 12.6. *Configuration window of the ROC curve box. The number and the label of the classes are specified. The stimulation that will trigger the calculation of the curve is also indicated*

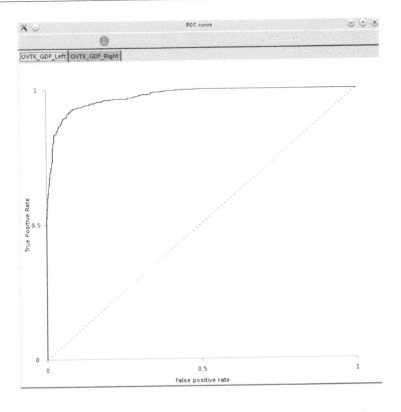

Figure 12.7. *ROC curve provided by the ROC curve box. Each tab contains the curve of a particular class*

12.3.1.4. *Kappa coefficient*

The kappa coefficient makes it possible to evaluate the performance of the classifier comparatively to those that a random classifier would yield. It thus takes the number of classes into account. It can be displayed using the *kappa coefficient* box (Figure 12.8).

12.3.2. *Validation data*

In order to know the performance of the of the classifier on new data, several approaches are available. The simplest to implement is based on a decomposition of the available data: train and test for large datasets and cross-validation for small datasets.

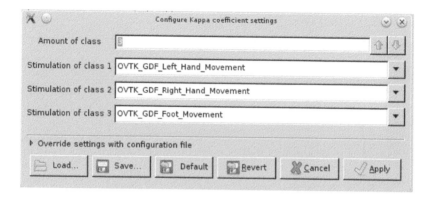

Figure 12.8. *Configuration window of the Kappa coefficient box. The number and the label of the classes are specified*

12.3.2.1. *Train and test*

The totality of the examples is divided into two parts: one will be used to learn the parameters of the model and the other will evaluate its performance with new data. In practice, a large number of examples are dedicated to learning; the amount of testing data must, however, be sufficient to obtain a statistically significant estimate. For example, 75% of the data could be employed to train the classifier parameters and evaluate it with the remaining 25%.

To access this evaluation mode in OpenViBE, it is necessary to capture two data sets. The first will be used by the learning scenario such as the one illustrated in Figure 12.2, whereas the second will be in an evaluation scenario such as that presented in Figure 12.3.

12.3.2.2. *Cross-validation*

Cross-validation is a commonly used process to estimate the performance of a classifier when the number of examples is small. Indeed, in this case, the low number of examples contained in the test set when applying a train-and-test type of decomposition does not provide a meaningful evaluation. Cross-validation uses a partitioning into k partitions of the data set dedicated to learning with $k = 10$ even $k = 5$. The classifier is trained using $k - 1$ partitions. Once the training completed, the partition that has been set aside is used to test the performance of the classifier with new data. To compensate for the fact that the evaluation focuses on a small number of examples, the operation is repeated k times using a different subgroup in the test and by training the parameters of the classifier with the $k - 1$ remaining groups.

In OpenViBE, cross-validation is directly integrated in the *classifier trainer* box. It is executed when the learning process is triggered by using the number of partitions in the parameters of the box (Figure 12.9). The process then calculates the average of the intermediate accuracies as well as the standard deviation.

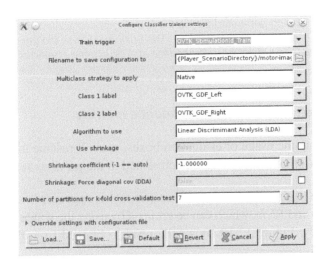

Figure 12.9. *Among the training parameters of the classifier trainer box, the number of partitions to be used for cross-validation can be seen at the end of the list*

Care should be taken in the case when using supervised training filters as common spatial filters and where the combinations of the values measured on the electrodes are determined for each class; the cross-validation will be biased because the filter will be trained on the full data set and not only with the partitions theoretically concerned by the learning phase.

```
Classifier trainer> Received train stimulation. Data dim is [1344x18]
Classifier trainer> Randomizing the feature vector set
Classifier trainer> k-fold test could take quite a long time, be patient
Classifier trainer> Finished with partition 1 / 10 (performance : 81.3433%)
Classifier trainer> Finished with partition 2 / 10 (performance : 85.0746%)
Classifier trainer> Finished with partition 3 / 10 (performance : 79.2593%)
Classifier trainer> Finished with partition 4 / 10 (performance : 85.0746%)
Classifier trainer> Finished with partition 5 / 10 (performance : 81.4815%)
Classifier trainer> Finished with partition 6 / 10 (performance : 85.0746%)
Classifier trainer> Finished with partition 7 / 10 (performance : 84.3284%)
Classifier trainer> Finished with partition 8 / 10 (performance : 80.7407%)
Classifier trainer> Finished with partition 9 / 10 (performance : 88.0597%)
Classifier trainer> Finished with partition 10 / 10 (performance : 82.2222%)
Classifier trainer> Cross-validation test accuracy is 83.2659% (sigma = 2.5362%)
Classifier trainer> Training set accuracy is 84.747% (optimistic)
```

Figure 12.10. *Tracing generated during the learning phase achieved by the classifier trainer box for a cross-validation, $k = 10$. The tracing contains the good classification rate for each partition, then the average rate and its standard deviation. The last line gives the rate of correct classification when all the data are used for learning*

12.3.3. *Illustration of the performance metrics*

To illustrate the usage of evaluation boxes, we will resume the problem of the classification of motor imageries presented in the previous section.

The result of these different performance metrics appears in a set of boxes (Figures 12.5 and 12.7), which can be grouped by using the windows managing tool. Similarly, Figure 12.10 shows the results obtained from the validation data sets.

12.4. Conclusions

A set of methods has been implemented in OpenViBE to provide classification training, to make its testing and its usage with future data possible. In the near future, regression methods will be added to allow for the prediction of a continuous value and not a class. Naturally, the skilled programmer can add his/her own algorithms particularly inspired by existing methods.

12.5. Bibliography

[CLE 16] CLERC M., BOUGRAIN L., LOTTE F. (eds), *Brain–Computer Interfaces 1*, ISTE, London and John Wiley & Sons, New York, 2016.

[HAS 97] HASTIE T., TIBSHIRANI R., "Classification by pairwise coupling", *Advances in Neural Information Processing Systems 10 (NIPS)* Denver, CO, pp. 507–513, 1997.

[PRI 94] PRICE D., KNERR S., PERSONNAZ L. *et al.*, "Pairwise neural network classifiers with probabilistic outputs", *Advances in Neural Information Processing Systems 7 (NIPS)*, Denver, CO, pp. 1109–1116, 1994.

13

OpenViBE Illustration of a P300 Virtual Keyboard

This chapter illustrates, by means of a P300 virtual keyboard application, several fundamental notions of BCIs: preprocessing, extraction of characteristics, classification and training. Without referring again to the details of these notions, since they have already been discussed in the first part of this book, this chapter proposes to the reader to appropriate them with a specific application. The P300 virtual keyboard application, described in section 3.2.1, flashes the symbols of a virtual keyboard displayed on a screen [FAR 88]. When a flash appears on the symbol that the user wants to select (target), their brain activity presents a particular response involving several neurophysiological phenomena, including the P300 wave (see section 4.3.2 of Volume 1). The real-time analysis of nerurophysiological signals and their classification allows detecting the presence or absence of the P300 wave in response to the flashes, and *in fine* to determine the symbol that the user wants to select.

This illustrative chapter offers the reader the possibility of appropriating the concepts and methods involved in a P300 virtual keyboard. "OpenViBE scenarios and electroencephalographic data sets to reproduce the examples presented in this chapter are available on the OpenViBE webpage: http://openvibe.inria.fr/brain-computer-interface-book/" Section 13.1 presents

Chapter written by Nathanaël FOY, Théodore PAPADOPOULO and Maureen CLERC.

the binary classification (target versus non-target) in the specific context of the P300 wave. Section 13.2 exposes the implementation of the processing chain in OpenViBE (see Chapter 10 and [REN 10]) as well as the totality of the software system that controls the P300 virtual keyboard.

13.1. Target/non-target classification

An evoked potential is a neurophysiological response to a stimulus marked in time. Evoked potentials are measured by segmenting EEG signals (Chapter 6 of Volume 1) into time windows whose beginning corresponds to the moment of the stimulation, and whose duration is typically of the order of 1 s. The signal segments obtained after segmentation are called *trials*. These are divided into two groups, target and non-target, depending on whether or not they are the evoked potential looked for.

13.1.1. *The average model*

A simple way to bring forward the signal of interest (evoked potential), and to attenuate the noise inherent to the measuring device, is to average the target trials signals between them, for each channel (electrodes). An *average* potential is thus obtained, in the form of a function depending on time, for each of the channels. Figure 13.1(a) shows target (in blue) and non-target potentials (in green), for the electrode P8, obtained by averaging the signals measured during a P300 speller calibration session.

The average evoked potential obtained by averaging the signals over several trials can be seen as an accurate representation of the evoked potential.[1] In reality, the raw signals, captured during an individual trial, present a high level of noise, as shown in the examples of raw targets and non-target signals in Figure 13.1(b). Given the noise present in each trial,[2]

---

1 It sometimes happens that the time that separates two stimulations is be less than the duration of the time window. In this case, taking the average between the trials does not always provide the best approximation and other methods are utilized to calculate the average potential, as that described, for example, in [RIV 09].

2 Noise designates here the variability of the signal around the average potential, which both refers to the measurement noise, and also to the neuronal activity not determined by target and non-target stimuli or even the variability of these intertrial signals.

data classification, for example the allocation to each test of a class (target or non-target), is a difficult task. Figure 13.2 shows the histogram of the values measured during the trials, for a specific time sample ($t = 352$ ms after stimulation), and for a specific electrode (P8). This histogram shows the distribution of the values around their average value. The shape of the histogram, which can be found for each time sample and for all the electrodes, justifies that target evoked potential (respectively, non-target) can be modeled by two multivariate normal laws, $\mathcal{N}(\boldsymbol{\mu}_1, \boldsymbol{\Sigma}_1)$ (respectively, $\mathcal{N}(\boldsymbol{\mu}_2, \boldsymbol{\Sigma}_2)$).

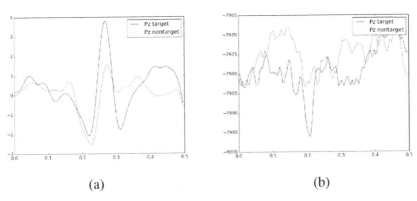

(a)   (b)

Figure 13.1. *a) Average of 66 target (in blue) and non-target (in green) signals in an electrode (Pz); b) Raw target (blue) and non-target (green) signals. For a color version of the figure, see www.iste.co.uk/clerc/interfaces2.zip*

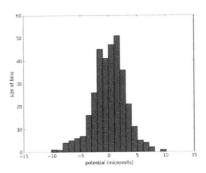

Figure 13.2. *Histogram of values captured by channel P8 at time t = 352 ms after stimulation, over a set of 330 trials of the non-target class*

In the context of this model, $\mu_1 = (\mu_{1,i}(t))_{1 \leq i \leq n_c, 0 \leq t < n_t}$ and $\mu_2 = (\mu_{2,i}(t))_{1 \leq i \leq n_c, 0 \leq t < n_t}$ represent the average evoked potential for n_c channels and n_t time samples. The matrices Σ_1 and Σ_2 model the variance of the measures around their mean value. The calculation of these matrices from the measurements of the signal shows a relative homogeneity within the classes (that is to say $\Sigma_1 = \Sigma_2 = \Sigma$), a property that is called homoscedasticity.

Such a model paves the way for classification methods specially adapted for this type of situation, such as linear discriminant analysis.

13.1.2. *Linear discriminant analysis and the overtraining issue*

As explained in section 9.1.3.1 of Volume 1, linear discriminant analysis (LDA) is suitable for binary classification within the Gaussian multivariate homoscedastic context. The classification of a vector of characteristics $\mathbf{x}$ consists of imposing a threshold on its scalar product with a weight vector $\mathbf{w}$. The test is classified as part of the "target" class if

$$\mathbf{w} \cdot \mathbf{x} > c$$

where

$$\mathbf{w} = \Sigma^{-1}(\mu_1 - \mu_2) \tag{13.1}$$

$$c = \frac{1}{2}(\mu_1^T \Sigma^{-1} \mu_1 - \mu_2^T \Sigma^{-1} \mu_2) \tag{13.2}$$

In order to talk about these formulae, we are going to examine the very simple case where only a single channel is considered and in which the average evoked potentials are constant, for example: $(\mu_1(t))_{0 \leq t < n_t} = (1, 1, ..., 1)$ and $(\mu_2(t))_{0 \leq t < n_t} = (-1, -1, ..., -1)$. In addition, consider that the time samples are independents[3] and with the same variance: $\sigma^2 \, Id$. In this example, $\mathbf{w} = \frac{2}{\sigma^2}(1, 1, ...1)$ and $c = 0$. Thus, the class is simply determined by the sign of the sum of the values of the trial vector $(x(t))_{0 \leq t < n_t}$. Now suppose that for

---

3 It should be noted that this assumption of independence can be done without loss of generality because Σ is symmetric, then it is diagonalizable in an orthonormal basis. We can always therefore refer to it.

a certain $t = t_0$, the difference in averages $|\mu_1(t_0) - \mu_2(t_0)|$ is greater than for the other ts (assume $\mu_1(t_0) = 3$ and $\mu_2(t_0) = -3$ to illustrate the idea), all other things being equal. The dissimilarity between the distributions being larger at t_0[4], the value taken by $x(t_0)$ is more significant than the other values for the classification, which is reflected by its more significant weight in the vector w (formula 13.1). Conversely, a greater variance at t_0 implies that it would be more difficult to dissociate the two distributions and $x(t_0)$ would be associated with a smaller weighting.

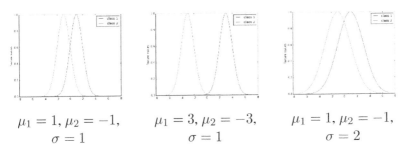

$$\mu_1 = 1, \mu_2 = -1, \qquad \mu_1 = 3, \mu_2 = -3, \qquad \mu_1 = 1, \mu_2 = -1,$$
$$\sigma = 1 \qquad\qquad \sigma = 1 \qquad\qquad \sigma = 2$$

Figure 13.3. *When the distance between the two classes is largest, all other things being equal, the LDA associates a greater weight to this characteristic. Conversely, a larger variance is associated with a smaller weight*

The calculation of the weights w and the threshold c is achieved from μ_i and Σ, and in practice, these latter are estimated from training data, acquired during a calibration phase, containing labelled trials. For example, with the P300 virtual keyboard, during a "calibration" phase the user must direct, their attention to a series of predetermined letters, making it possible to know for this dataset which flashes correspond to targets and non-targets. μ_1 and μ_2 are vectors of size $n_c n_t$ obtained by averaging the trials of each class in the training data, and concatenating the average potentials thus obtained for each electrode into a single vector. The matrix Σ is itself an $n_c n_t \times n_c n_t$ square matrix obtained by calculating the covariance matrix of the trials[5].

---

4 The dissimilarity between probability distributions is strictly measured by the Fisher information distance. In the space of one-dimensional Gaussians parameterized by (μ, σ), the Fisher distance between $\mathcal{N}(\mu_\infty, \sigma)$ and $\mathcal{N}(\mu_2, \sigma)$ increases with $|\mu_1 - \mu_2|$ and decreases with σ.

5 More specifically $\Sigma = Cov(X)$ where X is a matrix having in each row the $n_c n_t$ measurements for each trial.

The method described above works even better when the number of trials in the training dataset is large compared to the trial dimension $(x_i(t))_{i,t}$ (given by $n_c n_t$), in order to accurately estimate μ_1, μ_2 and Σ. Otherwise, there is a risk of overtraining. As already explained in section 9.1.2 of Volume 1, overtraining is an omnipresent issue in machine learning, which originates from a poor generalization from the training data, generally due to too small a number of examples when compared to number of characteristics that describe the example. To illustrate this phenomenon in a colorful manner, knowing that a blue square belongs to a class A and that a yellow circle belongs to a class B is insufficient to generalize the membership to one of the two classes considering a yellow square.

When the training data set is not extensive enough, as happens in BCI due to the experimental time necessary to acquire data, it is convenient to perform a reduction of dimensionality. This is where the methods of dimensionality reduction such as xDAWN come into play.

13.1.3. *Dimension reduction with xDAWN spatial filtering*

Spatial filtering with the xDAWN method is a dimensionality reduction method to be applied to the data before performing an LDA classification. It consists of determining linear combinations of channels that bring forward the interesting part of the signals with respect to noise [RIV 09].

In order for the LDA classification to operate in the best possible way, it is necessary that the distances between the averages of the classes $(\mu_{1,i}(t) - \mu_{2,i}(t)$ for $1 \leq i \leq n_c$ and $0 \leq t < n_t)$ be as large as possible, for the reasons mentioned above; on the other hand, the intraclass variance among trials should be as small as possible. The main point is therefore to find a linear combination of the channels weighted by the weights V that maximizes the energy of the signal $V^T(\mu_1 - \mu_2)^T(\mu_1 - \mu_2)V$ while minimizing the energy of the noise $V^T \Sigma V$. Here, μ_1 and μ_2 are $n_t \times n_c$ matrices obtained by averaging the trials in the training data, and Σ is an $n_c \times n_c$ square matrix obtained by calculating the covariance matrix of the trials.[6] The algorithm that is implemented in OpenViBE maximizes the quantity

$$\frac{||V^T(\mu_1 - \mu_2)^T(\mu_1 - \mu_2)V||}{||V^T \Sigma V||},$$

using a generalized eigenvalue decomposition method. The best spatial filters are given by the eigenvectors corresponding to the largest generalized eigenvalues. It should be noted that the expression that has to be maximized differs slightly from the original formula of the xDAWN algorithm (Volume 1, Chapter 7 formula [7.4] presented in section 7.4 of Volume 1) whose numerator includes the average of the target signals only.

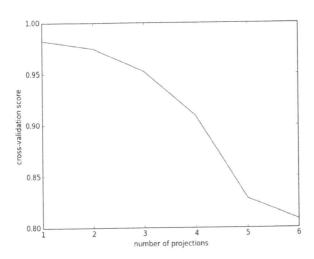

Figure 13.4. *Cross-validation score according to the number of projections*

Figure 13.4 shows the cross-validation score with respect to the number of selected filters. A small number of filters (between 1 and 3) are usually sufficient to capture all of the necessary information for the classification. The

---

6 More specifically, $\Sigma = Cov(X)$ where X presents in each row i the totality of the measured values in the training data trials, in the channel i. We should note the small differences in the definitions of μ_1, μ_2 and Σ compared to the above definitions.

error eventually increases with more filters because the additional projections only add noise that has no significant information, resulting in overtraining and poor generalization.

This method has proved to be very efficient in classifying evoked potentials. Spatial filtering has the double function of the discriminant signals, while minimizing noise. Indeed, the signals of interest have an increased correlation structure with the different sensors when compared to the noise (not related to the signal of interest). For example, the average potentials of the channels P7 and P8 represented in Figure 13.5 exhibit a relative similarity. The signals of interest therefore tend to add up in a more optimal manner through the sensors, whereas the noise has a greater tendency to be neutralized by summation.

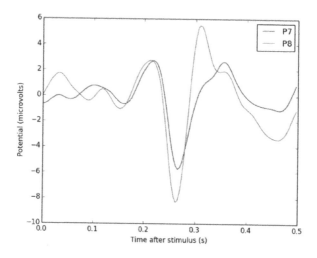

Figure 13.5. *P300 prototypes for channels P7 and P8*

Finally, we consider the effectiveness of the xDAWN method and present some of its limitations of the method. xDAWN appears to be ineffective from the moment it involves *cross-session* or *cross-subject* classification. In effect, the weight attributed to the channels depends directly on the level of noise present on canals. As a result, noisier channels are assigned low coefficients. The noise level is partly related to the way the electrodes have been placed on the scalp, their impedance and to other practical factors that vary from one session to another. Since the coefficients calculated by xDAWN are fixed, it is unlikely that a filter for one session will be optimal for the next session. New methods based on geometry information prove to be more robust against this type of situation.

13.2. Illustration of a P300 virtual keyboard

In this section, we present the tools available in OpenViBE to perform a classification of the evoked potentials, using the methods discussed in the previous section. The reader will thus be able to apply these methods with the data set available at the webpage http://openvibe.inria.fr/brain-computer-interface-book/. Finally, we present how the detection of P300 waves can be employed to build interactive applications such as the P300 virtual keyboard.

13.2.1. *Detection of P300 with OpenViBE*

OpenViBE provides access to tools which allow for the implementation of a signal processing chain for the classification of evoked potentials such as the P300, by making use of individual processing boxes that can be connected to one another. For the classification of the P300, the chain represented in Figure 13.6 is composed of:

– a fifth-order Butterworth bandpass filter (1–20 Hz);

– an xDAWN spatial filter;

– an LDA classifier.

It is necessary to calculate the parameters of the xDAWN spatial filter and the LDA classifier in advance in order to be able to use them in the signal processing chain. To this end, a calibration phase is carried out. In the context of the P300 speller, the subject is required to focus on the keyboard letters that are indicated in advance. A training dataset is thus constituted and the class of signals windows that it comprises, target or non-target. The signals that are acquired during this calibration phase are stored in a file. These signals are accompanied with event markers that indicate the exact time of each flashing of the letters, and a value reflecting whether this flash contains the letter stared at by the subject, thus constituting a label for the target versus non-target classification. These signals can then be utilized to compute parameters of the xDAWN spatial filter and the classifier. The two scenarios represented in Figure 13.8 allow reading of the recorded signals from the file and the calculation of the parameters. One of them computes the parameters of the xDAWN filter, and must be executed first; the other makes it possible to compute the parameters of the classifier and must be executed second because the latter requires the parameters of the xDAWN filter to operate.

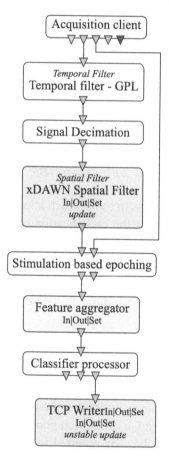

Figure 13.6. *OpenViBE processing chain for the detection of the P300*

The dataset made available (calibration.gdf) which was acquired during a calibration phase, can be utilized directly to compute the parameters of the xDAWN spatial filter and the classifier. Different metrics can be observed in the OpenViBE *logs* allowing evaluation of the effectiveness of the chain to classify the P300 waves, such as cross-validation. We are also giving the reader the possibility of accessing a modified version of the recording scenario represented on the left of Figure 13.7, which allows signals recorded in the format.gdf be read. The reader can also visualize the average evoked potentials in the electrode Pz, thus illustrated in Figure 13.7.

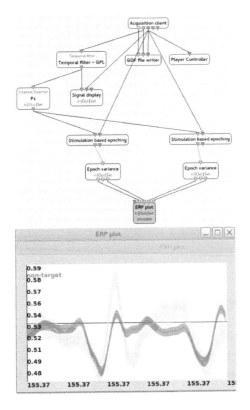

Figure 13.7. *Recording and visualization of averages and variances. Top: OpenViBE scenario for the recording and the online display of the average and the variance of the target and non-target signals. Bottom: Visualization of target and non-target evoked potentials in Pz by means of OpenViBE. The thickness of the line represents the variance of the noise at each point*

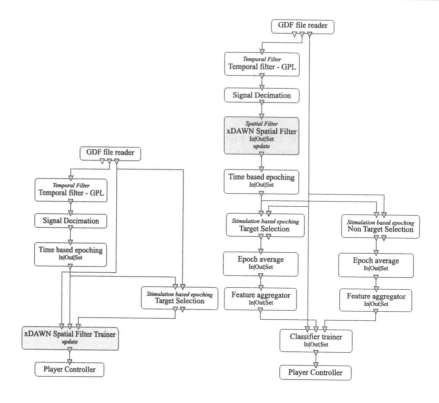

Figure 13.8. *OpenViBE scenarios involved in the detection of P300 waves. Left: Training scenario of the xDAWN spatial filter. Right: Training scenario of the LDA classifier*

13.2.2. *Implementation of a P300 speller*

The detection of P300 waves can be employed to build interactive applications such as a P300 virtual keyboard (or *P300 Speller*). Such a system relies on the combination of different elements described hereafter:

– a signal processing chain, including the acquisition of the signals and real-time classification, using OpenViBE;

– an external application displaying stimuli, interpreting the results of the classification by OpenViBE, and responsible for the interaction with the user.

The display of stimuli consists of briefly flashing certain letters on the virtual keyboard presented to the subject, as illustrated in Figure 13.9.

Figure 13.9. *P300 speller. The letter upon which the subject must focus her attention is the letter L. The stimulus illustrated in this figure is thus supposed to generate a P300 response*

The signals are acquired and classified by OpenViBE, which gives on output a value estimating the probability of a P300 occurring after each stimulation. This value is communicated to the external application via TCP/IP, allowing it to determine, after a certain number of flashes, the letter observed by the subject.

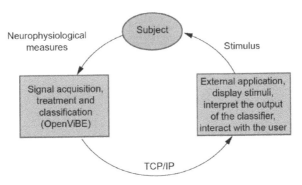

Figure 13.10. *Interaction between the different elements of the system*

Figure 13.10 summarizes the interactions between the different elements of the brain–computer interface system. The external application can be a P300 virtual keyboard or any other application, such as a video game, making use of the neurophysiological signals classification as a means of interaction.

13.3. Bibliography

[FAR 88] FARWELL L., DONCHIN E., "Talking off the top of your head: toward a mental prosthesis utilizing event-related brain potentials", *Electroencephalography and Clinical Neurophysiology*, vol. 70, no. 6, pp. 510–523, 1988.

[REN 10] RENARD Y., LOTTE F., GIBERT G. *et al.*, "OpenViBE: an open-source software platform to design, test, and use Brain–Computer interfaces in real and virtual environments", *Presence: Teleoperators and Virtual Environments*, vol. 19, no. 1, pp. 35–53, 2010.

[RIV 09] RIVET B., SOULOUMIAC A., ATTINA V. *et al.*, "xDAWN algorithm to enhance evoked potentials: application to Brain-Computer interface", *IEEE Transactions on Biomedical Engineering*, vol. 56, no. 8, pp. 2035 –2043, 2009.

14

Recreational Applications of OpenViBE: Brain Invaders and Use-the-Force

This chapter aims at providing the reader with two examples of open-source brain–computer interface (BCI) games that work with the OpenViBE platform. These two games are "Brain Invaders" and "Use-The-Force!" and are representative examples of two types of BCI: event-related potential (ERP) based BCI and oscillatory activity based BCI. This chapter presents the principle, design and evaluation of these games, as well as how they are implemented in practice within OpenViBE. This aims to provide the interested readers with a practical basis to design their own BCI-based games. These two games are described hereafter.

14.1. Brain Invaders

A P300-based BCI enables the user to successively select symbols among an available set, without relying on any motor command. The symbols can be of any kind, such as alphanumeric characters (for example for spelling) or icons (for example the elements of a menu in a computer application). These BCIs exploit the well-known oddball paradigm, in which an infrequent task-related item (the target symbol) elicits a P300 ERP [WOL 11]. By flashing symbols exhaustively, either one-by-one or in groups, it is possible to

Chapter written by Anton ANDREEV, Alexandre BARACHANT, Fabien LOTTE and Marco CONGEDO.

estimate the probability of each symbol being the one selected by the user. This is achieved by evaluating the P300 elicited by each symbol once it has flashed. The complete set of flashes must be repeated a number of times to obtain reliable ERP estimations by means of trial averaging. The distinctive advantages of P300-based BCIs are that the alphabet (the set of all available symbols) can be large (hundreds of symbols) and that 100% accuracy can in principle be obtained when allowing a sufficient number of repetitions. That is to say, with P300-based BCIs there is a direct trade-off between accuracy and speed of symbol selection. In the context of this chapter, the low transfer rate is not considered a limitation, rather a challenge for the player, along the line of the reasoning in [NIJ 09]. Nonetheless, we aim at video games progressing with a sustained pace. For this reason, we have implemented several improvements over the basic P300 BCI paradigm [CON 11].

Brain Invaders is inspired by the vintage *Space Invaders* game. Like most old-fashioned video game, Brain Invaders proceeds by levels. To finish a level, the user has to destroy a target alien, chosen at random within a grid of 36 aliens and which is indicated by a red circle at the beginning of the level. Aliens may be of different color. The target alien is always red. Aliens move with patterns that are specific to each level. A repetition of flashes consists of 12 flashes of groups of six aliens chosen in such a way that after each repetition each alien has flashed exactly two times. After each repetition, the system assigns to each alien the probability of being the target according to the signal processing and classification method implemented in the OpenViBE platform and destroys the alien with the highest probability. If this alien is the target, the level ends, otherwise this alien is eliminated and another repetition of flashes starts. The process is continued until the target alien is destroyed or until eight non-target aliens have been destroyed, after which another level starts. The current number of attempts per level is indicated by coloring the bullets on the bottom of the screen. During the game, the cumulative score is shown to the player. The points obtained at each level are inversely proportional to the number of repetitions necessary to destroy the target. Figures 14.1(a) and (b) show the welcome screen and simplest level, respectively, in which the aliens move altogether from the left to the right of the screen as in the original game Space Invaders; Figures 14.1(c) and (d) show more complex levels, where aliens move according to elaborated patterns and several distracting aliens are colored green or red, like the target. The flashing time is fixed and should be set in between 60 and

150 ms. The interstimulus interval is randomly drawn from an exponential distribution with mean 100 ms and bounded in the range of 20–500 ms by drawing a random number until it falls in this range. The destruction is almost instantaneous after the last flash. Then, a 2s break is allowed to relax and move freely, after which the new level starts. One game session is composed of 12 levels.

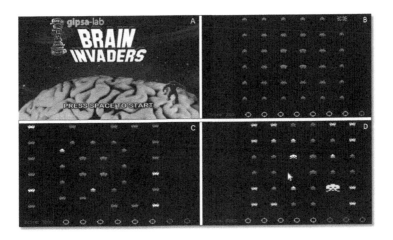

Figure 14.1. *Screenshots of Brain Invaders user interface*

14.1.1. *Results*

We present several results issued from an extensive evaluation of Brain Invaders performed at GIPSA-lab in Grenoble. Twenty-four subjects performed one session of Brain Invaders. Seven of these subjects performed seven more sessions, twice a week, for a total of eight sessions. Each session consisted of two runs of Brain Invaders, one using the typical training-test procedure (non-adaptive mode) and the other without any training using an initialization and an adaptation scheme (adaptive mode). In the non-adaptive mode, the BCI is trained in a training session and the training is used to calibrate the classifiers to be used in the test session. In the adaptive mode, the BCI is initialized with a training obtained on a user database and then continuously learn from the subject while the subject is playing. The two runs looked exactly identical to the subjects, in that in both cases a training session preceded a test session; however, the training session was not used for calibration in the adaptive mode. The order of the two runs was randomized and the design was double-blinded; at any time neither the subject nor the experimenter could know in what mode the BCI was running. Data were acquired with a Porti amplifier (TMSi, The Netherlands) using 16 electrodes positioned at Fp1, Fp2, Afz, F5, F6, T7, Cz, T8, P7, P3, Pz, P4, P8, O1, Oz, O2, referenced by the amplifier to a hardware common average, using a cephalic ground and sampled at 512 Hz. In online operation and for offline analysis, EEG data were band-pass filtered in the range of 1–20 Hz and downsampled to 128 Hz.

We present both some online results and offline results, the latter in order to compare the Riemannian minimum distance to mean (MDM) classifier [CON 2013], which is used by Brain Invaders, with two popular state of the art algorithms [LOT 07]: xDAWN [RIV 11] and the stepwise linear discriminant analysis (SWLDA) [FAR 88]. For xDAWN, the two most discriminant spatial filters were retained. EEG data were then spatially filtered, decimated to 32 Hz and vectorized so as to classify the obtained 32 × 2 features with a regularized linear discriminant analysis, using an automatic setting of the regularization parameter [LED 04, VID 09]. For the SWLDA, EEG data were decimated to 32 Hz and vectorized so as to feed the classifier with the obtained 32 × 16 features.

We begin by presenting several offline results of the performance pertaining to the non-adaptive mode, including the classic training-test setting and the cross-subject and cross-session initialization comparing several classifiers. We also present the online results obtained in the adaptive and non-adaptive mode. These latter results are the most relevant as they report the actual performance achieved by the Riemannian MDM algorithm in real operation. All performance results for this experiment are reported in terms of area under the curve (AUC).

14.1.2. *Offline results: "classic" training-test mode*

Figure 14.2 shows the grand average (seven subjects × eight sessions) AUC accuracy criterion for the three classification methods obtained training the classifiers on the training run and testing on the test run ("Classic" column). Paired *t*-tests revealed that the mean AUC obtained by the MDM is significantly greater than the mean AUC obtained by the SWLDA method ($t_{(55)} = 3.377$, $P = 0.001$) and equivalent to the mean AUC obtained by xDAWN.

14.1.3. *Offline results: cross-subject initialization*

These results are obtained using a leave-one-out method. Figure 14.2 shows the grand average (seven subjects $\times$ eight sessions) AUC accuracy criterion for the three classification methods obtained when training the classifiers on the test data of all subjects excluding the one on which the performance are computed ("Cross-subject" column). As compared to the classic mode, the average AUC with cross-subject transfer learning is significantly lower for all classification methods ($P < 0.002$ for all of them). This is an expected result as no information at all about the subject actually using the BCI is provided to the classifiers. Paired *t*-tests comparing the average performance of the three classification methods in the cross-subject mode reveal that the average AUC obtained by the MDM is marginally higher than the average AUC obtained by the SWLDA ($t_{(55)} = 1.676$, $P = 0.099$) and by xDAWN ($t_{(55)} = 1.755$, $P = 0.085$).

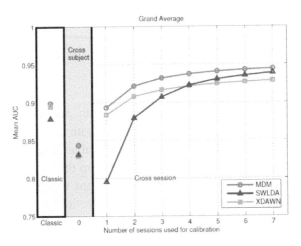

Figure 14.2. *Classic (training-test), cross-subject and cross-session offline AUC performance for the P300-based Brain Invaders BCI experiment. Results are the grand average of seven subjects playing eight sessions of Brain Invaders*

14.1.4. *Offline results: cross-session initialization*

These results are also shown in Figure 14.2 ("cross-session" column). The mean AUC is obtained by initializing the classifier with any possible combination of S number of sessions among the eight available sessions and testing on the remaining 8-S sessions. The results are given for S in the range of 1–7 and correspond to the average of all subjects and all combinations (whose number depends on S). The MDM algorithm proves superior both in the rapidity of learning from previous subject's data and in the performance attained for all values of S, although for $S = 7$ the performance of the SWLDA approaches the performance of MDM. Note that xDAWN, which is a spatial filter approach, performs fairly well even when only one session is available for training, but its performance grows slowly as more data are available for training. This is because the spatial filter is influenced negatively by the difference in electrode placements across sessions and, in general, by all factors that may change from one session to the other. On the other hand, the SWLDA classifier performs poorly when only one session is available for training; however, it learn fast as the number of available sessions increase. This is because the SWLDA, being a "hard machine learning" approach, tends to perform well only when a lot of training data are available. So, xDAWN possesses fast learning capabilities, but lacks good transfer learning, while the opposite holds for SWLDA. The MDM algorithm possesses both desirable properties.

14.1.5. *Online results: adaptation*

Finally, we show the actual online results for the adaptive and non-adaptive mode of functioning. Let us reiterate that the adaptive and non-adaptive runs were performed in a double-blinded fashion and randomized order. In online operation, starting from the second repetition the MDM uses the cumulated distance of all repetitions to select the alien with the highest probability. Hence, the number of repetitions needed to destroy the target (NRD) is a direct measure of performance: the lower the NRD, the higher the performance. The generic classifier is calibrated using online data from the preceding sessions. The individual classifier is trained in a supervised way (the labels are known) during the experiment after each repetition. Of course, the current repetition (used to select the target) is added to the training set only after the classification output is used in order to avoid biasing the results. The weights of the initial classifier (generic) based on a database and the classifier training online on the subject while s/he is playing (individual) are set according to the current number of repetitions, that is the individual classifier is weighted as alpha = min(1, Nrep/40) and the generic classifier as (1-alpha); in this way, the generic classifier is not used anymore after 40 repetitions. This value has been set arbitrarily based on pilot studies.

Figure 14.3 shows the mean and standard deviation NRD as a function of levels for the first session performed by all 24 subjects. As we can see, the non-adaptive MDM features a non-significant negative slope ($P = 0.087$), meaning constant performance across levels, whereas the adaptive MDM features a significantly negative slope (p=0.009), meaning that the performance increases as the algorithm learns from the data of the subject. This result shows that the adaptation is effective in leading the user toward good performances.

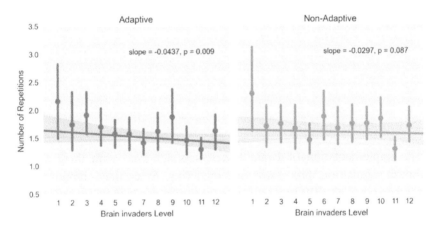

Figure 14.3. *Adaptation results. Mean (disks) and standard deviation (bars) number of repetitions necessary for destroying the target (NRD) for the 24 subjects across the 12 levels of the first session of Brain Invaders, for the adaptive run (left) and the non-adaptive run (right). On top of the plots is printed the slope of the means and its P-value for the two-tailed test of the slope being significantly different from zero*

Figure 14.4 shows the histogram and percent cumulative distribution of the NRD for all 24 subjects and all 12 levels of Brain Invaders game. The cumulative distribution at the third repetition is 94.44% for the non-adaptive mode and 95.49% for the adaptive mode, that is to say on the average of all levels and subjects about 95% of the times three or less repetitions suffice to destroy the target. These results demonstrate that our adaptive system without calibration yields performances equivalent to the traditional system with calibration, already at the first session.

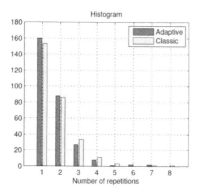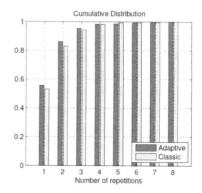

Figure 14.4. *Comparison of the performance of the adaptive and non-adaptive BCI as a function of the number of repetitions. Raw histogram (left) and percent cumulative distribution (right) of the number of repetitions necessary to destroy the target (NRD) for all 24 subjects and all 12 levels of the first session of Brain Invaders game*

14.2. Implementation

The implementation of Brain Invaders is achieved with three software modules: acquisition, processing and rendering. Since they communicate to each other via a TCP/IP protocol, they may run on a single computer or on distinct computers in any combination:

– *acquisition*: this is the OpenViBE acquisition server [REN 2010]. It is in charge of acquiring the data from the EEG machine, streaming the data, correcting for possible amplifiers drifts and sending the data to the OpenViBE platform [REN 10] (http://openvibe.inria.fr/) for analysis;

– *processing*: the OpenViBE platform performs data analysis online. At the end of each repetition, it computes the probability of each alien being the target and sends to the rendering application the indices of the alien with the highest probability;

– *rendering*: a dedicated application serves as user interface. The classification results computed by OpenViBE are sent to this application using a VRPN network protocol. Once the result is received in the form of a selected alien, the alien is destroyed on the screen.

14.2.1. *Artifact management*

As an option, Brain Invaders can continuously receive control values from OpenViBE (through a VRPN network protocol). These values can be used for online EEG artifact monitoring. Upon reception of a signal flagging the presence of an excessive EEG artifact, we can freeze Brain Invaders application, display a pause message and wait until a continue signal is received (no EEG artifact is present). We have implemented an online artifact monitoring using the Riemannian Potato method [BAR 2013]. In practice, we do not use this feature as pausing the game is annoying for the subject. As a matter of fact, the Riemannian MDM method is very efficient, thus its functioning in the presence of small artifacts encountered routinely in real-life experimental sessions is satisfactory.

14.2.2. *Brain Invaders in OpenViBE*

Figure 14.5 shows the workflow implemented in OpenViBE for running Brain Invaders in adaptive mode. The EEG signal is first filtered in the band-pass region (1–20 Hz) using the OpenViBE's *Temporal filter – GPL* box. Then, it is downsampled with a factor of 4 from 512 to 128 Hz because of the *signal decimation* box. The *target* and *non-target* boxes accept as inputs the EEG signal and the triggers. The first uses only triggers that correspond to a flashing group containing the target alien, while the second uses only triggers that correspond to flashing groups not including the target alien. Both boxes output 1 s epochs of EEG starting at flashing onset (the ERPs) that is provided as input. The *adaptive MDM* box performs the adaptive classification (the mix of generic and individual classifier as previously explained). The box outputs a decision, that is the alien to be destroyed, which is sent via the *VRPN server* box to Brain Invaders rendering application. The MDM box is implemented in the language Python. Two more OpenViBE boxes exist: *Train MDM* and *Process MDM*. These two boxes are the non-adaptive versions of the *MDM box* (Figure 14.5). For example, they can be used for motor imagery with five movements.

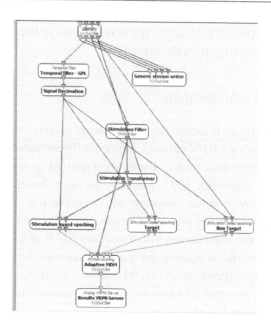

Figure 14.5. *Screenshot of the OpenViBE scenario for running Brain Invaders in adaptive mode*

An additional application called "Brain Invaders Launcher" is also provided. This application configures Brain Invaders and OpenViBE and starts the two automatically for user convenience. The application allows the user to define a certain number of important runtime parameters.

14.2.3. *Notes on technical issues*

The implementation of P300 BCI-based video games encounters a number of difficulties, the most important one being the *drift* problem. The drift refers to the fact that at least two clocks are involved in the implementation of a BCI-based video game: the clock of the computer running the user interface (and possibly tagging the data) and the clock of the EEG amplifier. The differences between the paces of the two clocks accumulates over time and results in a larger and larger time difference. In order to tag the EEG data to know the exact stimulation time (when the symbols are flashing), we need to mark the EEG sample corresponding to stimulus onset. This is then needed to extract the (time-locked) event-related potential generated by the stimulus.

Sending a flash command to the screen and tagging the EEG data stream cannot be executed at the same time. The difference between the two should be as small as possible, but, above all, should be as constant as possible from tag to tag. Also, the time interval between the moment the command is sent and the moment the monitor actually displays the flashes is variable, especially on LCD monitors. The best way to verify the precision of the tagging is to use a light diode stuck on the screen and compare the time difference between the actual flash onset as seen by the diode and the time of the tagging command. The variability of the tag timestamp is known as the jitter phenomenon. The larger the jitter, the lower the signal-to-noise ratio of averaged ERP and the lower the classification accuracy achievable by the BCI. There are two possible ways to perform data tagging, named here "Hardware Tagging" and "Software Tagging". In Hardware Tagging, the computer running the user interface sends via parallel port a trigger (a sort of message) to the EEG machine at the moment of the stimulus presentation. The EEG machine synchronizes the trigger with the flow of incoming EEG data. This type of tagging is very precise (error $= \pm 2$ ms in our testing and negligible jitter). Drift is not of concern when Hardware Tagging is used, so the overall jitter is very low in this case. In Software Tagging, tags are sent internally (by software) from the user interface application to the EEG data acquisition server application (for example the OpenViBE Acquistion Server). Software Tagging has the advantage of not requiring a cable connection from the rendering application to the EEG machine and of working with any computer and EEG machine, however the overall jitter is much larger (tens of milliseconds on the average at the best according to our tests). When using software tagging the drift problems must be addressed very carefully. In OpenViBE, drift can be corrected with the built-in functionality of the OpenViBE AS called "Drift correction". Unfortunately, the current implementation of the drift correction does not work satisfactorily for all EEG amplifiers. Thus, testing of the drift for the available EEG hardware is a mandatory step if software tagging is used.

14.3. Use-The-Force!

The second OpenViBE-based video game that we present in this chapter is the game entitled "Use-The-Force!", a game that comes with the OpenViBE platform. The game environment corresponds to the inside of a "Star Wars^{TM}" mother ship, in which the player can see a virtual spaceship, namely a

Tie-Fighter (see Figure 14.6). The purpose of the game is to lift the Tie-Fighter up by using the BCI. This task establishes an analogy between the use of the BCI and the use of "the Force" in the Star Wars^{TM} movie. As such, the application was named "Use-The-Force!". More precisely, the player can lift the Tie-Fighter up by imagining or executing foot movements, those being recognized by the BCI system. The Tie-Fighter is lifted-up at a speed and height proportional to the strength of the beta event related synchronization (ERS, see Chapters 3 and 4 from Volume 1) a.k.a. Beta rebound, following the end of the real or imagined foot movement [PFU 1999]. This BCI, its design and properties as well as its OpenViBE implementation are described below.

Figure 14.6. *A user playing with an early prototype of the "Use-The-Force" game, in an immersive virtual reality room ((c)Hubert Raguet/Photothèque CNRS) [LOT 08]*

14.3.1. *The BCI system*

The BCI used for "Use-The-Force!" is a simple self-paced one. It is based on a single EEG channel (either monopolar or Laplacian), located at position Cz and, as mentioned above, aims at detecting a beta ERS, appearing posterior to the real or imagined foot movement. To detect this postmovement beta ERS, a single band power feature is extracted in the beta band (16–24 Hz) for the last second of data. This feature is extracted every 100 ms and the last four consecutive features are averaged (with a moving average) in order to produce a smooth control signal (CS).

To detect the beta ERS, and hence, the foot movement, based on the resulting CS, we use a simple threshold Th. If the computed CS is higher than this threshold Th, a foot movement is detected (intentional control state) and a command is sent to the application. If the CS is lower than the threshold Th, the non-control state is detected and no command is sent to the application. This design enables the user to control the BCI in a self-paced way. The value of Th is simply determined according to the mean μ and standard deviation σ of a CS epoch obtained while the subject is in a resting state, according to the equation Th = $\mu+3\sigma$. This threshold determination procedure is similar to the one used in another virtual reality application based on BCI [LEE 07]. It should be noted that Th is determined without using any example of real or imagined foot movement. As such, this BCI does not learn the mental state to be detected.

14.3.1.1. *Evaluation*

A first, simple version of the game was evaluated with 21 naive subjects in a challenging situation: a first-time session, using a single EEG electrode (no Laplacian filter), and during a public exhibition [LOT 08]. Results showed that, without training, half the subjects could control the game by using real foot movements. A quarter of the subjects could control the spaceship by using imagined foot movements. The results of subjective questionnaires filled out following the system's use showed that the whole application appeared enjoyable and motivating to the users.

A more recent version of the game uses more electrodes, namely electrodes FCz, C1, Cz, C2 and CPz to build a Laplacian derivation over Cz, which leads to improved performances. While this new setup has not been formally evaluated, informal observations suggest that about 90% of naive users could control the spaceship using real foot movement and more than 50% of them using imagined movements.

14.3.2. *Implementation with OpenViBE*

In order to design the "Use-The-Force!" BCI game with OpenViBE, two scenarios are necessary: a first scenario to calibrate the BCI, that is to identify the value of the threshold Th to use to detect the postmovement Beta rebound, and a second scenario to detect this beta rebound online and interact with the three-dimensional (3D) game.

The first scenario is represented in Figure 14.7. It aims at instructing the user to start a resting phase, according to a sound being played and a picture representing a relaxing landscape being displayed, and to measure the mean and standard deviation of the beta band power of this user in electrode Cz (ideally after Laplacian filtering). The threshold to detect the beta rebound is then computed as the mean of the beta band power at rest plus three times its standard deviation. The instructions to the user are created using the *Lua Stimulator* box to send OpenViBE stimulations indicating the beginning and end of the rest period, and the *sound player* and *display cue image* boxes that will play the sound and display the image instructing the user to start/stop resting. The beta band power in Cz was computed with the *channel selector* and *spatial filter* boxes to apply first a Laplacian filter, then the *temporal filter* box to band-pass filter the data in the 16–24 Hz band (the beta band), then the *time-based epoching* (to extract 1 s long time windows), *simple DSP*, *signal average* and *epoch average* boxes, to square the signal, average it over the 1 s time window and average it again over the last four time windows, respectively (to smooth the signal).

The online scenario is displayed in Figure 14.8. It uses the same boxes as the calibration scenario to compute the smoothed beta band power over Laplacian channel Cz. It uses new boxes though, to first apply the computed threshold Th to the beta band power. This is done by cropping the signal below the threshold value (that is every band power lower than the threshold value will be set to 0) using the *crop* box, and shifting it by subtracting the threshold from the resulting signal using the *simple DSP* box. In this way, the resulting signal – the control signal – will be zero when the beta band power is below the threshold, and positive when it is over the threshold, that is when a beta rebound is detected. This CS is then transmitted to the actual 3D application, using the VRPN protocol. As for "Brain Invaders", the rendering of the game is done in an external application, not part of OpenViBE (although in the case of the "Use-The-Force!" game, this external application is provided with the OpenViBE platform). The OpenViBE designer thus communicates with this external application via VRPN, by sending stimulations (instructions) to this application using the *button VRPN server* box, which sends button press or button release events according to the received OpenViBE stimulations, and the *analog VRPN server*, which sends a continuous value to the application, in this case, the CS. On its side, the rendering application moves the spaceship according to the CS it receives via the analog VRPN protocol: if the received CS is zero, the spaceship does not move; if it is positive, the spaceship is lifted from the ground up to an height proportional to the CS. The higher the CS, and thus the bigger the Beta rebound, the higher the spaceship is raised.

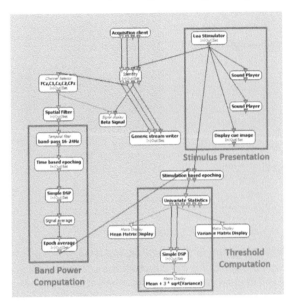

Figure 14.7. *OpenViBE scenario to calibrate the "Use-The-Force!" game, that is, to compute a threshold on the beta band power of the user, defined as the mean of this beta power at rest plus three times its standard deviation. The scenario also includes stimuli (pictures and sounds) to instruct the user when to start and stop resting so that the threshold can be computed*

14.3.3. *Conclusion on Use-The-Force!*

The Use-The-Force! BCI-based game is a simple and easy to setup BCI-game based on oscillatory EEG activity. While its gameplay value is limited, it is an interesting and practical demonstration of a BCI-based video game, and therefore a useful starting point to build more advanced and complex BCI games.

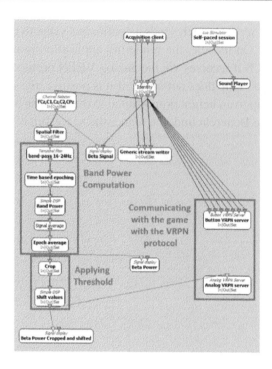

Figure 14.8. *OpenViBE scenario to run the actual "Use-The-Force!" game, after it is calibrated. This scenario computes the beta band power of the user in the Laplacian Cz channel, thresholds it to detect a possible beta rebound following executed or imagined foot movement, and transmits the resulting command to an external 3D application (rendering and animating the spaceship) using the VRPN protocol*

14.4. Conclusions

In this chapter, we have presented two examples of BCI-based video games: "Brain Invaders" and "Use-The-Force!". We have described their principle, design and characteristics, as well as their implementation with OpenViBE.

"Brain Invaders" and "Use-The-Force!" exploit two different types of brain signals and thus two different kinds of BCI: ERP-based BCI and oscillatory activity (that is ERD/ERS) based BCI. As such, we hope that they will provide the readers with a useful and potentially inspiring basis to design new and more advanced BCI games. Regarding "Brain Invaders", our development is open source and available at: https://bitbucket.org/toncho11/openvibe-gipsa- extensions. The "Use-The-Force!" game is delivered with the OpenViBE installer and/or source code, that is it is also free and open source like OpenViBE.

14.5. Bibliography

[ALL 03] ALLISON B.Z., PINEDA J.A., "ERPs evoked by different matrix sizes: implications for a brain computer interface (BCI) system", *IEEE Transactions on Neural Systems and Rehabilitation Engineering*,vol. 11, no. 2, pp. 110–113, 2003.

[BAR 13] BARACHANT A., ANDREEV A., CONGEDO M., "The Riemannian potato: an automatic and adaptive artifact detection method for online experiments using Riemannian geometry", *Proceedings of the TOBI Workshop IV*, Sion, Switzerland, 2013.

[CON 13] CONGEDO M., EEG Source Analysis, HDR presented at Doctoral School EDISCE, University of Grenoble, 2013.

[CON 13] CONGEDO M., BARACHANT A., ANDREEV A., "A new generation of Brain-Computer interface based on Riemannian geometry", arXiv:1310.8115, 2013.

[CON 11] CONGEDO M., GOYAT M., TARRIN N. *et al.*, "Brain Invaders: a prototype of an open-source P300-based video game working with the OpenViBE platform", *Proceedings of the 5th International BCI Conference*, Graz, Austria, pp. 280–283, 2011.

[FAR 88] FARWELL L.A., DONCHIN E., "Talking off the top of your head: toward a mental prosthesis utilizing event-related brain potentials", *Electroencephalography and Clinical Neurophysiology*, vol. 70, pp. 510–523, 1988.

[GIB 08] GIBERT G., ATTINA V., MATTOUT J. *et al* "Size enhancement coupled with intensification of symbols improves P300 Speller accuracy", *4th International Brain-Computer Interface Workshop and Training Course*, Graz, Austria, 2008.

[JIN 11] JIN J., ALLISON B.Z., SELLERS E.W. *et al.*, "Optimized stimulus presentation patterns for an event-related potential EEG based brain-computer interface", *Medical & Biological Engineering & Computing*, vol. 49, no. 2, pp. 181–191, 2011.

[LEE 07] LEEB R., FRIEDMAN D., MUELLER-PUTZ G.R. *et al.*, "Self-paced (asynchronous) BCI control of a wheelchair in Virtual Environments: a case study with a tetraplegic", *Computational Intelligence and Neuroscience*, 2007.

[LED 04] LEDOIT O., WOLF M., "A well-conditioned estimator for large-dimensional covariance matrices", *Journal of Multivariate Analysis*, vol. 88, pp. 365–411, 2004.

[LOT 07] LOTTE F., CONGEDO M., LÉCUYER A. *et al.*, "A review of classification algorithms for EEG-based brain-computer interfaces", *Journal of Neural Engineering*, vol. 4, no. 2, pp. R1–R13, 2007.

[LOT 08] LOTTE, F., RENARD, Y., LÉCUYER, A. "Self-paced Brain-Computer interaction with virtual worlds: a qualitative and quantitative study out-of-the-lab", *4th International Brain-Computer Interface Workshop and Training Course*, Graz, Austria, pp. 373–378, 2008.

[NIJ 09] NIJHOLT A., BOS D.P.O., REUDERINK B., "Turning shortcomings into challenges: Brain-Computer interfaces for games, *Entertainment Computing*, vol. 1, no. 2, pp. 85–94, 2009.

[PFU 99] PFURTSCHELLER G., DA SILVA F.H.L., "Event-related EEG/MEG synchronization and desynchronization: basic principles", *Clinical Neurophysiology*, vol. 110, pp. 1842–1857, 1999.

[REN 10] RENARD Y., LOTTE F., GIBERT G. *et al.*, "OpenViBE: an open-source software platform to design, test and use Brain-Computer interfaces in real and virtual environments", *Presence: Teleoperators and Virtual Environments*, vol. 19, no. 1, pp. 35–53, 2010.

[RIV 09] RIVET B., SOULOUMIAC A., ATTINA V. *et al.*, "xDAWN algorithm to enhance evoked potentials: application to brain-computer interface", *IEEE Transactions on Biomedical Eng ineering*, vol. 56, no. 8, pp. 2035–43, 2009.

[TOW 10] TOWNSEND G., LAPALLO B.K., BOULAY C.B. *et al.*, "A novel P300-based brain-computer interface stimulus presentation paradigm: moving beyond rows and columns", *Clinical Neurophysiology*, vol. 121, no. 7, pp. 1109–1120, 2010.

[VID 09] VIDAURRE C., KRÄMER N., BLANKERTZ B. *et al.*, "Time domain parameters as a feature for EEG-based brain computer interfaces", *Neural Networks*, vol. 22, pp. 1313–1319, 2009.

[WOL 11] WOLPAW J., WOLPAW E.W., *Brain-Computer Interfaces: Principles and Practice*, Oxford University Press, Oxford, 2011.

PART 4

Societal Challenges and Perspectives

15

Ethical Reflections on Brain–Computer Interfaces

The general objective of Brain–Computer Interfaces (BCIs) is to interface our central nervous system (CNS) with artificial systems to restore lost functions following a disease or an accident. Since the CNS is generally understood as the most intimate seat of thought, consciousness, and of personality, this area of research raises fundamental ethical issues.

To what extent do the possible applications of BCI systems of today belong to reality or fiction? Who can benefit from these technologies and for what purpose? Where should the border be situated between rehabilitation and performance enhancement? For what applications are invasive implants justifiable? How should the hope aroused in patients awaiting for new technologies be managed? What are the problems related to the safety and the security of BCIs? Can legal consequences from their use be expected and anticipated? From a fundamental point of view, can BCIs modify the identity of a person? In the long term, can they lead to a redefinition of the human species?

This debate has traditionally been at the citizen initiative, either through the media, or through actions of organizations. Here, the opportunity is given to

Chapter written by Florent BOCQUELET, Gaëlle PIRET, Nicolas AUMONIER and Blaise YVERT.

researchers to present their own reflection on their research in order to share their thoughts not only with their colleagues, but also with the general public.

The objective of this chapter is not to make judgments on any particular development or study but to raise a number of questions (about animals, about human beings, about the human species) that seem important to bear in mind when conducting research, in order to include them in a responsible process with regards to society and human beings in general.

15.1. Introduction

BCIs are an emerging technology that aim to establish a direct communication between the brain and a computer or a machine in order to directly control effectors, objects or software from thoughts [CHA 99, BIR 99, WES 00, SER 02, HOC 06, HOC 12, COL 13]. These approaches thus offer a new interaction mode between living individuals and machines, which contrasts with those commonly used today such as touch or vocal modes.

With neuroprosthetics, the objective of BCIs is to interface the CNS with arrays of electrodes or sensors allowing recording of neuronal activity and/or delivering controlled electrical stimulations to the CNS to recover of a function. These systems can be developed at different scales (from microscopic to macroscopic) depending on the chosen interfacing level (from microelectrodes interfacing individual cells to macroelectrodes recording wider populations, or even whole cortical areas). It is thus possible to distinguish between non-invasive interfaces – based on electroencephalography, magnetoencephalography or even functional magnetic resonance imaging – and invasive interfaces requiring the implantation of micro- or macroscopic electrodes in the CNS.

These technologies are developed for multiple purposes, which can be divided into three families. The first group is that of clinical applications. It includes the majority of studies currently undertaken that aim to propose new therapeutic routes in the case of sensory or motor disabilities or neurodegenerative diseases [for example BEN 91, RAU 02, MAR 02, HOC 06, GUE 09]. The second family is that of fundamental research employing these technologies as a means to explore in a novel manner the functioning of the CNS, for example adaptation, plasticity and learning processes involved when using a BCI system [FET 69, CAR 03, GAN 09, GAN 11, JAC 06, FET 07, MOR 08, SAC 12, ENG 13] or neurofeedback processes [LAC 07, MER 14]. Finally, the third family includes the applications not included in fundamental research nor in clinical research, such as military applications [TEN 12], or even consumer applications such as the game and recreation industry [CON 11, BON 13] (see also Chapters 5 and 14).

It seems now quite likely that, within several years, these technologies will have more and more applications, that they will become available on the market and thus impact our society. Although the consequences of these technologies on our society remain difficult to predict, several questions can be formulated on ethical, legal, political, economic, philosophical, moral and religious levels[1].

Ethical reflection cannot remain silent before the multiple goals that are assigned to BCIs [VEL 12], as it aims at providing tools to discern the right choices of a scientific approach.

Whatever the reasons that scientists would wish to use to justify their actions, the role of ethics very generally looks like it consists of accompanying the emergence of novelty, of challenging it, but also of alerting us of its possible risks. The reflection can be conducted in parallel or jointly, by the developers of these technologies, the experts in ethical issues, the end-users of these technologies, or the citizens in general. An interactive multidisciplinary reflection, even if difficult to implement, is likely to be the most fruitful.

In all cases, an ethical argumentation method is required. Several methods are available and a large number of authors compete against each other. Nowadays, whereas in applied ethics discussions may focus on what is good or not, in moral philosophy discussions rather focus on the arguments that make it possible to justify an ethical choice than on this choice itself [CAN 04].

---

1 See, for instance, the work of the European Parliamentary Technology Assessment (EPTA http://eptanetwork.org) that evaluates the social, economic and environmental impacts of the new technologies being developed.

An agent may indeed wish to justify its action by referring to the good, the duty or the usefulness. Aristotle defines the good and happiness. If the good is thought of as existing objectively, the action should then be directed toward it in order to be considered as good, and the virtuous agent will then have a good chance to be happy. But if we start to doubt the objectivity of the good and, correlatively, happiness, we will perhaps think that it is necessary to rely on a more impartial judge that we will call duty [KAN 85]. Good will, then, is the will that acts under the influence of no particular interest, but by pure duty. To act morally, that is to say by pure duty, we only need to turn toward one's inner self and follow what consciousness, inner but objective, dictates, the point being that everyone perceives the same duty. Yet, if we believe that the indication of a concrete direction is difficult with such a reference to duty, we might wish to turn toward what experienced people deem most useful, to what we like most and affects us the least [MIL 63]. The agent will thus seek to maximize the usefulness for himself, or for him and a group of others, or for him and all other ethical agents, and to minimize everything that may cause uselessness or pain. His decisions will thus seek to maximize a risk/benefits ratio, extended either to himself, or to those that surround him, or to all human beings (anthropo-centered ethics), or to all sentient beings – human beings and animals – (patho-centered ethics), or to all living beings (bio-centered ethics), or to all ecosystems (eco-centered ethics), or yet to our whole planet (geo-centered ethics). The question of the ethics perimeter therefore begins with the answer to the issue of identifying which entities fall under ethical considerability [GOO 78].

It is possible to consider three subjects of ethical questionings associated with BCIs, dealing, respectively, with the animal, human being, and human species. We will try to address at these three levels the various families of BCI technologies: rehabilitation and care solutions for disabled patients, advancement of fundamental research in the understanding of brain mechanisms, and the development of new markets, including consumer products based on more or less invasive BCIs.

15.2. The animal

As BCIs typically require preclinical animal experimentations, research on animals are for many researchers the occasion for a real ethical questioning.

15.2.1. *The fight against pain, suffering and anxiety in animals*

European legislation considers as a value for all European Union (EU) member countries to minimize as far as possible animal pain, suffering and anxiety. Anyone visiting an animal facility today in a state-of-the-art laboratory will be struck by the resemblance between the respect shown toward a patient or a human subject and the respect shown toward an animal: animal facility officials and researchers experimenting with animals place extreme importance on the welfare of animals; the traceability of practical actions on animals is total; the operating room to operate on any rat or any non-human primate under anesthesia assimilates in all respects to an operating room for human beings. Trials on animals are submitted to an ethics committee of animal experimentation, and application files for experimentations on animals may sometimes be thicker than that of applications submitted to ethical committees or committees for the protection of people, which oversee any experimentation on human beings. The remarkable parallelism of the procedures eventually goes hand in hand with the idea that humans and animals are all beings capable of feeling suffering, which should be minimized as much as possible in one and in the other, as stated, among other things, in the new directive of the European Commission[2]. Recently, a manifesto was signed by 24 scholars, entitled "For an evolution of the legal system of the animal in the civil code recognizing its nature as a sentient being".

15.2.2. *Reflection on the difference between human beings and animals*

Since the suffering of animals has been taken into consideration at the same level as that of human beings, the difference between the human being and the animal has no longer the evidence that it had formerly, as if the legitimacy of the former to use the latter is no longer as straightforward as it used to be. Although for a large number of people, death does not have the same meaning for a human as for an animal, as shown, for instance, in the

---

2 Directive 2010/63 of the European Commission enjoins all member countries to restrain the most possible pain, suffering and anguish in animals upon which scientific experiments are carried out, recommendation translated in France by the decree No. 2013-118 of February 1, 2013 relating to the protection of animals used for scientific purposes, amending the rural code.

extremely codified practice of bullfighting for those who are still making sense of it, the decline of the idea that a human life would have to confront the question of transcendence, jointly with the often exclusive domination of sensitivity as a sign of our time, increase the discomfort of the researcher. For example, the researcher practicing an experimental approach leading to the sacrifice of an animal that he had to live with day after day for several weeks may feel some discomfort faced with the lethal procedures that he has to employ, going along with the idea that it is difficult for a sentient being to cause another to suffer for the main benefit of the former. "Why is it him, and not me?", implicitly questions the researcher. Thus, the researcher prepares himself everyday a little more in order to be able to justify, to himself, to the public, and to militants of the animal cause, more or less violent, that it is not possible to expect care or knowledge – knowledge to enable care, or knowledge to understand – without carrying out trials on animals. There are therefore different contexts for justification to be distinguished according to whether the experiments have clearly defined clinical objectives, or objectives not so clearly significant at the time they are performed (the latter being no less paramount, because they benefit both the progress of the knowledge that mankind has of the world with regard to its surroundings, and future medical solutions or protective ones of any living species).

15.2.3. *Animals are not things*

Nevertheless, this does not prevent that a few borderline cases be distinguished. For example, if the animal becomes a simple game, such as the cockroaches that can be controlled to move forward at will in any direction using a box that interacts with a circuit glued on their backs and to which their antennae have been connected[3], what usefulness then justifies this application of BCIs? In this case, human domination is exercised, without any battle honors nor the representation of a metaphysical difference between the animal and the human being, but for the simple leisure industry which, in an ethically questionable manner, transforms animals into toys. Is the usefulness relying on economic and commercial factors relevant in this case? What limits should be enforced to these approaches; that today involve cockroaches or rats [TAL 02], but with nothing to prevent thinking that they may one day involve human beings? Should humans be superior to animals, must their

---

3 Backyard Brains: The RoboRoach.

domination of them, as for the case of domestication, be exerted at the expense of the living nature of animals? Indeed, animals being intelligent and sentient beings [BEK 00, PAU 05, REZ 07, WAR 07], as recently officially recognized in France[4], they should not feel pain or suffering or anxiety when manipulated, and their condition must be respected.

15.3. Human beings

Just like animals, human beings are directly concerned by BCIs, which can have a major impact on their well-being. Numerous ethical questions emerge when considering the use of BCIs, be they invasive or not, and this is particularly so because their applications are still at the research stage, still immature. These questions concern in the first place patients who agree to participate in BCI research protocols.

15.3.1. *Addressing the hope aroused*

Indeed, BCI studies often suggest real prospects for improvement among heavily handicapped patients, for whom there is no other alternative at the moment. Moreover, the sole word improvement may well give rise to many expectancies, some being real and reasonable in the context of a well-proven technique, and some being more distant and limited to future patients, and thus totally unrealistic for the patients participating to a study and hoping for immediate benefits for themselves. It is thus conceivable that caregivers, sometimes still students, may experience discomfort before the wide gap that may exist between the expectation of the patients and what can be offered to them in return for being included in a study designed to test a paradigm, a material, or a hypothesis, not aiming at improving the status of a real person [CLA 06, LID 09]. For health professionals, the challenge posed by this gap consists of knowing how to address the hope encouraged by these new technologies among "expecting" patients, that is in individuals whose state is so serious that they have reached the point to expect everything from medicine, the progress of which is now considered so important that patients

---

4 The French National Assembly has recognized on October 30, 2014, that animals were "sentient living beings", thus aligning the civil code with the penal code and the rural code; the amendment was rejected by the Senate on January 22, 2015, and then confirmed by the National Assembly on January 28, 2015.

tend to put on practitioners the hopes that they once placed in nature or in God's healing. Today doctors are supposed to know, they are supposed to have the power to give patients their health back. In this context, the physician can still choose, following a tempered paternalism, to tell the truth to a sick person or not to tell it, according to what he perceives the patient can or cannot hear, or wants or does not want to hear, and the practitioner then respects any refusal to hear or to know. Addressing this hope becomes even more significant when the effectiveness of non-invasive BCI systems remains limited, and when a choice has to be made to resort or not to a surgery for testing a more invasive system. Although the present results obtained with invasive interfaces offer extremely promising perspectives with a growing number of degrees of freedom that can be controlled simultaneously [HOC 12, IFF 13, WOD 14], they nevertheless remain modest [DIE 10] and great importance is still given to more conventional techniques for the compensation of handicaps using interfaces based on residual movements [BRU 10, PIN 03, TAK 11, TRE 10]. However, these approaches are themselves limited, and the hypothesis currently favored through the development of new generations of BCI systems is that direct interfacing of the SNC in the long run should offer better rehabilitation prospects.

15.3.2. *Risk/benefits ratio*

Any BCI application must be conducted in accordance with the principles of the patients' autonomy, of their informed consent, as well as the practitioners' commitment about the beneficence of their acts, sworn during the oath to respect the code of medical ethics[5,6,7]. In the case of invasive BCIs, for which it is necessary to proceed with a surgical implantation of electrodes in the brain, the primary concern, more or less consciously Hippocratic, is to not harm[8]. It assumes the implementation of a framework for thought analogous to a scale that allows weighing the various expected

---

5 In France: Article R4127-109 of the public health code.

6 Good Medical Practice 2013, http://www.gmc-uk.org/static/documents/content/GMP_.pdf.

7 Directive 2001/20/EC of the European Parliament and of the council of April 4, 2001.

8 The principle of not doing harm is equally defended by those who Ruwen Ogien refers to as maximalists in ethics, and by those (to whom he belongs) who he refers to as minimalists. These minimalists, in order to restrict the increase in the duties that they assimilate to a "moral police" (Mill), agree only on a very small number of ethical principles. In the end, R. Ogien admits only one of them, that of not harming others. He thus excludes the moral duties to oneself and

benefits, and adjusting them with the list of the different damages, inconveniences or only possible risks. This risk-benefit approach is now adopted by ethics committees assessing the relevance of the protocols under consideration. Despite the criticism which argues that a risk/benefit ratio consists of adding terms so radically heterogeneous between themselves as pleasures and pains, converted to positive or negative units, which as such can be added within a sum, the principle of the risk/benefit ratio, originated in utilitarian philosophy, corresponds to the intuition that it should be possible to anticipate the result of an action. This principle, yet logically refuted, thus manages to appear as intuitively true, which it may well be if we do not forget that this is only an approximation. Although a well-controlled surgical procedure, opening a skull comprises significant risks [KOU 15, GRA 05, LEG 13] and thus cannot be intuitively justified unless there is a real prospect for improvement of the patient's condition, which could not be achieved by other means. Immediately, a whole arborization of possible cases becomes available, which strongly complicates the establishment of a positive risk/benefit ratio. At least the intuitive framework remains – if not logically justifiable: we cannot morally accept to open the skull of another human unless the risks being taken are balanced by the prospect of an expected improvement.

15.3.3. *Informed consent and patient involvement*

It may be then tempting for the investigator of a clinical trial to limit descriptions in the fear that no patient will agree to participate in a research protocol, which would have the consequence of slowing it down. Allowing patients to imagine that a purely cognitive trial would be beneficial to them and eventually therapeutic would therefore constitute a form of deceit, whatever the intention, maximizing the omnipotence of the one who knows

---

the positive duties – so-called paternalistic – to others. This minimalism is also what makes him support the decriminalization of the consumption of narcotic drugs and of assisted suicide for those who request it [OGI 07]. It might be objected that it is debatable that consent be the ultimate criterion of morality, and that it would not be possible to harm oneself, and much more, that it is contradictory that consent be the ultimate criterion of morality, and that it would not be possible to harm oneself. Because in order to consent, we should be able to choose, and the choice, in some cases, will focus on what will engage or not the possibility to harm oneself. This implies, by following minimalists, that sometimes the choice or the consent, is not actually one.

but says nothing. Confronted with the large gap that may exist between the aspiration of a patient to participate in a study from which he expects an immediate benefit, and the preparatory question that the researcher aims to solve by advancing into uncharted territory, it thus seems unethical to let patients fantasize about promises greater than those the trial can deliver. This is true even if the fact of explaining to patients that they are considered for a protocol that will not benefit themselves (purely cognitive or therapeutic research protocol with more distant implications for other future patients) will slow down the recruitment of patients in this protocol. The truth of the relationship between physicians and their patients comes at this price. Misleading someone is generally not ethical. Misleading someone who is weakened and trustful appears even worse.

This trustful relationship is even more important where, in the case of invasive interfaces where patients are implanted for an indefinite period, they therefore become a major active participant of the research protocol, whose involvement is central to its success. Indeed, unlike short protocols in which patients are only involved transitorily, when chronically implanted in the long term [HOC 12], their commitment and often that of their family become considerable. As a result, patients become real contributors to the study, especially when they will not benefit directly from a BCI system that remains at a research and development stage.

15.3.4. *Repairing versus replacing*

Another ethical behavior complements the obligation of not doing harm and not deceiving. It consists of trying, whenever possible, to repair instead of trying to replace. In a society where the act of throwing away and replacing supersedes in many situations making the effort to understand where the problem comes from and to repair it, the rehabilitation approaches can also be confronted with this choice: understanding versus reproducing. Although the first option requires investing in fundamental research in order to extract new knowledge that will produce therapeutic results in the long term, the second option, more pragmatic, consists of investing in application research to recover a lost function in a better timeframe. Applicative research often reaches its goals more quickly due to more significant financial investments it can benefit from: the current technological advances, combined with an increasingly accurate observation of life, make it sometimes easier to replace a failing organ than repairing it [ATA 06, MEY 11, RON 11]. For example, some patients who have lost the use of a limb which is still present, have made the choice for it to be amputated and to substitute it with a functional bionic limb [BOW 11, BOW 12]. BCIs are also confronted with this rule. Yet, we can observe an evolution of the rehabilitation approaches that tend to increasingly take advantage of the remaining functional residues of the damaged CNS, and therefore on repairing rather than replacing. For instance, while the first BCI studies for motor rehabilitation used artificial limbs [CHA 99, HOC 12], the works being carried out aim to reconnect several sections of the central and/or peripheral nervous systems by means of recording and stimulation systems in order to reactivate directly the paralyzed limbs by thought [MOR 08, NIS 13]. Eventually, these repair approaches should lead not only to more efficient rehabilitation strategies, since they recycle the residual functional physiology of the body, but also to cheaper approaches than replacement, which requires expensive technological products for the substitution. The avenue to repairing everything is nonetheless still long, and the choice between responding to the patients' emergency and gradually filling the lack of knowledge – even if it means that it may take many years before they will be sufficient to be used in care – remains a broad ethical issue for any scientist aspiring to work for the common good.

15.3.5. *Accessibility of BCIs*

This issue is also linked to the problem of the financial cost of the commercial solutions for rehabilitation. In order to be available for people with disabilities whose financial resources are often limited because of a larger precarity[9] and a smaller salary on average[10], these technologies require low-cost production in the long term. Especially for BCIs, for which some current prototypes are reaching very high costs, this implies that the research being undertaken involves a financial constraint allowing them to become accessible to the greatest number of people for whom they have been originally developed.

---

9 http://www.inegalites.fr/spip.php?page=article&id_article=549.
10 http://www.agefiph.fr/content/download/458673/10310252/.

15.3.6. *Modulating brain activity with BCIs: what are the consequences?*

Several studies suggest that using a BCI system leads to a modification of the neural substrate of the areas involved in the practiced tasks. For example, in macaques, the preferential direction properties of motoneurons of the primary motor cortex appear to have been altered in the long term when learning a specific BCI task [CAR 03, GAN 09, GAN 11]. In humans, neurofeedback allows a subject to see in real time his brain activity, as for example with the BrainTV environment [LAC 07] (see Chapter 4). This methodology makes it possible to envisage in the long run cognitive therapeutic solutions in psychiatry, with which patients can learn to control their brain activity in order to correct their behavioral state [MER 14]. Similarly to the repeated physiotherapy sessions that allow correcting of motor behavior, this kind of approach would eventually enable a mental, social or emotional behavior to be corrected, or even to modify significant personality traits [MER 14]. Beyond the clinical applications, neurofeedback (see Chapter 13 of Volume 1, [CLE 16]) could be used for other purposes, such as improving performance, and in particular attention, at work or in daily life. BCIs may indeed be employed to monitor or even strengthen vigilance states at work [BLA 10], and could help people improve their concentration on repetitive tasks that they are carrying out in a continuous fashion, such as for the security control of luggage in airports [MUL 08]. Depending on the objective, the ethical question of the usefulness of these practices, whose impact may concern people themselves or a third-party beneficiary, can then be raised [VLE 12]. In any case, it seems important that the subject remains free to choose whether or not to participate in these learning protocols.

15.3.7. *Reliability and safety of BCIs*

Given the rapid advances in BCI technologies, it is reasonable to assume that in the relatively near future, they will be parts of the daily lives of patients outside a protective clinical environment. User patients who want to be autonomous in their daily life, will thus need a BCI system which is both safe and reliable.

The system must be safe so as not to be disturbed accidentally or maliciously by the external environment. In addition, BCI systems transmit neural signals reflecting the thoughts and intents of action of their users, who may not wish to see these intimate and personal data being accessed by strangers. Therefore, BCI systems ought to be protected, and this all the more that they will increasingly rely on wireless technologies [GUE 09, BOR 13, MES 14], where data can be more easily intercepted and likely to be disturbed by the external environment. In the event that this security problem needs to be seriously addressed, it is however not specific to BCIs only [MIY 12, FAI 14]. Numerous increasingly "intelligent" objects integrating embedded electronics and control software already occupy a large part of our daily life, including in a clinical context (for examples pacemakers or insulin pumps).

The system must also be reliable in order not to hurt its end-user or those that surround him or her, or even damage its environment. Indeed, neural signals may often be subject to fluctuations, which must be taken into account so as not to produce dangerous commands. This requires robust algorithms constraining the operation of the effector within predetermined limits, and thus limiting the actions that users can produce so that they cannot hurt their surrounding environment.

15.3.8. *Responsibility when using BCIs*

This issue is related to the responsibility involved when using a BCI system: who should be held responsible for an accident caused by means of a BCI system? The user, the designer, or the distributor? This issue already gives rise to discussions that are all the more important given the widening spectrum of possible applications of BCI. There are uncertainties at multiple levels: the machine can incorrectly record or wrongly interpret the brain activity of the subject, but the brain activity of the subject can also be unconscious and not volitional. Subjects may also not fully control how their brain activity is interpreted and transformed into action (as a result of the algorithms being employed), which does not make them totally responsible for the actions that they would perform using a BCI system. Grübler [GRU 11] then observes that, in this case, the moral responsibility may or may not be attributed to users, depending for example on whether the system makes use of the signals that they emit intentionally or unconsciously, or whether the signals are used to initiate an action of the machine or only to modulate the action of a machine already operating. Other authors consider that the responsibility is rather shared between users and the machine, thus leaving a gap of liability where it is not possible to determine who is responsible [LUC 08], while some think the opposite, that modes of standard reflection and pre-existing laws can be applied to the case of BCIs [CLA 09, HAS 09]. However, the usual principle of analysis of the causal chain that consists of identifying whether the error comes from the user or from the machine seems harder to apply in the case of BCIs.

Before these devices are put on the market, some propose to implement certain rules such as the obligation to measure and to assess the reliability of BCIs [GRU 11]: this consists of determining if the error rate impacts only the frustration of users or if the device can cause harm to its users or even to third parties (for instance a BCI able to control a wheelchair that could knock over bystanders). In order to prevent possible accidents, in addition to the certifications asserting the liability of vendors to whom a system will have to be submitted in order to be verified as being safe, the usage of a BCI interface could also be assessed in terms of security by issuing some sort of "license to use" – similar to driving licenses – adapted to each context of usage (home, public places, etc) in order to certify that they really are in control of the actions that they perform through the BCI system and thus assume their responsibility as end-users. In all cases, the legal system should anticipate the emergence of BCIs in our daily lives so as to adapt itself accordingly.

15.4. The human species

Brain–machine interfaces, whose main objective is the rehabilitation of functions in people suffering from severe disabilities, such as simply walking or talking again, remain largely uncommon today. On the other hand, other types of interfaces between man and machine multiply at high speed in our everyday environment: touchscreens, speech or gesture recognition, facial recognition, augmented reality, etc. These non-invasive interfaces have been quickly democratized and integrated by society to the extent that they transform our daily life. Although the scientific limitations (concerned with physics, computer science, technology, or biology) of BCI applications are still huge [DIE 10], it is estimated that their first applications could appear on the market within a few decades [BLA 10, NIJ 13, VEL 12], knowing that this time scale could be easily shortened or lengthened depending on many uncertain parameters (technological locks, scientific discoveries, investors, etc.). In this context, can we expect in the foreseeable future a strong influence of BCIs on the functioning of societies, or even on humanity itself?

15.4.1. *BCIs as bridges between the real and the virtual*

In a context in which society has been highly modified by the ever growing presence of the virtual, gradually brought into everyday life by video gaming, it is interesting to ask oneself the question of the influence that BCIs will, in turn, have on the relationship between humans and real and virtual worlds. Video games and virtual reality systems allow an individual to move from the real world to an imaginary world by means of a keyboard, a touch screen, or virtual reality headsets. Although for some disabled people games offer the possibility of having the same capabilities as the other players, allowing them to reduce their sense of handicap, several studies and news stories have highlighted the drifting risks of these practices, making attractive to the players a life in an alternative virtual and immaterial world devoid of the constraints and communitarian rules of the real world, sometimes to a point where this virtual life becomes preferable to real life and eating or sleeping are neglected[11,12]. Since BCIs create new bridges between the real and the virtual worlds, an ethical question is to know whether they will only strengthen this dematerialization or derealization of life [GUI 11]. These technologies indeed allow to directly transform a mental image into a virtual action, for example by controlling video games from thoughts [CON 11, BON 13].

Nevertheless, by their primary purpose, BCIs mainly allow the transformation of a mental image into a concrete action in the real world by converting an imagined action into an action actually executed by an effector, especially in the case of motor rehabilitation (robotic arm, exoskeleton, computer), but also in the case of some games (see, for example, the games MindFlex and Force Trainer[13]). Thus arises the issue of identifying what applications mankind intends to give to these technologies allowing for a new

---

11 http://www.uqat.ca/blogue/index.php/2013/03/19/addiction-aux-jeux-video-un-reel-danger-aux-multiples-consequences.

12 http://www.huffingtonpost.fr/2012/07/19/addiction-jeux-video-tuer_n_1687034.html.

13 These games use a rudimentary BCI to control the displacement of a ball by thought and are actually already marketed.

mode of control for the real: only for therapy and entertainment, or also to acquire new capabilities [BRU 07, BER 08]?

15.4.2. *BCIs as future means of enhancement?*

Human beings have always sought to explore all the possibilities that were offered to them to increase their capabilities, for example by creating machines extending their abilities (moving quickly, flying, seeing at a distance, etc.), or by resorting to treatments extending their life. The boundary between therapy and enhancement is becoming increasingly blurred. In a world where the cult of performance is ever present, the choice of enhancement is attractive: for example, in the pharmaceutical field, although the majority of drugs aim to heal, for many years some substances have been used for the purpose of improving performance: physical performance, cognitive performance, sexual performance, etc. Surgery once reserved for the medical field is now used for aesthetics. The ever finer knowledge of neurobiological mechanisms also paves the way for the pharmacological improvement of performances [FAR 02]. Other technologies are also used for enhancement: some prostheses become today so efficient that they could allow people using them not only to circumvent their disabilities, but also to surpass and to reach physical performances enhanced and superior to the "norm" [CAM 08].

Because BCIs are still far from reproducing the natural performance of the human body, they have not yet reached a stage allowing a person to be enhanced. However, some works suggest that this is potentially possible. For instance, a recent study shows how sensitivity to infrared light can be introduced in rats through an implanted neuroprosthesis [THO 13]. Other studies in humans suggest that BCI approaches can be used to improve certain cognitive performance such as attention [GOM 14] or short-term memorization [BUR 15]. Let us thus deliberately consider the hypothesis that these technologies could provide, on the long term, significant perspectives of improvement over the faculties that we naturally have. This would impact the military field, where soldiers would improve their efficiency during their missions, but also all individuals eager to surpass themselves in their both private and professional lives. Even if this desire for enhancement for different purposes is not new, the potential of new technologies makes it possible to envisage a rupture of the level of enhancement that is offered. So far this level has been maintained within the limitations, obviously slightly enhanced, of the body. The hybridization of the body with machines opens avenues toward a scaling of enhancement possibilities, which could result in a rethinking of the definition of the human.

15.4.3. *The risk of transhumanism?*

Such prospects feed the hopes of transhumanist movements, which take the idea of human enhancement by technologies to the extreme, by advocating the fusion of man and machine to overcome not only disabilities, pain and diseases, but also any physical limitation of the body, such as aging and death, all being fatalities perceived as unnecessary and unwanted [GOF 15, HOT 15]. To achieve the improvement program of our nature [MOR 99b], two transhumanist pathways can be distinguished [GOF 15, p. 159]: the computing and robotics path [MOR 99a] and the biological path [KUR 05]. According to these movements, humans could find an extension of the human condition by merging with advanced technologies and thus controlling their own evolution toward a new augmented transhuman species. These perspectives are based on the fact that progress seems to follow an exponential development that could reach a critical point that some transhumanist theorists call "singularity" [BEN 10]. They borrowed this term from mathematicians in order to symbolize the emergence point of a transhumanity, where human beings will be put back in their rightful place relative to very complex machines that will continue the evolutionary adventure with or without them [BES 09, KUR 05]. Transhumanists thus meet posthumanists, who deconstruct the privilege of humans with regard to all other subjects, especially animals or machines, which they feel unjustified [HAR 91, SLO 00, GOF 15]. It should be noted however that BCIs do not *a priori* oppose man and machine, moving indeed along the lines of a hybridization of the living and the artificial. Those who would want to employ them to improve the human species should be aware that BCIs would thus adhere more to a transhumanist perspective rather than to a posthumanist perspective. The "Nano-Bio-Info-Cogno – NBIC – report", very often cited and developed by the engineer Mihail Roco and the transhumanist sociologist William Bainbridge [ROC 03], was already based on the transhumanist concept of *convergence* of the different fields of research, providing humanity with access to a level of progress never achieved so far. This progress, for some transhumanists, could now reach the "total prosthesis", enabling the instantaneous and comprehensive understanding of human intentions by the machine, the establishment of transparent communication between two individuals communicating brain to brain without symbolic mediation, and the complete transfer of the human spirit onto a machine [NEE 15, p. 393, LEB 11]. Although these perspectives sound very futuristic, they are however the focus of serious reflections and are largely financed. For example, several major industrial players in new technologies finance the Singularity University[14], which provides decision makers, managers, politicians and scientists from around the world, with education and training programs aiming at anticipating the emergence of a technological singularity in order to take maximum advantage from it.

The question may arise of whether these futuristic assumptions are not specifically intended to attract capital investors, themselves encouraged by the expectations of the general public [NEE 15, p. 396]. The advent of such a future could lead, as feared by the German philosopher Jürgen Habermas [HAB 01] concerning cloning, to a multitiered society, where technologically advanced populations would take precedence over non-enhanced populations – lacking means, for example – thereby becoming "disabled" because of their originally "normal" condition. Finally, the dream of a matter extending without major ontological distinction from the atom to the elephant, including humans and computers, appears as nothing more than a materialist hypothesis with a monist pretention (a single principle of matter explaining everything that exists), which does not seem obvious at first and deserves further discussion, notably for all those who continue to support the thesis of the impossible confinement of the spirit to the brain [BER 19, CHA 96], or of the emergence of the spirit [KIM 93, KIM 05].

15.4.4. *Freedom and BCI*

If the human species develops new technologies, it is to exploit and take advantage of them for its well-being. If the singularity principle proves to be true, mankind may become prisoner of the technologies that it will have developed for itself. Are we not already dependent on a large number of them,

---

14 http://singularityu.org/community/founders/.

such as the means of communication by which we expect others to be reactive without delay and at any time?

BCIs therefore require consideration of the issue of freedom. Due to their functioning, these approaches consist of the real-time decoding of some of our intentions. While early works focused on motor intentions within a rehabilitation framework, the same methods are now striving, even if the goal is still far from being fully achieved, to decrypt more intimate information, such as perceived speech [MES 08], stored memories [RIS 10] or even dreams [HOR 13]. Despite these advances being significant and beneficial because they allow to better understand the functioning of our CNS, they provide the opportunity to explore specific information that people used to be free to keep for themselves. Will developed systems still be able to stop operating as soon as the user wants so? What usage, good or bad, will be made of the data collected about the user? The prospect that BCI technologies can easily be transposed beyond the field of research for social, economic [ULM 14], political, military or even legal purposes [WOL 10], gives rise to the major ethical issue of their impact on the freedom of the individual or more generally of the human species. As suggested by Tennison *et al.* [TEN 12], if an enhancement technology may, for example, benefit an employer, which could be a company looking for employees more focused on their work or an army aspiring for more effective soldiers [KOT 10], what freedom will then be left to an employee – faced with an employer or with the competition of those who have made the choice for enhancement – to comply to it or not? Subsequently, when a technology will have spread more widely to become a standard in everyday life, what freedom will an individual have, and more largely humans in general, to avoid it?

15.5. Conclusions

15.5.1. *A choice to be made*

In the past, Stoic philosophers opposed things that depend on us (our thoughts, our wills) and things that do not depend on us (everything that happens to our body, a number of events too contingent, unstable and fluctuating for us to attach on them any wisdom). Descartes somehow takes back this distinction by opposing the unlimited nature of our will to the limited nature of our knowledge and our body [DES 41].

As a result, we are now facing two major assumptions: either we consider the human being as existing within the limitations of a body, to which all technological innovations must biologically comply; or we think of the human being as a collection of dynamics of undefined progress of which the body is only the contingent support, and the technological innovations that we add to it will not have any constraints other than to extend, and optimally favor these dynamics of indefinite progress. These two assumptions allow distinguishing between the technological innovations that strive to serve more the purposes of the body from those that serve more the purposes of the will. However, the constraints that apply to technological innovations are not the same if these innovations aim at serving a body rather than a will. Serving a body requires respecting its functioning, its normativity, its limitations. Serving a will does not seem bound by the same constraints, the same limitations and the same internal normativity.

The continuation of these dynamics of indefinite progress may, at a given time, outweigh the respect for identity. Those who are more concerned about progress than identity would argue against the importance of identity, provided that human beings explore all possibilities available to them, since mankind originates from a history that does not cease with it [HUX 57, HAR 07].

All the threats to human beings, either external or internal, may become the subject of history, be they, for example, climates or the resistance to antibiotics. Since the emergence of new dangers has driven mankind to try to protect itself from them, it is possible, without even talking about its nature, to describe a few steps of its evolutionary history, where it learns to live in society, educates and strives to increase its knowledge. As a result, ethics itself can be considered to be what has emerged in the evolutionary history of primates as a certain result of natural selection. The possession of an ethic would thus constitute a selective advantage, allowing adaptation to living together [RUS 91]. Some go even further and believe that it is possible to describe the specific brain basis of morality. Joshua Greene supports the thesis according to which the distinction between deontologism (duty moral) and consequentialism (utilitarianism) is based on the distinction between the psychological schemas driven by emotion, and those driven by cognition, selected according to the situations that we ought to address [GRE 01].

In this context, ethics, the final product of natural selection, would no longer be either true or false, but simply well adapted to social life by favoring gregarious behaviors. In this case, the evolution of human beings would thus not necessarily imply that of ethics, and there would be no need to resort to an ethic of progress – ethics applied to progress, raising the question of whether this progress is ethical, or if it belongs to the ethic of evolving according to this progress – to reflect on the distinction between what would be ethical and what would not.

15.5.2. *The need for constant ethical vigilance of BCIs*

Nevertheless, it appears paramount that an ethical reflection, both open and demanding, accompanies the current research in order to ask the important questions that will help enlighten minds.

The issue of the welfare of the human species cannot oppose, in a probably too simplistic manner, bioconservatives and bioprogressists. The call for an international reflection group dedicated to these issues will certainly produce, as is the case for 60 years of global bioethics, some recommendations that will become laws governing these new technologies and their applications, but will not unfortunately always prevent that capital investors will sometimes gravitate toward the best opportunities.

Therefore, all the key players of these new technologies (including public and private researchers, investors, vendors, distributors), after all discussions, recommendations, and bioethics laws addressing these questions, should probably prepare themselves to carefully examine the arising *pro* and *contra* arguments, without being able to rely on some allegedly higher ethical authority, since none of such is better, for them and for all, than the one that their own consciousness represents.

15.6. Bibliography

[ATA 06] ATALA A., BAUER S.B., SOKER S. *et al.*, "Tissue-engineered autologous bladders for patients needing cystoplasty", *Lancet*, vol. 367, pp. 1241–1246, 2006.

[BEK 00] BEKOFF M., "Animal emotions: exploring passionate natures current interdisciplinary research provides compelling evidence that many animals experience such emotions as joy, fear, love, despair, and grief—we are not alone", *BioScience*, vol. 50, no. 10, pp. 861–870, 2000.

[BEN 91] BENABID A.L., POLLAK P., GERVASON C. *et al.*, "Long-term suppression of tremor by chronic stimulation of the ventral intermediate thalamic nucleus", *The Lancet*, vol. 337, pp. 403–406, 1991.

[BEN 10] BENDERSON B., *Transhumain*, Payot, Paris, 2010.

[BER 19] BERGSON H., *L'Energie spirituelle*, Alcan, Paris, 1919.

[BER 08] BERGER F., GEVERS S., SIEP L. *et al.*, "Ethical, legal and social aspects of brain-implants using nano-scale materials and techniques", *NanoEthics*, vol. 2, no. 3, pp. 241–249, 2008.

[BES 09] BESNIER J.-M., *Demain les posthumains. Le futur a-t-il encore besoin de nous?*, Hachette, Paris, 2009.

[BIR 99] BIRBAUMER N., GHANAYIM N., HINTERBERGER T. *et al.*, "A spelling device for the paralysed", *Nature*, vol. 398, pp. 297–298, 1999.

[BLA 10] BLANKERTZ B., TANGERMANN M., VIDAURRE C. *et al.*, "The Berlin Brain–Computer Interface: non-medical uses of BCI technology", *Frontiers in Neuroscience 4*, 2010.

[BON 13] BONNET L., LOTTE F., LÉCUYER A., "Two brains, one game: design and evaluation of a multi-user BCI video game based on motor imagery", *IEEE Transactions on Computational Intelligence and Artificial Intelligence in Games*, vol. 5 no. 2, pp. 185–198, 2013.

[BOR 13] BORTON D.A., YIN M., ACEROS J. *et al.*, "An implantable wireless neural interface for recording cortical circuit dynamics in moving primates", *Journal of Neural Engineering*, vol. 10, no. 26010, 2013.

[BOW 11] BOWDLER N., "Bionic hand for 'elective amputation' patient", *BBC News*, May 18 2011.

[BOW 12] BOWDLER N., "Woman considers hand removal for bionic replacement", *BBC News*, March 2012.

[BRU 07] BRUCE D., Report on an expert working group on converging technologies for human functional enhancement, NanoBio-RAISE EC FP6 Science and Society Coordination Action, 2007.

[BRU 10] BRUNNER P., JOSHI S., BRISKIN S. *et al.*, "Does the 'P300' speller depend on eye gaze?", *Journal of Neural Engineering*, available at: http://www.pubmedcentral.nih.gov/articlerender.fcgi?artid=2992970&tool=pmcentrez&rendertype=abstract, 2010.

[BUR 15] BURKE J.F., MERKOW M., JACOBS J. *et al.*, "Brain computer interface to enhance episodic memory in human participants", *Frontiers in Human Neuroscience*, vol. 8, 2015.

[CAM 08] CAMPORESI S. "Oscar Pistorius, enhancement and post-humans", *Journal of Medical Ethics*, vol. 34, no. 639, 2008.

[CAN 04] CANTO-SPERBER M., OGIEN R., *La Philosophie morale*, Presses universitaires de France, Paris, 2004.

[CAR 03] CARMENA J.M., LEBEDEV M.A., CRIST R.E. *et al.*, "Learning to control a brain-machine interface for reaching and grasping by primates", *PLoS Biology*, vol. 1, no. E42, 2003.

[CHA 96] CHALMERS D., *The Conscious Mind: In Search of a Fundamental Theory*, Oxford University Press, Oxford, 1996.

[CHA 99] CHAPIN J.K., MOXON K.A., MARKOWITZ R. *et al.*, "Real-time control of a robot arm using simultaneously recorded neurons in the motor cortex", *Nature Neuroscience*, vol. 2 no. 7, pp. 664–670, 1999.

[CLA 06] CLARKE A. "Qualitative interviewing: encountering ethical issues and challenges", *Nurse Researcher*, vol. 13, no. 4, pp. 19–29, 2006.

[CLA 09] CLAUSEN J., "Man, machine and in between", *Nature*, vol. 457, p. 1080–1081, 2009.

[CLE 16] CLERC M., BOUGRAIN L., LOTTE F. (eds), *Brain–Computer Interfaces 1*, ISTE London and John Wiley & Sons, New York, 2016.

[COL 13] COLLINGER JL, WODLINGER B, DOWNEY J.E. *et al.*, "High-performance neuroprosthetic control by an individual with tetraplegia", *The Lancet*, vol. 381, pp. 557–564, 2013.

[CON 11] CONGEDO M., GOYAT M., TARRIN N. *et al.*, "Brain Invaders: a prototype of an open-source P300- based video game working with the OpenViBE platform", *5th International Brain-Computer Interface Conference*, pp. 280-283, 2011.

[DES 41] DESCARTES, *Méditations métaphysiques*, Quatrième méditation, 1641.

[DIE 10] DIETRICH D., LANG R., BRUCKNER D. *et al.*, "Limitations, possibilities and implications of Brain-Computer Interfaces", *3rd Conference on Human System Interactions*, pp. 722–726, 2010.

[ENG 13] ENGELHARD B., OZERI N., ISRAEL Z. *et al.* "Inducing gamma oscillations and precise spike synchrony by operant conditioning via brain-machine interface", *Neuron*, vol. 77, pp. 361–375, 2013.

[FAI 14] FAIRCLOUGH S.H., "Physiological data must remain confidential", *Nature*, vol. 505, p. 263, 2014.

[FAR 02] FARAH MJ, "Emerging ethical issues in neuroscience", *Nature Neuroscience*, vol. 5, pp. 1123–1129, 2002.

[FET 69] FETZ E.E., "Operant conditioning of cortical unit activity", *Science*, vol. 163, pp. 955–958, 1969.

[FET 07] FETZ E.E., "Volitional control of neural activity: implications for brain-computer interfaces", *Journal of Physiology*, vol. 579, pp. 571–579, 2007.

[GAN 09] GANGULY K., CARMENA J.M., "Emergence of a stable cortical map for neuroprosthetic control", *PLoS Biology*, vol. 7, no. 7, 2009.

[GAN 11] GANGULY K., DIMITROV D. F., WALLIS J.D. *et al.*, "Reversible large-scale modification of cortical networks during neuroprosthetic control", *Nature Neuroscience*, vol. 14, pp. 662–667, 2011.

[GOF 15] Goffi J.-Y., "Transhumain", *in* Hottois G, J.-N. Missa, L. Perdal (eds), *Encyclopédie du trans/posththumanisme, L'humain et ses préfixes*, Vrin, Paris, pp. 156-163, 2015.

[GOM 14] Gomez-Pilar J., Corralejo R., Nicolas-Alonso L. F *et al.*, "Assessment of neurofeedback training by means of motor imagery based-BCI for cognitive rehabilitation", *36th Annual Conference of the IEEE Engineering in Medicine and Biology Society*, Chicago, August 2014.

[GOO 78] Goodpaster K., "On being morally considerable", *Journal of Philosophy*, vol. 75, pp. 308–25, 1978.

[GRA 05] de Gray L.C., Matta B.F., "Acute and chronic pain following craniotomy: a review", *Anaesthesia*, vol. 60, pp. 693–704, 2005.

[GRE 01] Greene J., Sommerville R.B., Nystrom L.E., *et al.* "An fMRI investigation of emotional engagement in moral judgement", *Science*, vol. 293, pp. 2105–2108, 2001.

[GRU 11] Grübler G., "Beyond the responsibility gap", *AI & Society*, vol. 26 no. 4, pp. 377–382, 2011.

[GUE 09] Guenther F.H., Brumberg J.S., Wright E.J. *et al.*, "A wireless brain-machine interface for real-time speech synthesis", *PLoS One,*, vol. 4, p. e8218, 2009.

[GUI 11] Guillebaud J.-C., *La vie vivante*, Les Arènes, 2011.

[HAB 01] Habermas J., *Die Zukunft der menschlishen Natur*, Suhrkamp Verlag, Frankfurt am Main, 2001.

[HAR 07] Harris J., *Enhancing Evolution. The Ethical Case for Making Better People*, Princeton Univiversity Press, Princeton, 2007.

[HAR 91] Haraway D., *Simians, Cyborgs and Women: The Reinvention of Nature*, Routledge, New York, 1991.

[HAS 09] Haselager P., Vlek R., Hill J. *et al*, "A note on ethical aspects of BCI", *Neural Networks: the Official Journal of the International Neural Network Society*, vol. 22, no. 9, pp. 1352–1357, 2009.

[HOC 06] Hochberg L.R., Serruya M.D., Friehs G.M. *et al.* "Neuronal ensemble control of prosthetic devices by a human with tetraplegia", *Nature*, vol. 442, pp. 164–171, 2006.

[HOC 12] Hochberg L.R., Bacher D., Jarosiewicz B. *et al.*, "Reach and grasp by people with tetraplegia using a neurally controlled robotic arm", *Nature*, vol. 485 no. 7398, pp. 372–375, 2012.

[HOR 13] Horikawa T., Tamaki M., Miyawaki Y. *et al.*, "Neural decoding of visual imagery during sleep", *Science*, vol. 340, no. 6132, pp. 639–642, 2013.

[HOT 15] Hottois G., J.-N. Missa, Perdal L.(eds), *Encyclopédie du trans/posththumanisme, L'humain et ses préfixes*, Vrin, Paris, 2015.

[HUX 57] Huxley J., "Transhumanism", in *New Bottles for New Wine*, Chatto & Windus, London, 1957 .

[IFF 13] IFFT P.J., SHOKUR S., LI Z. *et al.*, "A brain-machine interface enables bimanual arm movements in monkeys", *Science Translational Medicine*, vol. 5, no. 210ra154, 2013.

[JAC 06] JACKSON A., MAVOORI J., FETZ E.E., "Long-term motor cortex plasticity induced by an electronic neural implant", *Nature*, vol. 444, pp. 56–60, 2006.

[KAN 85] KANT E., *Fondements de la métaphysique des murs*, 1785.

[KIM 93] KIM J., *Supervenience and Mind: Selected Philosophical Essays*, Cambridge University Press, Cambridge, 1993.

[KIM 05] KIM J., *Mind in a Physical World. An Essay on the Mind-Body Problem and Mental Causation*, Massachusetts Institut of Technology Press, 2005

[KOT 10] KOTCHETKOV I.S. HWANG B.Y., APPELBOOM G. *et al.*, "Brain-computer interfaces: military, neurosurgical, and ethical perspective", *Neurosurgical Focus*, vol. 28, no. E25, 2010.

[KOU 15] KOURBETI I.S., VAKIS A.F., ZIAKAS P. *et al.*, "Infections in patients undergoing craniotomy: risk factors associated with post-craniotomy meningitis", *Journal of Neurosurgery*, vol. 122, no. 5, pp. 1113–1119, 2015.

[KUR 05] KURZWEIL R., *The Singularity is Near. When Humans Transcend Biology*, Penguin Books, New York, 2005.

[LAC 07] LACHAUX J.P., JERBI K., BERTRAND O. *et al.*, "BrainTV: a novel approach for online mapping of human brain functions", *Biological Research*, vol. 40, pp. 401–413, 2007.

[LEB 11] LEBEDEV M.A., TATE., A.J., T.L. *et al*, "Future developments in brain-machine interface research", *Clinics*, vol. 66, no. 1, pp. 25–32, 2011.

[LEG 13] LEGNANI F.G., SALADINO A., CASALI C. *et al.*, "Craniotomy vs. craniectomy for posterior fossa tumors: a prospective study to evaluate complications after surgery", *Acta Neurochirurgica*, vol. 155, no. 12, pp. 2281–2286, 2013.

[LID 09] LIDZ C.W., APPELBAUM P.S., JOFFE S. *et al.*, "Competing commitments in clinical trials", *IRB*, vol. 31, no. 5, pp. 1–6, 2009.

[LUC 08] LUCIVERO F., TAMBURRINI G., "Ethical monitoring of brain-machine interfaces", *AI and Society*, vol. 22, no. 3, pp. 449–460, 2008.

[MAR 02] MARGALIT E., MAIA M., WEILAND J.D. *et al.*, "Retinal prosthesis for the blind, *Survey of Ophthalmology*, vol. 47, pp. 335–356, 2002.

[MER 14] MERCIER-GANADY J., LOTTE F., LOUP-ESCANDE E. *et al.*, "The mind-mirror: see your brain in action in your head using EEG and augmented reality", *Proceedings – IEEE Virtual Reality*, pp. 33–38, 2014.

[MES 08] MESGARANI N., DAVID S.V., FRITZ J.B. *et al.*, "Phoneme representation and classification in primary auditory cortex", *Journal of the Acoustical Society of America*, vol. 123, pp. 899–909, 2008.

[MES 14] MESTAIS C., CHARVET G., SAUTER-STARACE F., "WIMAGINE®: wireless 64-channel ECoG recording implant for long term clinical applications", *IEEE Transactions on Neural Systems and Rehabilitation Engineering*, vol. 23, no. 1, pp. 10–21, 2015.

[MEY 11] MEYER A., SLAUGHTER M., "The total artificial heart", *Panminerva Medica*, vol. 53 no. 3, pp. 141–54, 2011.

[MIL 63] MILL J. S., *L'utilitarisme*, 1863.

[MIY 12] MIYASAKA M., SASAKI S., TANAKA M.., "Use of Brain-Machine interfaces as prosthetic devices: an ethical analysis", *Journal of Philosophy and Ethics in Health Care and Medicine*, no. 6, pp. 29–38, 2012.

[MOR 99a] MORAVEC H., *Robot: Mere Machine to Transcendent Mind*, Oxford University Press, 1999.

[MOR 99b] MORE M., "A letter to Mother Nature", in MORE M., VITA-MORE N., *The Transhumanist Reader: Classical and Contemporary Essays on the Science, Technology, and Philosophy of the Human Future*, John Wiley & Sons, Inc., 2013, 1999.

[MOR 08] MORITZ C.T., PERLMUTTER S.I. FETZ E., "Direct control of paralysed muscles by cortical neurons", *Nature*, vol. 456, pp. 639–642, 2008.

[MUL 08] MÜLLER K.-R., TANGERMANN M., DORNHEGE G. *et al.*, "Machine learning for real-time single-trial EEG-analysis: from brain–computer interfacing to mental state monitoring", *Journal of Neuroscience Methods*, vol. 167, pp. 82–90, 2008.

[NEE 15] NEERDAEL D., " Interfaces cerveau-machine", in HOTTOIS G, J.-N. MISSA, PERDAL L. (eds), *Encyclopédie du trans/posththumanisme, L'humain et ses préfixes*, Vrin, Paris, pp. 388–397, 2015.

[NIJ 13] NIJBOER F., CLAUSEN J., ALLISON B.Z. *et al.*, "The asilomar survey: stakeholders' opinions on ethical issues related to Brain-Computer interfacing", *Neuroethics*, vol. 6, pp. 541–578, 2013.

[NIS 13] NISHIMURA Y., PERLMUTTER S.I., FETZ E.E.,"Restoration of upper limb movement via artificial corticospinal and musculospinal connections in a monkey with spinal cord injury", *Frontiers in Neural Circuits*, vol. 7, no. 57, 2013.

[OGI 07] OGIEN R., *L'éthique aujourd'hui. Maximalistes et minimalistes*, Gallimard, Paris, 2007.

[PAU 05] PAUL E.S., HARDING E.J., MENDL M., "Measuring emotional processes in animals: the utility of a cognitive approach", *Neuroscience & Biobehavioral Reviews*, vol. 29, pp. 469–491, 2005.

[PIN 03] PINO A., KALOGEROS E., SALEMIS E. *et al.*, "Brain Computer interface cursor measures for motion-impaired and able-bodied users", *International Conference on Human-Computer Interaction*, vol. 4, pp. 1462–1466, 2003.

[RAU 02] RAUSCHECKER J.P., SHANNON R.V., "Sending sound to the brain", *Science*, no. 295, pp. 1025–1029, 2002.

[REZ 07] REZNIKOVA Z., *Animal Intelligence*, Cambridge University Press, Cambridge, 2007.

[RIS 10] RISSMAN J., GREELY H.T., WAGNER A.D., "Detecting individual memories through the neural decoding of memory states and past experience", *Proceedings of the National Academy of Sciences*, USA, vol. 107, pp. 9849–9854, 2010.

[ROC 03] ROCO M., BAINBRIDGE W., Converging technologies for improving human performance. Nanotechnology, biotechnology, information technology and cognitive science, National Science Foundation sponsored Report, Kluwer Academic Publishers, Dordrecht, 2003.

[RON 11] RONCO C., DAVENPORT A., GURA V., "The future of the artificial kidney: moving towards wearable and miniaturized devices", *Nefrologia*, vol. 31, pp. 9–16, 2011.

[RUS 91] RUSE M., "Une défense de l'éthique évolutionniste", in CHANGEUX J.-P., (ed), *Fondements naturels de l'éthique*, Odile Jacob, Paris, pp. 35–64, 1991.

[SAC 12] SACCHET M.D., MELLINGER J., SITARAM R. *et al.*, "Volitional control of neuromagnetic coherence", *Frontiers in Neuroscience*, 6, 2012.

[SER 02] SERRUYA M.D., HATSOPOULOS N.G., PANINSKI L. *et al.*, "Instant neural control of a movement signal", *Nature*, vol. 416, pp. 141–142, 2002.

[SLO 00] SLOTERDIJK P., *Die Domestikation des Seins. Für eine Verdeutlichung der Lichtung*, Suhrkamp, Frankfurt, 2000.

[TAK 11] TAKAHASHI J., SUEZAWA S., HASEGAWA Y. *et al.*, "Tongue motion-based operation of support system for paralyzed patients", *Proceedings of IEEE 12th International Conference on Rehabilitation Robotics*, 2011.

[TAL 02] TALWAR S.K., XU S., HAWLEY E.S. *et al.*, "Behavioural neuroscience: rat navigation guided by remote control", *Nature*, vol. 417, pp. 37–38, 2002.

[TEN 12] TENNISON M.N., MORENO J.D., "Neuroscience, ethics, and national security: the state of the art", *PLoS Biology*, vol. 10, no. e1001289+, 2012.

[THO 13] THOMSON E.E., CARRA R., NICOLELIS M.A., "Perceiving invisible light through a somatosensory cortical prosthesis", *Nature Communications*, vol. 4, no. 1482, 2013.

[TRE 10] TREDER M. S., BLANKERTZ B., "Covert attention and visual speller design in an ERP-based Brain–Computer interface", *Behavioral and Brain Functions*, vol. 6, 2010.

[ULM 14] ULMAN Y.I., CAKAR T., YILDIZ G., "Ethical issues in neuromarketing: I consume, therefore I am", *Sci Eng Ethics*, vol. 1, pp. 1271–1284, 2014.

[VEL 12] VELLOSO G.T., "Bridging present and future of Brain–Computer Interfaces: an assessment of impacts", IET Working Papers Series 09/2012, Universidade Nova de Lisboa, 2012.

[VEL 12] VELLOSO G.T., "Brain-Computer interface (BCI): a methodological proposal to assess the impacts of medical applications in 2022", *Enterprise and Work Innovation Studies 8*, pp. 57–81, 2012.

[VLE 12] VLEK R., STEINES D., SZIBBO D. *et al.*, "Ethical issues in Brain-Computer interface research, development, and dissemination", *Journal of Neurologic Physical Therapy*, vol. 36 no. 2, pp. 94–9, 2012.

[WAR 07] WARNEKEN F., HARE B., MELIS A.P. *et al.*, "Spontaneous altruism by chimpanzees and young children", *PLoS Biol*, vol. 5, pp. e184, 2007.

[WES 00] WESSBERG J., STAMBAUGH C.R., KRALIK J.D. *et al.*, "Real-time prediction of hand trajectory by ensembles of cortical neurons in primates", *Nature*, vol. 408, pp. 361–365, 2000.

[WOD 14] WODLINGER B., DOWNEY J.E., TYLER-KABARA E.C. *et al.*, "Ten-dimensional anthropomorphic arm control in a human brain-machine interface: difficulties, solutions, and limitations", *Journal of Neural Engineering*, vol. 12, no. 1, 2014.

[WOL 10] WOLPE P.R., FOSTER K.R., LANGLEBEN D.D. "Emerging neurotechnologies for lie-detection: promises and perils", *American Journal of Bioethics*, vol. 10, pp. 40–48, 2010.

16

Acceptance of Brain–Machine Hybrids: How is Their Brain Perceived *In Vivo*?

16.1. The ethical problem

The social acceptance of brain–machine interfaces is now part of the technological debate concerning humans enhanced by implants inserted into the body [HUM 95]: the end of handicaps, or at least a greater autonomy of very dependent people, seems possible by providing them with the means for the communication and expression of their subjectivity through interfacing with machines. Despite the persisting fear of robotic dehumanization, in the posthumanist context of the convergence of biological and technology systems, the equipment embedded inside and on the body itself becomes more acceptable. For the philosophers criticizing the technical progress of the theories of Foucault [ROU 08], this hybridization represent a way of manipulating these individuals in a market through the trade of body parts [LAF 14, p. 34]. It is true that these hybrid individuals could be perceived as guinea pigs, were it not for the fact that the experimental protocol respects the word of the subject by using its expression only as a testimony of the scientific success.

This chapter underlines how this singular expression of the connected brain is not a passive acceptance of the implant but a new reconfiguration of its physical activity based on an original space. Accepting an implant defines

---

Chapter written by Bernard ANDRIEU.

a new social status against the stigmatizing confinement of an individual immobilized by a wheelchair: by becoming hybrid [AND 08], the implanted individual is no longer stigmatized as a patient or a disabled person who would otherwise depend entirely on others regarding the management of everyday tasks like feeding and communicating. Individuals are now able to come forward to speak not only to thank their physicians but also to give their side of the story about their motor rehabilitation. Is their word original in the eyes of the expert who successfully achieved the implant into the body of the disabled person?

However, if the hybridization of human bodies with the spirit and the body of machines has become more commonplace due to the service provided to the daily life of disabled people, a number of ethical issues arise regarding intracranial implants: threats to the physical integrity of an individual caused by the penetration and installation in their skull of an implant; the disappearance of private thought and mental intimacy due to advertising and neuroinformatics outsourcing in the interface of mental content; physical intrusion and new aesthetics of body image due to implants on top of the skull. This post-Foucault interpretation of neurobiopower only makes sense if we were actually to generalize this neuroinformatics transparency. Nevertheless, in the case of disabled individual with implants, the new control which these implants will give seems, at least for the time being, acceptable.

A new perception of oneself provided by an implant produced by the perception of one's living body and becomes visible and measurable for the individual through the external action of the body on screens and other interfaces. Without directly feeling their brain, the implanted individuals discover a new mode of action through the mental work of their brain: visualize one's EEG activity on a screen, act through thinking when the body is immobile, trigger motion by activation, awaken in oneself an activity, develop a mental attention.

What are the conscious experiences of brain–computer interfaces (BCI) patients of their living brain activated by stimulation and attention? If the activation of the brain is triggered before being aware, how is this immediate action of the brain perceived in the body that cannot be felt? The living brain is active as demonstrated in the processing of its signals and in the recording of its activity but implanted individual claim to feel this activity through the implant.

16.2. The method

Knowing that one is equipped with an implant that acts as an interface and ensures an interaction between one's brain and the perceived environment modifies the self-perception of the subject both from the point of view of the redefinition of the body image and from the point of view of new motor functions that we define as remotely motor because they are carried out remotely, through the mediation of a mental intention captured by the implants and its translation into an action by a robotic arm or in a computer. One of the ethical challenges of this evaluation on what BCI patients perceive using implants is the absence of spontaneous declarations, because we have access to their feelings only through laboratory results that are put online. By means of spontaneous verbatim, a conversation or an oral or physical expression can be recorded and studied in order to clarify how the cranial BCI implants in the skull of the disabled person produces a specific experience of mobility in a paralyzed body. The verbatims that we investigate are produced in the context of American university laboratories that have developed and achieved these implants in disabled patients. If these patients were not participating in a study, we would know nothing of the corporal experiences of these implanted patients because the staging of their performance, through videos produced by the research teams, makes them express themselves more or less freely, as we shall see further on.

It is true that without these implants we would know nothing of the modifications of the remote-motor experiences of the hybridized person. Moreover, the relationship between the physical body and the relay of neuromotor intension is established:

– on the one hand, by means of a physically evaluable efficacy (such as demonstrated by the scientific results and showed in video form) that establishes a new mode of action previously impossible because of the neuropathological limitations of the subject; an assessment of the physical performance is no longer based on the muscular effort but on the work of attention training that requires extensive learning;

– on the other hand, the implanted individuals discover the idea of a body which they never knew in the case of a congenital disability or that was lost after an accident, such as for the pioneer Matt Nagle who became tetraplegic in the C3 category (above C3 there is complete paralysis of the respiratory muscles) following an assault. The expression of this discovery of a new body should be recognized in the verbatim by the singularity of the adjectives and other attributes of a subject that thus define a new field of motor and social action.

Through the video documents, scientific articles and the verbatim that we have transcribed, we can distinguish three different ethical levels in the acceptance by the equipped person:

– a primarily scientific and technical acceptance by a narrator in the video and during the experiment. The video is a scientific report of the experiences that follows a temporality. The experimentation [KAU 07] consists of three parts: the first two training parts and the third of evaluated tests. The film demonstrates the acceptance of the protocol and only the smooth sequence of events (failure is never visible in these video films despite the success rate being in average only of 50%). Everything is built in the narrative of the film to demonstrate the continuity of the steps;

– therefore, Cathy Hutchinson's performance with Hochberg's team is based on 158 trials over 4 days; she was able to achieve her target ("touch the target", note the verb *touch* in English refers to the physical body whereas it refers here to an effort of concentration on the target) in 48.8% of cases when using a DLR robotic arm and hand and 69.2% with the DEKA arm and hand. Thus, the isolated character of the performance in the video, certainly successful, does not appear in the verbatim nor in the body language of the subject, or at least the choice of images does not make this apparent. First-person speech (associative and/or subjective) is possible in the associations of patients who share the same pathologies: the progress of the implantation, in light of more traditional techniques in improving the lives of people with disabilities, has a double function: on the one hand, it is the opportunity to here from hybrid individuals turned heroes in the eyes of the scientific community and of other disabled persons; on the other hand, the exemplary nature of these pioneers intends to encourage other people likely to be implanted in the future and to create a new sense of community of these hybrids. By taking the opportunity to speak out, expressed through the use of "I", the subject may indicate how the living brain is felt less in itself but in the effects of the connection on the new motor functions;

– the language of the living body of the paralyzed person is expressed in the videos by expressive gestures that manifest the affective and emotional life of the subject, sometimes in spite of himself, losing control of what is produced by his living body. The smile shared with the members of the laboratory or the peacefulness recovered by the possibility of communicating through the body with the surroundings are signs of expression of the living body that incarnates through movement not only the technological success but the relational well-being.

16.3. Ethics of experimentation: Matthew Nagle, the first patient

First implanted in 2004, Matt Nagle (1980–2007) had quadriplegia at category 3, although he had not lost his ability to speak. He became quadriplegic following a brawl during which he was wounded in the spine by a knife, which left him disabled. He was the first volunteer to come forward for an implantation and thus became a hero as a clinical pioneer. He faced the ethics of experimentation both in the process and in the mode of communication, less well-understood than the other clinical cases that will follow him.

In the book *The Man with the Bionic Brain: And Other Victories over Paralysis* [MUK 12], physician-researcher and rehabilitation specialist Jon Mukand, medical director of the Southern New England Rehabilitation Center and clinical research associate at the Brown University and Tufts University, uses an image of his patient, Matt Neagle, on the cover. He describes the context of the implantation by defending the theory of a "bionic brain", similarly to the other works on the bionization of the arms and legs. On being chosen for the cover of Nature, Matthew Nagle declares "I was happy that *Nature* put me on the cover" [MUK 12, p. 286]. But behind the facade of the success and the scientific awards of the team, the living conditions of the pioneer degraded. Mukand reverses the perspective by showing the bugs in the system, the difficult connection between the biological and the neurobiological systems and the interface with the machine. Matthew's body, which benefited from stem cell research to restore his functions, was not able to adapt successfully.

Figure 16.1. *Matthew Nagle on the front cover of Nature*

In the movie *Brain Gain*, Matthew Nagle declares, "I can't put it into words. It's just – I use my brain. I just thought it. I said, 'Cursor go up to the top right.' And it did, and now I can control it all over the screen. It will give me a sense of independence". The control of the movement of the cursor is immediately associated with the technical efficiency and the sense of independence thus acquired.

However, in this bit of verbatim that is accessible to us, the three levels of the corporal experience can be extracted (Table 16.1).

	New corporal schema of the living body	New first person experience	New social ethics
Matthew Nagle	"I use my brain. I just thought it. I said, 'Cursor go up to the top right.'"	" And it did, and now I can control it all over the screen"	" It will give me a sense of independence"

Table 16.1. *Verbatim of M. Nagle's body experience*

In a hybrid body network, the artificial connection between the brain and thought is proven by means of the mental exercise of the subject who must use his thoughts to carry out and complete a task. By declaring "I use my brain", Matthew Nagle confirms a direct link between brain and thought, of which he was not aware earlier since he seemed to be subjected to its thought contents without their resulting in physical motor functions. The brain appears to act directly according to the will of the subject. He uses here "I use" to emphasize first-person control of his brain, through the effect of an activation caused by attention: the attentional effectiveness thus obtained makes the subject believe that he has direct access to his brain, the technological intermediary being in reality an action by proxy.

In the first experimental recording, of 1 min 51 s, from July 13, 2006 directed by ITN, Matthew Nagle appears in an experiment with the robotic hand that he commands from his brain: "I am going to close the hand: close, open", he stands in front of his screen and can open his post, move a slider to adjust the volume of his TV and choose his television channels. In this film, he does not express any subjective speech about his experiences other than his new technical and remote motor power by showing it with a smile. His satisfaction is clear and he manages to make movements that he could not previously do.

In the movie produced for CBS, completed the same day, he has more time to express a personal thought in a face-to-face interview with the journalist: beyond his personal situation he knows that he represents "hope for the people in 'his' situation". For himself, he hopes he will be able to "walk" and thus to recover from the accident, although he acknowledges that "this is a dream". The hope aroused by this direct connection of the brain with the outside world thus begins to challenge the conventional representation of motor functions. Why not consider, as DARPA developed for amputee veterans [AND 13], a bionic connection whose results are convincing regarding the upper limbs. By directly involving the brain, a new concept of the motor unit becomes representable: that of a direct connection between the brain and the nervous system that makes the biological continuity of the body network no longer necessary but increases the capacities by rebuilding the disability through its substitution with neurotechnology hybridization.

16.4. Body language in performance

The body language of the face, unlike language as a whole, is quicker and more spontaneous notably among quadriplegic individuals who cannot express themselves with the whole body due to the immobilization of paralysis. The expression of this body language is not always controlled, and the novelty of requiring motor control can overwhelm the quadriplegic person. Cathy Hutchinson[1], 58 years old and unable to move for 15 years, can be seen in this video, aired in the context of the "new posthumanist singularity". This would be proof of the successful connection between machine and brain, from a third-person point of view. The video presents the act of controlling the robotic arm so as to drink through a straw (Figure 16.2) while one can see the concentration of her gaze and the tension of the face, at the moment of drinking, which she has perfectly anticipated, opening the mouth, the face is relaxed and smiles, clearly expressing satisfaction through her body language. Dr. Leigh Hochberg, engineer and neurobiologist at the Brown University and at the Harvard Medical School was thus able to declare: "The smile on her face was something that I and my research team will never forget"[2].

This satisfaction is at first internal, even though she cannot move and make use of her hands; then it becomes external at the end of the movie when the applauses of the scientists join in with her joy, she turns and looks at the camera to share the success of the performance. The acceptance of hybridization here is emotional, the living body translates how much the subject is satisfied with the result obtained: if the scientific performance is successful a feeling of well-being invades the whole face and the neck. The scientific performance is understood here as a new performativity of the living body able to understand itself in a new body space: the extension of the body schema is thus integrated into a global greening of the body and of the world.

This corporeal world is based on the hybridization of the biological body and of the technological extension by direct connection: this hybridization is spontaneous in the language of the living body which, without being intentional, is sensitive to the technological extension. The ability to manifest

---

1 http://www.youtube.com/watch?v=X8SD8jSFlQI.

2 http://www.dailymail.co.uk/sciencetech/article-2145314/Paralysed-woman-able-drink-cup-coffee-robot-arm-thanks-mind-reading-brain-implant.html.

a bodily joy is here based on the feeling of belonging to a new corporeal world: not that of the abled-bodied that would allow recovering a body schema, nor that of disabled people immobilized in their chair. Cathy Hutchinson clarifies this point, using eye-tracking technology to select some words on the computer screen; her returning to the world of the able-bodied as a key player: "I am part of the community again. The privacy back is wonderful. I have my life back". Body language thus provides a greater social acceptability because in its performance it expresses the participation of the subjects in the effects they produce on their environment. The scientific marketing of the laboratory must here be distinguished from Cathy Hutchinson's personal will, caught between the benefits of her new situation and the awareness of what she represents as a hope for the community of quadriplegics.

Figure 16.2. *Cathy Hutchinson moves robot arm using implant technology*

16.5. Ethics of autonomous (re)socialization

The ethics of autonomous (re)socialization implies that BCIs promote greater continuity between the hybrid body schema and social relationships with others. There are no illusions here of restoring integral communication, but the BCI hybridization restores a mode of less self-centered communication for the patient because the connection is hetero-centered toward the computer connection that will translate the thoughts of the person into actions in the outside world beyond the limits of their paralyzed body. The technique can thus transpose the inner and mental voice of the subject into an external voice understandable by others.

Despite not being able to talk, Cathy Hutchinson thus testifies in a video, in a in a 51 s message that we transcribe here, which she has transmitted through the movement of her eyes with eye-tracking on a screen that rebuilds her voice for the *Brain Injury Association of Massachusetts*[3]:

> "Fifteen years ago I had a brain stem stroke while gardening. I was not given a choice of my long-term care. I lived in a nursing home for 15 years. I feel very happy and satisfied to hear how this has helped other people and I hope to have all states to follow suit. I just love it. I feel like I am part of a community again. The privacy back is wonderful. I have my life back, I see my family more frequently and I can be involved in the community without the restricted nursing home regulations, I couldn't ask for more. Thank you for raising public awareness and informing families and disabled people that they have a choice".

The direction of the message, expressed in the first person under the form of moral testimony after being equipped, is addressed to the community of other persons with disabilities: she particularly indicates the communicative and social progress of the implantation. The new socialization brought through the equipment releases her from the dependence of the specialized care home in which she lived until then and "I see my family more frequently and I can be involved in the community without the restricted nursing home regulations":

This autonomy is an autonomous resocialization through the involvement in communicating with her family members: she is no longer directly dependent on intermediaries to communicate with her family. Confronted with disability and with the announcement of the diagnosis, the sense of a social and neurophysiological fate leaves little choice to Cathy, she expresses it in a vivid way by comparing it with what is possible today: "Fifteen years ago I had a brain stem stroke while gardening. I was not given a choice of my

---

3 http://www.youtube.com/watch?v=gVp0ygZWTmI.

long-term care. I lived in a nursing home for 15 years". This awareness of time is divided into three temporalities: before the disability, during the disability and with hybridization. Cathy does not speak about her previous handicap as if it still exists today: not because it has disappeared but because it has a new meaning, undoubtedly by becoming a tool through which she perceives herself differently.

	New corporeal schema of the body	New first-person experiences	New social ethics
Cathy Hutchinson	"I feel very happy and satisfied to hear how this has helped other people and I hope to have all states to follow".	"I can see my family more frequently and I can be engaged in my community without a strict obedience".	"I couldn't ask for more thank you for raising public awareness and informing families and disabled people that they have a choice".

Table 16.2. *Verbatim of C. Hutchinson's body experience*

Cathy seeks to raise public awareness by informing people that a new situation is becoming feasible for a person as disabled as herself: "I couldn't ask for more, thank you for raising public awareness and informing families and disabled people that they have a choice". Associating her successful path with other implantable patients must be relativized regarding to the actual possibility of implantation. This difference between the performed and successful operations and the global dissemination of information to all disabled persons must be nuanced. This dissemination of films resorts to volunteers such as Jan Scheuermann, a quadriplegic of 53 years old who has been suffering from spinocerebellar degeneration for 13 years, and who manifested herself following the broadcast of this type of film: "I always said except for this walking thing I'm in great health, I saw a video, I opened it and watched a man in a wheelchair having his brain hooked up; and he controlled the electronic arm and he was learning to move it. At the end of the story they said they were looking for volunteers and as soon as it was over we called. I didn't know where it was going to end up. I'm going to feed myself chocolate before this is over"[4].

An ethics of the living body: sensory feedback

---

4 http://www.youtube.com/watch?v=76lIQtE8oDY.

Sensory feedback is a concept that could be applied if recovering the remote neuromotor action in the body was attestable as the taste of chocolate that Jan Scheurmann recovers at the end of her neuromental gesture. In this case, sensory feedback achieves the following loop: remote neuromotor intention – robotic arm approach – biological feedback of chocolate. Nevertheless, sensory feedback can also be reversed as in Tim Hemmes's case who was able to touch the hand of his girlfriend by using the robotic arm that he was stretching toward her, controlled by his remote neuromotor intent: remote neuromotor intent – direction of the robotic arm – touching his girlfriend's biological hand of with the robotic hand. Jan Scheuermann declares that her implantation could enable him for the first time "I'm moving things. I have not moved things for about 10 years", to move things, which she was unable to do for 10 years. Moreover, the essential point is not to act on things but to feel them again with the recovery of the motor action on the perception of taste, or of tactile sensations. Here, sensory feedback is not a perception of one's own body to the extent where there is no recovery of the body schema as a whole. So far, the robot arm coming back to her face, her mouth in this case, gives her a sensation that she provides to herself by means of the remote neuromotor action:

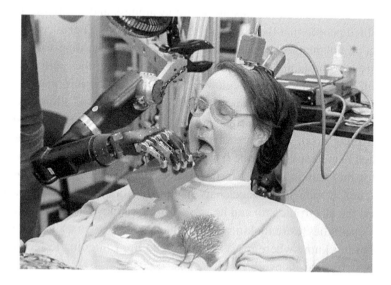

Figure 16.3. *J. Scheuermann neuromotor intention*

Sensory feedback for Jan Scheuermann originates from the new dexterity that transmits information by directing the orientation of her attention toward an object. She personifies her brain saying "my brain knows what things to move to make that happen"[5]. This intentional attribution to the brain seems to be felt directly by the implanted subject. The brain becomes a thinking substance that directly analyzes the movement of things and thus guides the activity of the robotic arm.

	New corporeal body schema	New first-person experience	New social ethics
Jan Scheuermann	"Now I just look at the target and Hector goes there. It's not a matter of thinking which direction anymore. It's just I wanna do that and my brain knows what things to move to make that happen. It's just fabulous and I'm enjoying every second of it".	"I can make a difference for people in the future. So I'm excited to think that our work here in the lab will inspire more people to come forward and for the work to continue".	"I can make a difference for people in the future so I'm excited to think that our work here in the lab will inspire more people to come forward and for the work to continue".

Table 16.3. *Verbatim of J. Scheuermann's body experience*

Jan Scheuermann's enthusiasm, "It's just fabulous, I'm enjoying every second", defines a new 1st-person experience: the body becomes alive through the focusing of the brain on precise goals, establishing a sense of direct action. Becoming an intentional subject again, likely to aim for goals through thinking reflected in the body implementation, restores a loop: brain-thinking-computer translation-robot action- satisfaction.

Tim Hemmes's case, implanted after a motorcycle accident at the age of 30, achieves an additional step no longer by touching objects or materials but by recovering the tactile sensation of his friend through his implantation: "For 12 days at his home and nine days in the research lab, Mr. Hemmes began the testing protocol by watching a virtual arm move, which triggered neural signals that were sensed by the electrodes. Distinct signal patterns for

---

5 http://www.youtube.com/watch?v=76lIQtE8oDY.

particular observed movements were used to guide the up and down motion of a ball on a computer screen. Soon after mastering the movement of the ball in two dimensions, namely up/down and right/left, he was able to also move it in/out with accuracy on a 3-dimensional display. "During the learning process, the computer helped Tim hit his target smoothly by restricting how far off course the ball could wander," Dr. Wang said. "We gradually took off the 'training wheels,' as we called it, and he was soon doing the tasks by himself with 100 percent brain control" [WAN 13].

To this motor skill, a sensory experience specific to the BCI interface is added; even if the device is obviously a robotic hand controlled by Tim Hemmes's brain, the interaction between his friend's biological hand and that of the robotic arm is perceived by the two humans, Tim and his friend, as a real and intentional physical contact.

Figure 16.4. *Tim Hemmes in intercorporeality with his girlfriend via his tactile prosthesis*

Affectivity could therefore be transmitted through this technological means, the sensory feedback from the contact is imagined by Tim Hemmes while his girlfriend can feel the intensity and substance of the contact. This contact of both hands also renews the autonomous resocialization in an ethics of sharing a common experience. Unlike technical socialization that is possible through the relay of the computer by the remote neuromotor functions of the implanted subject, the sensory feedback restores the affective loop of of sentimental information transmission.

In the movie[6] filmed at the Medical Center of the University of Pittsburg, Tim Hemmes expresses himself after 2 min, after the scientists Mike Boninger and Andrew Schwartz, who had previously conducted the procedure with a monkey, and also Elizabeth Tyler-Kabara, the neurosurgeon in the operating room.

As with other people with implants, Tim Hemmes pictures his interface in a social dimension but also gives it an emotional value: social continuity finds in the communication of emotions a way of developing an ethics no longer of compassion but of sharing.

16.6. Conclusions

The *in vivo* perception of the brain in BCI, as evidenced by the analysis of the verbatims, is based on an experienced illusion. Kant refers to it to as the natural illusion: in the transcendental dialectic of the Critique of Pure Reason, he defines it as a "natural and unavoidable illusion, that relies itself on subjective principles and presents them as objective principles". Thus, the BCI feeds this illusion because the hybrid subject feels the effectiveness of the interface, under the subjective impression of controlling the objective information of the computer that will result in a technical action in the surrounding world. Social ethics is more objective than subjective because in being hybridized, the subjects communicate less as pioneers turned heroes by the laboratories, than as examples within a community of disabled peers who will benefit, individually from these advances.

The step is achieved on the ontological level: it is no longer enough to have a body to control one's brain, but brain activity can be recorded to act by means of another body which is not disabled. This duplication of the disabled body by an additional body, obviously technological and robotic, is nonetheless connected to the will of the subject. Can we go as far as the theory of Marc Jeannerod (1935–2011) of the voluntary brain?: "I learn to know myself by watching myself acting" [JEA 09, p. 269]. By watching my brain acting for me, I validate its action as mine by attributing it to my conscious intention: the BCI interface reinforces this mental belief that my conscience acts upon my brain to control the robotic arm.

---

6 http://www.youtube.com/watch?v=yff20TlHv34.

16.7. Bibliography

[AND 08] ANDRIEU B., *Devenir hybride*, Preface Stelarc, 2008.

[AND 13] ANDRIEU B., "Vétérans amputés: Se déshandicaper par la capacibilité sportive", in BUNARU D., LE BRETON D., (eds), *Corps abîmés*, P.U. Laval, Presses de l'Université Laval pp. 141–152, 2013.

[JEA 09] JEANNEROD M., *Le cerveau volontaire*, Odile Jacob, Paris, 2009.

[HUM 95] HUMPHREY D.R., HOCHBERG L.R., "Intracortical recording of brain activity for control of limb prostheses", *Proceedings of the Rehabilitation Engineering Society of North America*, Vancouver, Canada, pp. 650–658, 1995.

[KAU 07] KAUHANEN L., JYLÄNKI P., LEHTONEN J. *et al.*, "EEG-based brain-computer interface for tetraplegics", *Computional Intelligence and Neuroscience*, vol. 2007, no. 23864, 2007.

[LAF 14] LAFONTAINE C., *Le corps-marché, La marchandisation de la vie humaine à lère de la bioéconomie*, Le Seuil, Paris, 2014.

[MUK 12] MUKAND J., *The Man with the Bionic Brain: And Other Victories over Paralysis*, Chicago Review Press, Chicago, 2012.

[ROU 08] ROUVROY A., *Human Genes and Neoliberal Governance. A Foucauldian Critique*, Routledge-Cavendish, London, 2008.

[WAN 13] WANG W., JENNIFER L. COLLINGER A.D. *et al.*, "An electrocorticographic brain interface in an individual with tetraplegia", *PLoS ONE*, vol. 8, no. 2, 2013.

16.8. Appendix (verbatim video retranscriptions)[7]

Jan Scheuermann's verbatim[8]

Jan Scheuerman: I always said that, apart from this walking thing, I am in great health. I saw a video, I opened it and watched a man in a wheelchair have his brain hooked up and he controlled an electronic arm and he was learning to move it. At the end of his stay they said they were looking for volunteers and as soon as it was over we called. I didn't know where it was going to end up. I'm going to feed myself chocolate before this is over!

I was a very healthy person, and one day I was walking a lot that evening and I felt like that my legs were dragging behind me. The same thing happened a week later. Then it started happening more and more frequently. I had no idea

---

7 Mr Fintan Gallagher is gratefully acknowledged for providing these verbatim trasnscriptions.
8 Source: http://www.youtube.com/ watch?v=76lIQtE8oDY.

what was going to happen, what the prognosis was. So we made plans to move back to Pittsburgh. When I got to Pittsburgh I saw a doctor at UPMC. He did his tests, and three or four months later pronounced that I had spinocerebellar degeneration. I can move my neck and my head, and that's about it.

Dr Michael Boninger: With Jan we're hoping to achieve the ability to control an arm and a hand in space. The ideal scenario would be that she could move to a place in space, orient her wrist, and then have a variey of different grasps with her hand, so that she could pick up different objects like a coke bottle or a set of keys or a fork.

Jan: I can't wait to do this – to be part of medical science, pushing technology onward. For me, because I haven't been able to move my arm for 10 years, so just to be able to physically move something else... I can't wait, this is going to be so cool...

Dr. Elizabeth Tyler-Kabara: These are electrodes that have 96 contacts, and then they're literally injected into the surface of the brain. That just allows the electrodes to penetrate the surface so that you can record the responses of individual neurons as well as populations of neurons, and so in this case we implanted two. These are implanted along a motor strip and we really tried to target this so that we would place one centered in the areas that were activated when she was imagining using her hand, and then, place the second one in the area that was activated when she imagined using her shoulder. A few days after surgery, we went over to the rehab hospital and we took the system with us so that we could plug her in. We were just curious to find out whether or not we could record anything that sounded like a neuron.

Dr. Andrew Schwartz: When we hooked her up for the first time and we had her think about moving her little finger, right then we knew we'd done everything really well and that we had a really good circumstance so that we could do good recordings, and that Jan was going to work out really well.

To Jan: So now go ahead and try moving your wrist. Wow! There we go! [success on the screen]

Jan: Every day, as we get closer, and then we drive up the road to come to the lab, I'm thinking: "Oh good! What are we going to do today? What's going to be new?" And every time we do something new, it's challenging at first, and then when I get 28 out of 30 or whatever the score is, and they say

"That was all you – that wasn't the computer doing it – that was all you", I just can't stop smiling, it's so cool. I'm moving things! I have not moved things for about 10 years!

Team: All right! Very fast. There we go!

Dr. Jennifer Collinger: Initially we started out with her doing 3-dimensional control of the hand, and she's controlling the end-point position of the arm, moving forward/back or up/down, left or right – that kind of thing. And so, since she was making good progress at that, we decided to try to start adding orientation of the wrist, rotating in all three directions, and then also adding in grasp. So that's where we are focusing now on – 7-dimensional control of the end-point position, orientation and grasp, and really working on interacting with objects and being able to move them around her environment.

Jan: I used to have to think: up, clockwise, down, forward, back. Now I just look at the target, and Hector goes there. It's not a matter of thinking which direction anymore. It's just: I wanna do that, and my brain knows what things to move to make that happen.

Dr. Andrew Schwartz: Right now all Jan is doing is imagining moving the arm – exactly where she wants the arm to go – just like you or I would control our own arm. What we have done interestingly with Jan is that normally the computer controls a little bit, and Jan controls a little bit – at least that's how we started. Jan didn't want to know when we switched the computer control off – she didn't want to know when we weren't assisting her in the task, and almost as soon as she said that, we flipped all the controls off, so we gave her complete control of the arm. And then she controlled it perfectly.

Jan [as she succeeds in the task]: Yeah! Twenty out of twenty!

Team applause: Incredible! [etc.]

Jan: There are things I regret not doing when I was able – not sky-diving, but there are some adventures I would love to have had and I regret not doing them now. But this, this is the ride of my life. I keep saying, this is the roller-coaster, this is the sky-diving, it's just fabulous, and I'm enjoying every second of it.

Dr. Jennifer Collinger: From the beginning we've been really focused on how much control can you get of this arm, moving the hand and everything, but Jan's goal has really been to feed herself a piece of chocolate...

[applause, as Jan succeeds in feeding herself some chocolate]

Jan: One small nibble for a woman, one giant bite for BCI !

Dr Michael Boninger: I think the highlights of the study are watching Jan feed herself, watching Jan move objects, watching her complete tests that we normally have for people who are trying to recover function after a stroke, and having this beautiful fluid control of a robotic arm through thought.

Dr. Andrew Schwartz: It would be really great to get her to the point that she can actually feed herself enough food that she can satisfy herself and that it becomes routine. I guess I'm a little worried that she's eating just chocolate and cheese – we need to vary the diet a little bit.

Jan: Today I accomplished the goal that I set before the surgery even took place. They were asking if there was something special I wanted to do, like touch my children's cheek, or hold my husband's hand, and I said: my goal is to feed myself chocolate. And I did that today. I fed myself chocolate, and then string cheese and a red pepper...

Dr Michael Boninger: I watched Jan smile after completing a task, in a time close to what I could complete that task at, and you think we just have to take the next steps where we can make this a clinical tool, not just a research one.

Jan: It overwhelms me. I'm so glad I did this. I know some people will watch this down the road and say, "You know what? I could do that. I can't hold a job anymore. I can't even talk to my children or pick up a pen to write, but I can do that and I can make a difference for people in the future." So I'm excited to think that our work here in the lab will inspire more people to come forward, and for the work to continue.

Tim Hemmes's verbatim (6'30)[9]

Tim Hemmes: My life has changed dramatically since the accident. As of right now, there's nothing to cure paralysis, besides maybe a miracle. The first thing I'd do if I got my arms back? I would hug my daughter. It would be really nice to scoop something up in a spoon and feed myself again. This is going to go beyond spinal cord if this works. This is going to go MS. This is going to go stroke. This is huge. This is millions and millions and millions of people.

Tim Hemmes: I'm pretty much broken from the neck down, I guess you could say. The only thing that I have left that is untouched is my brain. And obviously I'm able to use it very good. I'm able to do this, to do that. There's no memory loss. So I opted for experimental surgery to go at the one thing that I still have.

Dr Michael Boninger: What we try to do is put a grid in place that's capable of recording signals from the brain. So when you think "I want to move", there's actually electrical impulses in the brain. We want to be able to record those electrical impulses and then decode what the electrical impulses mean, and use that to control an object or an arm. People thought for a long time that we might be able to tap into the brain, but it's only recently that we've gotten closer and closer. There's some great work going on here at the University of Pittsburgh by a gentleman named Andy Schwartz, and Andy has shown that he can get a monkey to control a robotic arm with an amazing degree of freedom by thought.

Dr. Andrew Schwartz: We've developed technology where we can implant an array of microelectrodes in the cerebral cortex of monkeys, and we can record activity from many neurons in the brain simultaneously, and from that signal we can extract the monkey's intention to move its arm, and now that we have that, we can intercept that signal and use it, instead of moving the monkey's own arm, use it to move a prosthetic arm.

What it takes to get it in people is a large team. So we've basically been, somewhat isolated in our laboratory, working on monkeys, proving the technology, making discoveries, validating the technology, developing new ways of doing this, and what we've been able to do recently is pass a lot of

---

9 Source: http://www.youtube.com/watch?v=yff20TlHv34.

this knowledge that we've gained to clinical colleagues. They came in the laboratory, learned a lot of what we're doing, and then took it back to the clinic and developed the technology that's appropriate for humans.

DrElizabeth Tyler Kabara: (largely unintelligible).

Tim Hemmes: Two days after the surgery, we plugged me in and started to basically train the computer to my brain, the way I'm thinking. The computer doesn't know up, down, right, left – it just knows the signals that I'm thinking. For the first couple of days, it was just: what's up, what's down. How I do it is, I look at the ball at the top, and through my peripheral vision I see the ball that's moving. So I'm focusing on the target, and almost with my mental eyes, or whatever you want to call it, lifting up, trying to get that ball to go up, or trying to get it to go down. So I'm focusing on the target while watching the moving ball with my peripheral. It's like a one-player video game. I'm trying to beat my own score, because there is a scoring. There's a certain percentage. Each time I do it, it's out of 16 balls, and I wanna know the number. If it's 13, I want 14, or I want 15. So it's just a challenge to myself. One thing I found out that if I focus too hard, it doesn't work right. It has to be very natural.

Team: That's pretty good. It's not too bad.

Tim Hemmes: We're making such ground on this, every single day. Every other day we're just doing leaps and bounds, and knowing that we're doing that, if I had another week or two weeks or a month, where would we be then? We've already done stuff that's unprecedented. I've been doing stuff, I've been told, with 3-D cursor control, [that elsewhere they've been doing over a year or over two years] they haven't got the type of control and percentages that I've got in a day, literally a day.

The highlight was 45 minutes ago – I got to use the robotic arm for the first time, and I got to reach out and touch my girlfriend for the first time in 7 years. *[Robotic arm, controlled by Tim, reaches out and touches his girlfriend's hand.]* Reaching out and touching my girlfriend for the first time, and holding her hand – that was mighty.

Dr. Andrew Schwartz: You really did start to sense that, for instance, his girlfriend had taken it as an emobodied hand of Tim's and was actually feeling the extension of Tim's body scheme to that hand. But what we really want to do, and what we think of in terms of the way we act on the environment, is we're generating behavioral output, so the only way you can express yourself – what's going on in your mind, what you're thinking about – is by moving. And what we want to do when we give these immobilized patients this device, we want to enable them to express what's going on, we want them to be able to output their behavior into the real world.

Dr Michael Boninger: For this research to move forward right now, what we need is a number of different things. We need great scientists – the team that we had working on this experiment, a multi-disciplinary team of neurosurgeons, engineers, neurologists, occupational therapists, all working together – that needs to continue, and I'm sure we can continue that. We need funding – we've been fortunate, we've received funding from the National Institute of Health, from the VA, from the Department of Defense, and from UPMC – all of which is critical to this going forward. And we need participants, like Tim, and we need people who are willing to step forward and say, I understand that I have a role, and I can push the science forward. It's not going to help them tomorrow, but it could help them a few years down the road.

Team laughter: All right! There you go! *[Tim demonstrates robotic hand movements]*

Tim Hemmes: I believe in my heart that this is the future and anybody out there who has the courage and the want to try to do this, you gotta go for it and hopefully it will help you just as much as I believe it's gonna help me.

17

Conclusion and Perspectives

17.1. Introduction

In this two-volume work (see [CLE 16]), we have been able to discover what Brain–Computer Interfaces (BCIs) are, how they work, what are the applications of these technologies and how to design and use them in practice. In this context, we have investigated the neuroscientific foundations of BCIs, that is the knowledge of brain structures and electrophysiological phenomena involved in controlling a BCI, and this for different types of BCIs, such as invasive/non-invasive and active/reactive/passive. We then studied different algorithms for preprocessing, processing, describing or even classifying brain signals (notably electroencephalogram (EEG)) in order to design a BCI. We have seen that these algorithms and machines are far from being sufficient and that the user is essential and must be taken into account, particularly concerning man–machine interaction, neurofeedback, and human learning. We then explored different BCIs and applications, more particularly, for establishing a diagnosis or communication with people presenting consciousness disorders, for allowing patients with severe motor disabilities to communicate and for real time visualization of brain activity or novel video-game interactions. In addition to BCI principles and applications, we have also reviewed various practical aspects, such as sensors, the organization of an EEG experiment, the patients' needs or software implementation.

Chapter written by Maureen CLERC, Laurent BOUGRAIN and Fabien LOTTE.

Finally, the ethical and philosophical issues related to these technologies have been studied.

BCIs are currently a quickly developing technology, involving a large number of laboratories, and raising a very significant public awareness. However, despite the enthusiasm and interest for these technologies, it would be wise to ponder if BCIs are really promising and helpful, or if they are simply a passing fad, reinforced by their "science-fiction" side. An interesting tool to try to elucidate this is Gartner's "hype cycle" [LIN 03]. This "hype cycle" – in fact, rather a curve – presents the different stages that all innovative technologies undertake, representing the visibility of each technology over time. Five main steps can be identified, as illustrated in Figure 17.1:

1) the technology trigger;

2) the peak of inflated expectations, where much more is expected from the technology than what it can deliver, or even that it will ever deliver;

3) the trough of disillusionment, when the technology is ultimately considered to be useless, or at least much less useful than what it is or will ever become;

4) the slope of enlightenment where the true potential and the usefulness of the technology begins to be perceived;

5) the plateau of productivity, when the technology is finally used where it is useful.

The Gartner group is at the origin of this concept and each year positions different innovative technologies on the curve. This group estimates that in 2015, BCIs are located at the very beginning of this curve, that is immediately after the launch of the technology, about to climb toward the peak of exaggerated expectations[1]. In other words, we will witness increased expectations about BCIs, some of which will be completely unrealistic. These unreasonable expectations are already very visible in the mainstream media, which do not hesitate to talk about "mind reading", or even "telepathy", which is completely out of the scope of BCI. For the moment, there is no result suggesting that BCI may achieve such feats one day.

_____

1 www.gartner.com/newsroom/id/3114217.

Figure 17.1. *The "hype cycle": different stages through which an innovative technology evolves, representing the visibility of this technology over time (source: Jeremy Kemp at Wikipedia)*

The vision of the scientific community is different from that of the general public, and the former could place BCIs further on the curve, for example in the downward slope, moving toward the trough of disillusionment. Effectively, the current performance of BCIs makes them unable to compete with most of the standard interaction devices, such as mouses, keyboards, joysticks or eyetrackers. As a matter of fact, BCIs are slow, rather unstable, and unreliable, often making mistakes regarding the mental command sent by the user, and recognizing another command instead. Thus, some researchers do not necessarily anticipate a bright future for BCIs used for directly controlling an application (active/reactive BCIs) [NIJ 13]. Research funding agencies (notably European), probably guided by similar fears, have funded two successive projects to define each time a roadmap for BCI research, and thus to identify what would be the true usefulness of BCIs, beyond the exaggerated expectations [BRU 15]. From these two roadmaps[2], as well as from the work of the BCI research community (see, for example, [ERP 12]), it appears that research in BCI is a field in its very early stages, offering many promising perspectives and a large number of research directions to explore, equally from a fundamental, a practical and an application point of view. There is still much to understand about the brain, about measuring its activity

----

2 www.bnci-horizon-2020.eu/.

and about using a BCI. Basic research focusing on these points has the potential to greatly improve the performance of BCIs, which for the moment remains modest. Numerous practical aspects must notably be explored to make BCIs usable outside laboratories, by patients with motor disabilities, but also to put them into the hands of the general public, after making them commercially viable and ethically usable. These different points will help to promote the development of BCIs, and to reveal their usefulness. Finally, BCIs have until now been applied only in a relatively small number of contexts. Opening BCIs to other applications could reveal many other areas for which BCIs might be useful. In the following sections of this final chapter, we detail these fundamental, practical and applicative perspectives.

17.2. Reinforcing the scientific basis of BCIs

Before definitively being able to decide whether or not BCIs are a useful technology for any particular application, there is still a lot of basic research to be performed in order to fully understand their potential, and to what extent their performance may increase. It is even necessary to undertake research to strengthen the scientific bases of BCIs. This notably includes understanding the specificities of the patients using BCIs, the way users learn how to control BCIs, the reasons why some succeed and others not, and why their performances vary in all cases. It is also necessary to understand the sources of fluctuations in brain activity, and to know how to design features and classifiers that are robust to noise and to the non-stationarity of signals.

A key point to enable progress in the field of BCI would be to understand its action on brain function itself, through plasticity, as well as on the sensorimotor loops. It would then be possible to better control the effects of neurofeedback, and to implement actual strategies of motor or cognitive rehabilitation with BCIs. This calls for the use of neuroscientific models in the development of BCIs. It is possible that BCIs themselves will be employed to better understand the brain, a fundamental challenge for the 21st Century, to which we will return later.

Understanding users' specific needs is a necessity when aiming to develop solutions that are adapted to them. In particular, in order to develop BCIs that are useful to individuals with certain functional or sensory disabilities, it is necessary to work closely with clinicians, patients and their caregivers in order to understand the patients' needs and propose appropriate solutions.

As mentioned in the previous chapters, regardless of the type of BCI, it has been repeatedly noted that a significant proportion of users could not control a BCI at all, at least during initial testing [ALL 10] (this phenomenon is called the "BCI deficiency"). Moreover, even among the users who manage to control a BCI, their performance (usually measured in terms of rates of correct classification of their mental command) proves to be highly variable from one user to another, as well as for the same user over time, from one day to the other, or even throughout a single session. This variability in performance, like the "deficiency", is still very poorly understood. Many hypotheses have been advanced, and partially confirmed by results; among these factors one can mention the differences in the structure and in the orientation of the cortical areas, attention or fatigue variabilities, or even differences of cognitive profiles or personalities [GRO 11, AHN 15, JEU 15]. However, these factors (also known as BCI performance predictors) only succeed in predicting part of the performance variations, and a significant part of this variability still remains unexplained. Regarding BCI deficiency, research carried out on the subject has concerned mainly naive subjects, and this phenomenon has essentially not been studied in the long term: do people initially unable to use a BCI manage to use it following a potentially long training period? Knowledge about the learning processes in BCIs are moreover very limited [LOT 13]. How does a user learn to control a BCI? What information and what sensory input (feedback) should be provided to the users so that they learn best? What learning tasks should users perform to learn as best and as quickly as possible how to control a BCI, according to their expertise, to their cognitive characteristics and to their personality? All these points essentially remain to be discovered. Their elucidation would allow understanding the limitations of the current systems and contribute to their improvement, depending on the specificities of each user.

The cortex comprises almost 100 billion neurons, each connected on average to 10,000 others. The transfer of information between neurons operates by chemical connections via neurotransmitters. The brain responds to the perceptions that it receives at a given time depending on its level of attention and fatigue. These few elements suggest that the same experience reproduced after an interval of a few seconds will not produce the same activity at the neuronal level. The activity measured in EEG during repetitions of the same protocol indeed shows great variability.

Brain activity thus appears as very difficult to apprehend in a reproducible manner. Feature extraction methods seek the most stable useful information (see Chapter 7 of Volume 1, [CLE 16]). New methods that make use of the stable features based on the covariance of the signals are beginning to prevail [SUG 07, BÜN 09]. Feature extraction is preceded by preprocessing, for example by frequency filtering to extract the information from specific frequency bands. The relevant preprocessing however varies according to users, and methods should be developed in order to select the information tailored to everyone's characteristics. An additional challenge consists of not specializing too much the machine learning to current data, which will eventually evolve, but in being able to make it evolve by means of coadaptation methods.

Finally, it should be noted that the academic sector is not yet organized to provide structured training programs in the field of BCIs. A number of thematic courses are certainly proposed regularly[3] but they are not sufficient to ensure comprehensive and lasting training on the many actors of BCIs, whose great thematic diversity has been underlined in this book. Despite the difficulty of the task, we hope that researchers in BCIs will come together in the coming years to define a whole framework of fundamental knowledge and specialties, in initial and continuous training. The international scholarly society, the "BCI Society"[4] created in 2015 would be an appropriate framework where this could be considered.

17.3. Using BCI in practice

Current BCIs are still mostly prototypes tested in laboratories, and very few of them are really marketed and used regularly in hospitals or at home. Many efforts must therefore be made in translational research, to bring BCIs out of the laboratories. This notably includes making BCIs such that they can be properly employed in a comfortable and independent way by the patients

---

3 This book itself originates from an autumn school about BCIs, organized in Nancy in 2011 under the auspices of the NeuroComp research society.
4 www.bcisociety.org/.

who need them, to make them cheaper and user-friendly, both for patients and the general public, to make them marketable, to ensure that their use is ethical and beneficial to society.

One of the problems faced by the field of BCI is that there is very scarce feedback on their use, given that relatively little manpower is devoted to operating the systems developed in laboratories. The factors that limit usage are particularly related to the hardware (bulk, gel, wires), but also to the fact that the possibilities of these systems are still limited. It is time to bring out simple and useful applications of BCIs so that they can take the leap and be tested in real life situations. There are numerous patients who, having experienced a BCI would like to bring it back to their home to use it more. Communication BCIs based on the P300 provide a possible framework for simple devices. "Brain Painting"[5], a BCI that allows users to express their creativity by painting, is a very nice example of this [ZIC 13].

BCI solutions will have to be integrated, in order to require only a minimal number of actions from the end-user. As a first step, the needs of BCIs were related to neuroscience and therefore required from the industry sensors with limited noise, and with many channels. Invasive BCI projects hence brought sensors such as the one of the BrainGate project to be developed. Now, electrocorticography is preparing to follow the same path. In addition, the companies that traditionally develop EEG acquisition systems have begun to propose solutions for BCIs by usually adding software components for marking stimulations and for the analysis of evoked potentials (e.g. BrainProducts GmbH or ANT Neuro).

Among the companies interested in BCIs, 83% are SMEs and 14% are start-ups, indicating a near-absence of large companies[6]. Investors in BCIs belong to gaming, medical, automotive, aerospace and emerging technologies industries. Some commercial ventures entirely dedicated to BCIs are emerging. Some are focused on the hardware (for example NeuroSky or EMOTIV), and others on BCI software design (for instance Mensia Technologies based on OpenViBE). These companies are often involved as partners in research programs to identify new markets and to implement solutions. Target markets include entertainment (Mattel Inc.),

---

5 www.brainpainting.net.
6 www.bnci-horizon-2020.eu.

sports (HumanWaves), well-being (BitBrain) or solutions for augmentative and alternative communication (Extendix from g.tec). After the new sensors, these companies now offer services and comprehensive products aiming to make BCI systems user-friendly as well as affordable.

In order to popularize the usage of BCIs, and thus their development and their practical utilization, it is necessary to make them affordable and accessible. This means that systems for acquiring and analyzing brain activity should be made cheaper. Indeed, current medical grade EEG acquisition systems cost thousands or even tens of thousands of euros/dollars. Recently, affordable acquisition systems have appeared, with prices in the order of a few hundreds of euros/dollars (in particular Neurosky or Emotiv systems), but these are of questionable quality [DUV 12, HEI 09], and the number and the positioning of their sensors do not allow them to reach the performances achieved in the laboratory with medical systems. It is thus necessary to further lower their costs to provide quality systems including many sensors which are accessible to all. The recent OpenBCI initiative (www.openbci.com/) goes in this direction, providing good-quality amplifiers whose performance for BCI seems equivalent to those of medical systems, with a price 10–20 times lower [FRE 16]. Brain signal processing software must also be affordable, which is fortunately already practically the case as entirely free and open-source solutions are available (notably OpenViBE and BCI2000).

The usability of software and hardware elements is also to be considered. As a matter of fact, non-engineers and non-expert users of BCIs should ideally be able to use this technology, which is not the case with the current software, despite efforts in this direction. When will there be a BCI that can be automatically turned on, calibrated and used with a single click? From a hardware point of view, the gel used with the electrodes is still a hindrance to the installation and the utilization of EEG caps, and a challenge is to develop dry EEG electrodes with a signal quality equivalent to those using gel that can be positioned on the scalp as comfortably and as quickly as putting on a hat. Current research is going in the right direction [ZAN 11a].

17.4. Opening up BCI technologies to new applications and fields

So far, BCIs have been mostly used as communication and control systems in order to send direct commands to a machine or to a computer. However, there are many other potential applications where BCIs might be useful, or where they are already useful but are still little explored. This notably includes introducing BCIs as tools for experimental investigation in neuroscience and in psychology, for neuroergonomy or adaptive man-machine interfaces, as well as for many other applications based on passive BCI, and finally various forms of rehabilitation using BCIs. Many of these new alternative applications have been considered in the recent roadmap "BNCI Horizon 2020" [BRU 15]. In short, BCI technologies will be potentially useful well beyond applications aiming to directly control systems.

In cognitive neuroscience, the real-time interpretation of brain activity measurements opens the possibility of adaptive experiments, where certain parameters of the protocol (the nature or the temporality of the stimuli or instruction) are manipulated online based on the observations. Online adaptation reduces the experimental time, which is in fact common practise in psychophysics, where the behavioral responses of subjects are easy to measure. We have, for instance, discussed in Chapter 10 of Volume 1 [CLE 16] the optimization of stimuli to distinguish between different cognition models. This same principle could be useful in clinical neuroscience for the evaluation of disorders of consciousness.

In BCI control tasks, manipulating the link between mental state and feedback allows to observe the capacity of reconfiguration of the brain networks (plasticity), in the short or in the longer term. This is the subject of invasive experiments in animals [SAD 14] as well as non-invasive experiments in humans [PIC 11].

BCI technologies are a unique way to measure mental states of the user continuously and in real-time. Most methods and applications mentioned in this book leverage this possibility in order to associate a mental state voluntarily generated to a command to control a system. There are however many other potential uses. In particular, applications based on passive BCIs remain relatively little explored in comparison, despite their huge potential [ERP 12, ZAN 11b, FAI 14]. In fact, being capable of continuously measuring mental states such as the mental workload [MÜH 14b, WOB 15], error recognition [FER 08, FRE 14], visual comfort [FRE 15] or even attention [TRA 14, FRE 16] provides new tools, for example, for evaluating the ergonomic qualities of a human–machine interface. This is referred to as "neuroergonomy" [PAR 08], a term used to designate the use of tools based on neurophysiological measurements to assess whether an interface is ergonomic, for example if it is cognitively pleasant, easy to use or intuitive. These tools can give rise to new generations of interfaces, which will be evaluated and refined by means of these new measures based on BCI technologies. This area must therefore be developed, seeking to estimate new mental states in brain signals (for example frustration), and to apply these measures to concrete and practical cases. Being able to measure such mental states also offers a large number of very promising perspectives for neuroadaptive technologies, particularly in the field of education. Indeed, by measuring the mental workload or the attention of a user trying to acquire skills or knowledge, training tasks will be adapted to his mental state, to maximize the quality of learning. Being able to measure the emotions of users from their brain signals [MÜH 14a], although it is very difficult, opens up the possibility to offer content, tasks or media (for example video games, movies, teaching exercises) giving rise to a potentially optimal user experience. Finally, BCI technologies can also be used to take advantage of the perceptual abilities of the human brain. It is possible to use measures of visuospatial attention in view of reducing the reaction time of users by presenting to them the information at an appropriate location [TRA 13]. It is equally possible to identify in a stream of information (such as images) what information is relevant to the user, according to the brain responses of the user upon presentation of this information [SAJ 07]. This can, for example, be used to identify target images in a large quantity of images presented very quickly one after another to the user, and this more quickly than an image processing algorithm or a manual selection [SAJ 07]. One can imagine that this kind of method could be extended to analyze, sort and very quickly combine multiple data types in potentially very large databases. All these examples are in fact only a tiny part of the possible applications of BCI technologies, and many others could and should be explored.

The usage of BCIs for rehabilitation will increase in the coming years. Indeed, BCIs will soon be customizable to every user. Thus, whether for motor disabilities such as those caused by a stroke, or for cognitive impairments such as attention disorder or even stress, it will be possible to provide exercises to measure and monitor the progress of the user. The equipment could be rented, or even bought so that sessions can take place at home rather than in rehabilitation centers. The results of the working sessions will be automatically transmitted to the physician for a follow-up, even allowing remote calibration of the equipment for the next session.

17.5. Concern about ethical issues

As we have seen in Chapters 15 and 16, the development and the use of BCIs give rise to numerous ethical questions. On the one hand, this innovative technology must be developed by practicing what is called "responsible innovation" [NIJ 15] in order to ensure that BCIs will really benefit society, in full respect for people. The fear that this technology can inspire indeed potentially hinders its development, despite the benefits it can already bring. In fact, as soon as physiological signals are being measured, it is possible to potentially access information on users without their knowledge, or their consent (see for example [MAR 12]), which can scare off potential BCI users. A major step forward would be to guide the development and the research of BCIs to ensure their ethical use under all conditions.

On the other hand, well before new techniques and applications of BCIs become mature, ethical reflection must be engaged, so that society becomes aware of all of the new possibilities it offers. It is quite likely that society will decide to allow only some of the proposed possibilities.

17.6. Conclusions

BCIs provide a limited but somehow universal interface between a human and his environment, because they take advantage of some basic principles of brain function which are common to all human beings, irrespective of their culture, their social origin, their age, their gender and their state of health. This book will have shown the reader, we hope, the richness and the complexity of BCIs, as well as the many potential applications of this technology. Despite the already impressive amount of work on BCIs that has been carried out and published, BCI research remains a very young area, in which the majority of work and research are yet to come, with very promising potential results. For a large number of emerging technologies, decades have elapsed between the first research carried out on the subject and their daily usage. This is the case, for example, of the computer mouse or the Internet. Thus, it is reasonably possible to suggest that BCIs have a long life and many years of research in front of them. Now is the time to contribute to this research and to these developments.

17.7. Bibliography

[AHN 15] AHN M., JUN S.C., "Performance variation in motor imagery brain–computer interface: A brief review", *Journal of Neuroscience Methods*, vol. 243, pp. 103–110, 2015.

[ALL 10] ALLISON B., NEUPER C., "Could anyone use a BCI?", in TAN D.S., NIJHOLT A., (eds), *Brain-Computer Interfaces*, Springer, London, 2010.

[BÜN 09] VON BÜNAU P., MEINECKE F., KIRÁLY F. *et al.*, "Finding stationary subspaces in multivariate time series", *Physical Review Letter*, vol. 103, no. 21, p. 214101, 2009.

[BRU 15] BRUNNER C., BIRBAUMER N., BLANKERTZ B. *et al.*, "BNCI Horizon 2020: towards a roadmap for the BCI community", *Brain-Computer Interfaces*, vol. 2, no. 1, pp. 1–10, Taylor & Francis, 2015.

[CLE 16] CLERC M., BOUGRAIN L., LOTTE F. (eds), *Brain–Computer Interfaces 1*, ISTE London and John Wiley & Sons, New York, 2016.

[DUV 12] DUVINAGE M., CASTERMANS T., DUTOIT T., *et al.*, "A P300-based quantitative comparison between the Emotiv Epoc headset and a medical EEG device", *Biomedical Engineering Online*, vol. 765, 2012.

[ERP 12] VAN ERP J., LOTTE F., TANGERMANN M., "Brain-Computer Interfaces: beyond medical applications", *IEEE Computer*, vol. 45, no. 4, pp. 26-34, 2012.

[FAI 14] FAIRCLOUGH S.H., GILLEADE K., *Advances in Physiological Computing*, Springer, 2014.

[FER 08] FERREZ P., MILLÁN J., "Error-related EEG potentials generated during simulated Brain-Computer interaction", *IEEE Transactions on Biomedical Engineering*, vol. 55, no. 3, pp. 923–929, 2008.

[FRE 14] FREY J., MÜHL C., LOTTE F. *et al.*, "Review of the use of electroencephalography as an evaluation method for human-computer interaction", *Proceedings of PhyCS*, Lisbon, Portugal, 2014.

[FRE 15] FREY J., APPRIOU A., LOTTE F. *et al.*, "Classifying EEG signals during stereoscopic visualization to estimate visual comfort", *Computational Intelligence and Neuroscience*, Hindawi Publishing Corporation, vol. 2016, no. 2758103, pp. 1-11, 2016.

[FRE 16] FREY J., Leveraging human-computer interactions and social presence with physiological computing, PhD Thesis, Bordeaux University, 2016.

[GRO 11] GROSSE-WENTRUP M., "What are the causes of performance variation in Brain-Computer Interfacing?", *International Journal of Bioelectromagnetism*, vol. 13, no. 3, pp. 115–116, 2011.

[HEI 09] HEINGARTNER D., "Mental block", *IEEE Spectrum*, vol. 46, no. 1, pp. 42-43, 2009.

[JEU 15] JEUNET C., N'KAOUA B., SUBRAMANIAN S. *et al.*, "Predicting mental imagery-based BCI performance from personality, cognitive profile and neurophysiological patterns", *PLoS ONE*, p. 20, July 2015.

[LIN 03] LINDEN A., FENN J., "Understanding Gartner's hype cycles", Strategic Analysis Report no. R-20–1971, Gartner, Inc, 2003.

[LOT 13] LOTTE F., LARRUE F., MÜHL C., "Flaws in current human training protocols for spontaneous Brain–Computer Interfaces: lessons learned from instructional design", *Frontiers in Human Neuroscience*, vol. 7, no. 568, 2013.

[MAR 12] MARTINOVIC I., DAVIES D., FRANK M. *et al.*, "On the feasibility of side-channel attacks with Brain-Computer interfaces", *USENIX Security Symposium*, pp. 143–158, 2012.

[MÜH 14a] MÜHL C., ALLISON B., NIJHOLT A. *et al.*, "A survey of affective brain computer interfaces: principles, state-of-the-art, and challenges", *Brain-Computer Interfaces*, vol. 1, no. 2, pp. 66–84, 2014.

[MÜH 14b] MÜHL C., JEUNET C., LOTTE F., "EEG-based workload estimation across affective contexts", *Frontiers in Neuroscience*, vol. 8, 2014.

[NIJ 13] NIJBOER F., CLAUSEN J., ALLISON B. Z. *et al.*, "The asilomar survey: stakeholders' opinions on ethical issues related to Brain–Computer Interfacing", *Neuroethics*, vol. 6, no. 3, pp. 541–578, 2013.

[NIJ 15] NIJBOER F., "Technology transfer of brain-computer interfaces as assistive technology: Barriers and opportunities", *Annals of Physical and Rehabilitation Medicine*, vol. 58, no. 1, pp. 35–38, 2015.

[PAR 08] PARASURAMAN R., WILSON G., "Putting the brain to work: neuroergonomics past, present, and future", *Human Factors*, vol. 50, no. 3, pp. 468–474, 2008.

[PIC 11] PICHIORRI F., FALLANI F.D.V., CINCOTTI F. *et al.*, "Sensorimotor rhythm-based brain-computer interface training: the impact on motor cortical responsiveness", *Journal of Neural Engineering*, vol. 8, no. 2, p. 025020, 2011.

[SAD 14] SADTLER P.T., QUICK K.M., GOLUB M.D. *et al.*, "Neural constraints on learning", *Nature*, vol. 512, pp. 423–426, 2014.

[SAJ 07] SAJDA P., GERSON A., PHILIASTIDES M. *et al.*, "Brain–Computer interface", chapter in *Single-trial Analysis of EEG During Rapid Visual Discrimination: Enabling Cortically-coupled Computer Vision*, MIT Press, Cambridge, Massassuchets, 2007.

[SUG 07] SUGIYAMA M., KRAULEDAT M., MÜLLER K., "Covariate shift adaptation by importance weighted cross validation", *Journal of Machine Learning Reseach*, vol. 8, pp. 1027–1061, 2007.

[TRA 13] TRACHEL R., BROCHIER T., CLERC M., "Adaptive and warning displays with Brain–Computer interfaces: enhanced visuospatial attention performance", *IEEE/EMBS 6th International Conference on Neural Engineering*, San Diego, November 2013.

[TRA 14] TRACHEL R., Protocoles d'interaction cerveau-machine pour améliorer la performance d'attention visuo-spatiale chez l'homme, PhD Thesis, University of Nice Sophia Antipolis, 2014.

[WOB 15] WOBROCK D., FREY J., GRAEFF D. *et al.*, "Continuous mental effort evaluation during 3D object manipulation tasks based on brain and physiological signals", chapter in *Human-Computer Interaction–INTERACT*, Springer, pp. 472–487, 2015.

[ZAN 11a] ZANDER T.O., LEHNE M., IHME K. *et al.*, "A dry EEG-system for scientific research and brain–computer interfaces", *Frontiers in Neuroscience*, vol. 5, 2011.

[ZAN 11b] ZANDER T., KOTHE C., "Towards passive Brain–Computer interfaces: applying Brain–Computer interface technology to human-machine systems in general", *Journal of Neural Engineering*, vol. 8, no. 2, p. 025005, 2011.

[ZIC 13] ZICKLER C., HALDER S., KLEIH S.C. *et al.*, "Brain painting: usability testing according to the user-centered design in end users with severe motor paralysis", *Artificial Intelligence in Medicine*, vol. 59, no. 2, pp. 99–110, 2013.

List of Authors

Anton ANDREEV
GIPSA-lab, CNRS
Grenoble Institute of Technology
University Grenoble Alpes
France

Bernard ANDRIEU
EA Techniques et enjeux du corps
Paris Descartes University
France

Nicolas AUMONIER
EA Philosophie, Pratiques et Langage
University Grenoble Alpes
France

Eric AZABOU
Raymond Poincaré University
Hospital
Garches
France

Jean-Michel BADIER
INSERM
Aix-Marseille University
Marseille
France

Alexandre BARACHANT
Burke Medical Research Institute
New York
USA

Florent BOCQUELET
Inserm U1205
University Grenoble Alpes
France

Laurent BOUGRAIN
LORIA
University of Lorraine
Vandoeuvre-lès-Nancy
France

Salvador CABANILLES
Raymond Poincaré University
Hospital
Garches
France

François CABESTAING
CRIStAL
Lille University of Science and
Technology
France

Alison CELLARD
Inria Bordeaux-Sud-Ouest
Talence
France

Maureen CLERC
Inria Sophia Antipolis-Méditerranée
University Côte d'Azur
France

Marco CONGEDO
GIPSA-lab, CNRS
Grenoble Institute of Technology
University Grenoble Alpes
France

José DEL R. MILLÀN
École Polytechnique Fédérale de
Geneva
Switzerland

Nathanaël FOY
Inria Sophia Antipolis-Méditerranée
University Côte d'Azur
France

Julien JUNG
Centre de Recherches en
Neurosciences de Lyon
Inserm, CNRS
University of Lyon
France

Jean-Philippe LACHAUX
Centre de Recherches en
Neurosciences de Lyon
Inserm, CNRS
University of Lyon
France

Anatole LÉCUYER
Inria Rennes-Bretagne Atlantique
France

Pierre LELEUX
MicroVitae Technologies
Meyreuil
France

Jussi LINDGREN
Inria Rennes-Bretagne Atlantique
France

Thomas LONJARET
MicroVitae Technologies
Meyreuil
France

Fabien LOTTE
Inria Bordeaux-Sud-Ouest
Talence
France

Jacques LUAUTÉ
Centre de Recherches en
Neurosciences de Lyon
Inserm, CNRS
University of Lyon
France

Emmanuel MABY
Centre de Recherches en
Neurosciences de Lyon
Inserm, CNRS
University of Lyon
France

Jérémie MATTOUT
Centre de Recherches en
Neurosciences de Lyon
Inserm, CNRS
University of Lyon
France

Louis MAYAUD
Mensia Technologies
Paris
France

Dominique MORLET
Centre de Recherches en
Neurosciences de Lyon
Inserm, CNRS
University of Lyon
France

Théodore PAPADOPOULO
Inria Sophia Antipolis-Méditerranée
University Côte d'Azur
France

Gaëlle PIRET
Inserm U1205
University Grenoble Alpes
France

Guillaume SERRIÈRE
Inria Nancy-Grand Est
Villers-lès-Nancy
France

Blaise YVERT
Inserm U1205
University Grenoble Alpes
France

Index

Contents of Volume 1

Other titles from

in

Cognitive Science and Knowledge Management

2016

FORT Karën
Collaborative Annotation for Reliable Natural Language Processing

GIANNI Robert
Responsibility and Freedom
(Responsible Research and Innovation Set – Volume 2)

LENOIR Virgil Cristian
Ethical Efficiency: Responsibility and Contingency
(Responsible Research and Innovation Set – Volume 1)

MATTA Nada, ATIFI Hassan, DUCELLIER Guillaume
Daily Knowledge Valuation in Organizations

NOUVEL Damien, EHRMANN Maud, ROSSET Sophie
Named Entities for Computational Linguistics

SILBERZTEIN Max
Formalizing Natural Languages: The NooJ Approach

2015

LAFOURCADE Mathieu, JOUBERT Alain, LE BRUN Nathalie
Games with a Purpose (GWAPs)

2010

ALBALATE Amparo, MINKER Wolfgang
Semi-Supervised and Unsupervised Machine Learning: Novel Strategies

BROSSAUD Claire, REBER Bernard
Digital Cognitive Technologies

2009

BOUYSSOU Denis, DUBOIS Didier, PIRLOT Marc, PRADE Henri
Decision-making Process

MARCHAL Alain
From Speech Physiology to Linguistic Phonetics

PRALET Cédric, SCHIEX Thomas, VERFAILLIE Gérard
Sequential Decision-Making Problems / Representation and Solution

SZÜCSAndras, TAIT Alan, VIDAL Martine, BERNATH Ulrich
Distance and E-learning in Transition

2008

MARIANI Joseph
Spoken Language Processing

Printed and bound by CPI Group (UK) Ltd, Croydon, CR0 4YY

27/10/2024

14580238-0005